Beyond the Moment

Latinx: The Future Is Now
A series edited by Lorgia García Peña and Nicole M. Guidotti-Hernández

Books in the series

PJ DiPietro, *Sideways Selves: Travesti and Jotería Struggles Across the Americas*

Sony Coráñez Bolton, *Dos X: Disability and Racial Dysphoria in Latinx and Filipinx Culture*

Marcos Gonsalez, *Revolting Indolence: The Politics of Slacking, Lounging, and Daydreaming in Queer and Trans Latinx Culture*

Sharina Maíllo-Pozo, *Bridging Sonic Borders: Popular Music in Contemporary Dominican/Dominicanyork Literature*

Frank García, *Clicas: Gender, Sexuality, and Struggle in Latina/o/x Gang Literature and Film*

Regina Marie Mills, *Invisibility and Influence: A Literary History of AfroLatinidades*

Jason Ruiz, *Narcomedia: Latinidad, Popular Culture, and America's War on Drugs*

Rebeca L. Hey-Colón, *Channeling Knowledges: Water and Afro-Diasporic Spirits in Latinx and Caribbean Worlds*

Tatiana Reinoza, *Reclaiming the Americas: Latinx Art and the Politics of Territory*

Kristy L. Ulibarri, *Visible Borders, Invisible Economies: Living Death in Latinx Narratives*

Marisel C. Moreno, *Crossing Waters: Undocumented Migration in Hispanophone Caribbean and Latinx Literature and Art*

Yajaira M. Padilla, *From Threatening Guerrillas to Forever Illegals: US Central Americans and the Cultural Politics of Non-Belonging*

Francisco J. Galarte, *Brown Trans Figurations: Rethinking Race, Gender, and Sexuality in Chicanx/Latinx Studies*

Beyond the Moment

IRENE
MATA

Connecting Histories of Latinx Performance and Resistance

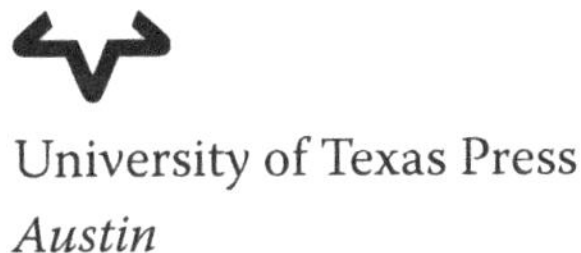

University of Texas Press
Austin

Printed in the United States of America
First edition, 2026

∞ The paper used in this book meets the minimum requirements of ANSI/NISO Z39.48-1992 (R1997) (Permanence of Paper).

Library of Congress Cataloging-in-Publication Data

Names: Mata, Irene, author.
Title: Beyond the moment : connecting histories of Latinx performance and resistance / Irene Mata.
Other titles: Latinx (Series)
Description: First edition. | Austin : University of Texas Press, 2026. | Series: Latinx: the future is now | Includes bibliographical references and index.
Identifiers: LCCN 2025029066 (print) | LCCN 2025029067 (ebook)
ISBN 978-1-4773-3356-3 (hardcover)
ISBN 978-1-4773-3357-0 (paperback)
ISBN 978-1-4773-3358-7 (pdf)
ISBN 978-1-4773-3359-4 (epub)
Subjects: LCSH: Performance art—Political aspects—United States. | Performance art—Social aspects—United States. | Hispanic American arts. | Arts—Documentation. | Hispanic Americans—Civil rights. | Noncitizens—United States—Social conditions. | Lowriders—Social aspects—United States. | Performing arts—Study and teaching—United States.
Classification: LCC NX456.5.P38 M38 2026 (print) | LCC NX456.5.P38 (ebook)
LC record available at https://lccn.loc.gov/2025029066
LC ebook record available at https://lccn.loc.gov/2025029067

doi:10.7560/333563

For my students, who never fail to help me learn and grow, and the artivists who create work that inspires our resistance and joy.

Contents

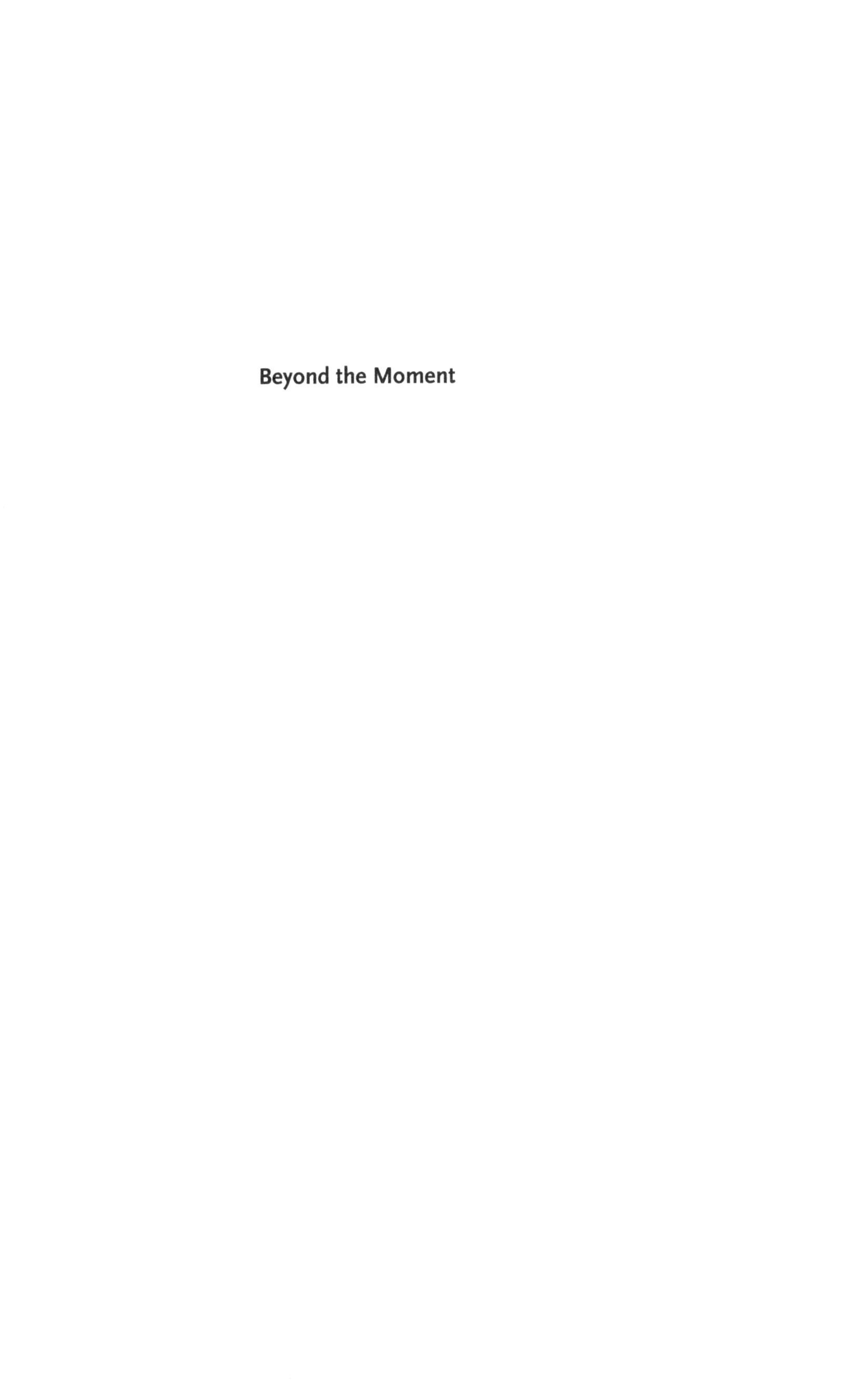

Beyond the Moment

INTRODUCTION
Ritual, Resistance, and Remembrance Onstage

I BELIEVE IN THE HOLY, I BELIEVE IN THE MAGIC, AND I BELIEVE IN THE TRANSMISSION THAT HAPPENS IN THE EPHEMERAL EXPERIENCE ON STAGE. THAT'S PRETTY MUCH THE PLACE I WORK FROM NOW. MY ALCHEMY IS IN CONNECTION, CAN THIS STORY POSSIBLY BE YOURS?

LUIS ALFARO, FACEBOOK POST, MAY 26, 2017

In May 2017, I had the good fortune of being in Chicago during the short run of Luis Alfaro's *St. Jude*, one of the performances in the Up Close and Personal series being staged by the Victory Gardens Theater. As my best friend and I waited in the lobby of the theater, a man politely approached us and asked if we would be willing to read a few lines during the performance. While surprised by the request, I was more in awe of the person making it, as it was the playwright himself, Luis Alfaro. I had first encountered the highly respected and acclaimed writer as an undergraduate student when I attended a theater panel in which he participated at the University of Texas at El Paso. I fondly remembered my professor introducing us to Alfaro, who showed generosity in interacting with his young fans. Almost two decades later, he was standing in front of me again, and while I wish I could say that I answered Alfaro's request with poise and calm, I acted just like that dumbstruck undergraduate: I froze.

My friend quickly agreed for both of us and explained that my awkwardness was due to my deep respect for him and his work. He laughed good-naturedly and handed us each a sheet with lines. He explained that we would read our lines in between sections of the performance and that he would cue us with the line listed at the top of the page. He thanked us and walked away to recruit more volunteers. After his departure, my friend gently laughed as I lamented my lack of cool and terrible impression, and we made our way into the performance space. Our interaction with Alfaro prepared me for the fact that the audience would be playing some kind of role in the performance, but nothing could have prepared me for the performance itself.

St. Jude is a solo show named after the hospital that treated Alfaro's father when he suffered a stroke.[1] The performance is a beautiful and painful story of family, trauma, loss, mourning, and survival. As an audience, we follow Alfaro down memory lane as he recounts his childhood, growing up in a family steeped in religion and tradition, an upbringing that made his queerness hard to embrace. He uses his father's illness as an opportunity to reconcile with his difficult history and to make sense of his own trauma and faith. Given that he was raised in a highly religious family, it is no surprise that religion plays a major role in the story, especially as it is at the root of so much homophobia. We learn from Alfaro that he grew up in both the Catholic Church and in Pentecostal Christianity, dividing his weekends between the revival tent and his duties as an altar boy. While his story is rich and complex, the physical setting is simple and clean. As he tells his story, slides are projected behind him: images of signs, maps, landscapes, and buildings. Alfaro alternates between standing center downstage at the podium and moving around the small stage as he speaks his monologue. On the podium is a large binder he occasionally turns to, similar to a pastor reading from sermon notes or a priest from the Bible. While the set is minimal, the impact of Alfaro's words and his delivery is anything but, and it is made more powerful by the organization of the performance itself.

The structure of the performance invoked the rituals of the two religious traditions that so deeply influenced Alfaro's childhood. In between his storytelling, Alfaro cued the selected audience member, and the volunteer delivered the lines they had been given. These supplements to his script inserted Alfaro's experience with his father's deteriorating health. Those of us who grew up Catholic recognized the exercise of audience participation as replicating the rite of parishioners reading from the scriptures, a part of the Catholic mass that makes up the Liturgy of the Word. Each reading was simply titled "First Reading," "Second Reading," and so forth, following the format of the Catholic practice of the parishioner proclaiming, "A reading from the holy gospel according to," and inserting the source of the text. The reading was followed by a communal singing of hymn excerpts, which were provided to the audience in the performance program. The spiritual and gospel songs that made up the *St. Jude* hymns included pieces popular in Pentecostal services, like "This Little Light of Mine" and "He's Got the Whole World in His Hands."[2]

I was struck by the brilliance of the invocation of these religious rituals in the telling of Alfaro's story. The performance space was transformed. By relying on well-known religious rituals and employing them to tell his queer story, Alfaro created his own sacred space in the theater. The space became his church—a church that challenges the homophobia and ostracizing of queer bodies and embraces the audience, bringing us into his congregation. The podium becomes a pulpit from which he can tell his story, making us active witnesses to his pain and trauma. By invoking the various rituals and transforming the stage into a sacred space of queer storytelling, Alfaro disrupts the assumed right of organized religion to dictate the meaning of queerness and make moral judgments on members of the queer community. He inserts his own spirituality and belief system into his queer narrative, undermining the power of the churches in which he grew up. His performance is a vital reminder that queer individuals can have faith and be guided by an ethics of care rooted in spirituality and love for others.

St. Jude is an extraordinary theatrical journey of personal loss and mourning, a process deeply affected by queerness and religion. Alfaro's strategy of taking structures that have harmed him and transforming them into storytelling tools of resistance was deeply meaningful and raised so many questions beyond the beauty of the performance. Oppressed communities have often turned to religion for comfort and support, but what happens when those structures of support replicate hierarchies of exclusion? What happens when those sites of comfort and community become sites of painful rejection? Alfaro's performance offered one strategy: We take what we can learn from them, deconstruct them to identify that which causes harm, and rebuild them into a new, more inclusive, and empowering structure.

St. Jude inspired me to think through how performance can offer us strategies of resistance to help our communities survive trauma and injustice. *St. Jude* is not just about Alfaro's personal experience and his process of healing. When he invited us into the performance, it became so much more. *St. Jude* became a site of communal learning through pain and healing. Using his personal story, Alfaro created a performance that offered his own narrative of loss and struggle to connect with the audience and encourage us to rethink how we've imagined the relationship between queerness and faith. One does not have to be religious or spiritual, and one can still admire and respect the transgressive use of religious rites and traditions in service of the queer community. I read Alfaro's performance as part of a wider strategy of performing identity and culture in service of community.

Years after attending the performance, *St. Jude* continues occupying space in my memory. I left the performance in awe of Alfaro's talent and his ability to move his audience—what he calls the alchemy of connection. The pain he expressed on the stage reverberated through my body, triggering my own sense of loss at my mother's death almost two decades earlier and answering his question: "Can this story possibly be yours?" (Alfaro). I was left emotionally depleted but intellectually inspired by the power of Alfaro's art and his storytelling strategies. After attending the performance, I was haunted by the experience as his narrative continued to run through my head. The more time passed, the more I appreciated the brilliance of the work. While the ephemerality of the performance limited my ability to interact with the piece once it was over, the impact of the performance stayed with me. My recollections were partially rooted in the small keepsakes I took home with me: the program, with the hymns we sang along with Alfaro, and the first and eighth audience readings.[3] These mementos functioned as tangible reminders of how Alfaro created meaning by subverting religious rituals. They also illustrate how the performance can go beyond the ephemeral and can ensure a form of connection with the audience. The readings and the hymns allow the text to go beyond the moment of performance, the moment of resistance, the moment of becoming. I turn to Alfaro's *St. Jude* and my layered engagement with the text to think through the practice of resistance and survival that performance offers communities of color—a practice that has the potential to go beyond the story of the individual and the moment of coming into being.[4]

Alfaro's text raised important questions for me as a student of theater and performance. How can we take scripts from the past and make something new out of them, something that goes beyond merely replication? How can we salvage, from earlier problematic performances of identity, enactments that can help marginalized communities in the present? How do we build on the current expressions of resistance to imagine, and work toward, a more just future? How can performance act as an intervention in the violent erasure of injustice and the historical amnesia around discrimination and oppression? How can we document our performances and processes to live and inspire after the embodiment of story on the stage? How can performance act in the service of community?

Beyond the Moment engages with these questions and expands on our understanding of the limitations and possibilities of performance. I discuss the power of performance, document how performance continues to be useful in challenging systems of oppression and creating art that inspires action, and argue for the mentoring potential of performance works. Like Alfaro's *St. Jude*, the texts I focus on are not simply entertaining or educating an audience. Through their insistence on active participation, they implicate the audience in the performance. These texts force us to confront uncomfortable truths about our previous moments of resistance and illustrate the limitations that are inherent in the type of social justice organizing that is not intersectional. They offer more inclusive visions of community activism and highlight the inherent potential of performance to move, to teach, and to inspire an audience. Theater scholar David Román reminds us that "performance in America matters," especially when we understand how the connection between contemporary performance and the past helps us "trace the remains of history within our present moment so as to better understand that present" (3–4).[5]

My reading of performance in this book is deeply influenced and inspired by the history of resistance and community at the root of so many works by Chicanx/Latinx writers and performers. This resistance is one born out of the necessity to shape our own identity formation outside of the conscripted meaning of Latinidad by a mainstream world. It challenges colonial legacies that erase the histories of our communities, defies the harmful images that have been used to reduce our communities to abject stereotypes, and offers oppositional representations of Chicanx/Latinx subjectivity. When I make reference to the Chicanx/Latinx community, I am not conflating the very real differences and tensions that exist within this diverse group of people. Instead, I am engaging with Rosaura Sánchez and Beatrice Pita's argument that the Latina/o/x identity is one "born in the context of difference and . . . marked by difference" and is composed of a heterogeneous, transnational, multiracial, and multilingual population (27).[6] Sánchez and Pita propose thinking of the Latinx community as a bloc to encourage a strategic form of solidarity that does not erase the tensions and contradictions that exist within the group but instead inspires working for common goals across differences.[7] I am also cognizant of the debate around language and the use of the *x* in "Chicanx/Latinx" and the more current use of the *e* in "Chicane/Latine." I choose to use the *x* because I want to denaturalize the gender binary and because I am strongly moved by the argument made by Alan Pelaez Lopez that the *x* in "Latinx" signifies a set of wounds based on the violence of colonization and not a simple linguistic trend. For Pelaez Lopez, the use of the *x* invites our reflection on how violence against LGBTQ+ individuals across our communities has been normalized.[8] By employing the term "Chicanx/Latinx," I gesture to a construction of community based on contradiction and tension but also a desire for solidarity; a community that has faced various forms of violence based on intersecting identities, our complicity in that violence, but also our resistance to that violence. When I write about community and resistance, I am inspired to think expansively about belonging within the Chicanx/Latinx community without losing sight of the imbalance of power and abuse of privilege that continues to exist within it. Community is complicated and always shifting, and my analysis of community resistance is rooted in the historical moments shaping our understanding of Chicanx/Latinx struggles for social justice.[9]

My analysis of the texts in the following pages is informed by an understanding of community as dynamic and contributes to the larger archive of cultural activism—cultural work that has been performed in community, with community, and in service of community. I am building on the foundation of Chicanx/Latinx theater scholarship built by Alberto Sandoval-Sánchez, Cherríe Moraga, Jorge Huerta, Carlos Morton, Tomás Ybarra-Frausto, and Yolanda Broyles-González, and the scholars who have further developed this legacy, including Alicia Arrizón, David Román, Rita Urquijo-Ruiz, Ramón H. Rivera-Servera, Israel Reyes, and the incomparable José Esteban Muñoz. My work contributes to an archived history of community mobilization in Chicanx/Latinx performance. By identifying the potential of archiving practices in the performance texts highlighted in this book, I also underscore the significance of theater as a means for community mobilization that can continue to function as a pedagogical apparatus past the ephemerality of embodiment. Through a focus on the materials and processes archived by artists and activists, the following chapters map out the message being conveyed by the performance, how it is being transmitted, and, more importantly, how the process of creation is captured and archived for future use. When I argue that a text goes "beyond the moment," I am gesturing toward the work's ability to, in the present, gesture backward (to the past) and forward (to the future).[10] Ultimately, the works featured in this study exemplify a form of textual mentoring and navigational storytelling that can be activated by communities for movements of resistance and liberation.

Performance as Cultural Organizing, and Cultural Organizing as Performance

As a word, "performance" carries with it multiple meanings that can be both simply descriptive and theoretically complex. "Performance" invokes a myriad of images, all depending on use and audience. A performance can be a professional activity, scripted and put on by one trained in the theater. It can be a group of fourth-graders struggling through their rendition of "Mary Had a Little Lamb" at their first orchestra concert. It can also be an action, a carrying out of a task or duty, the kind of action evaluated in professional performance reviews. These uses of "performance" are easily seen and understood. When we begin to discuss "performance" as it manifests in the communication of ideologies around identity, the word becomes much more complicated.

When we talk about the performance of identity, we aren't referencing a straightforward concept of putting on a concert or a play. As Judith Butler made clear in her theorizing of gender, performance is a vital component in the process of social construction—and not just of gender.[11] Our socialization into proper subjects of the nation is based on naturalizing the construction of multiple identity formations, which rely on repeatedly performing the manufactured behaviors ascribed to those identities.[12] The understanding of the performance can help disrupt those constructions. Once we recognize the artificialness of the performance, we can begin to take it apart and reject the essentialist logics that reduce identity to biology. Understanding and invoking performance in the context of identity becomes a way of disrupting imposed ideologies around gender and race and helps in challenging heteropatriarchal hierarchies of power.

Cultural production, in its many forms, plays a vital role in this ideological upending. For example, when we tune in to drag shows like *We're Here*, we witness drag artists like Shangela and Bob the Drag Queen teaching others how to put on the trappings of femininity in order to defy traditional performances of gender.[13] Suddenly, the idea of gender as a type of performance is made accessible to an audience that might never have questioned their understanding of femininity as an inherent trait. Used in the service of transgression, performance offers the possibility of resisting imposed subject formations and can foster opportunities for creating alternative understandings of identity. Viewing performance through such a framework allows us to see it all around us and to recognize its power to change our worldview. From the performance of Indigeneity and cultural heritage in *matachines* dancing to honor the Virgen de Guadalupe in the middle of Kansas, to the unapologetic performance of a fat Black feminism present in Lizzo's playing of James Madison's crystal flute, performance offers individuals a means of affirmation and a tool of resistance.[14] It is this spirit of defiance, and within this space of possibility, that situates my discussion of performance.

The use of performance in movements of resistance is an important part of Chicanx/Latinx histories of struggle and mobilization. As Cherríe Moraga powerfully argues, "Experience first generated through the body returns to the body in the flesh of the staged performance. In this sense, for me, it is as close to direct political activism as I can get as an artist, for theater requires the body to make testimony and requires other bodies to bear witness to it" (45). Like many, I learned about the Chicano civil rights movement through the reading of Teatro Campesino and Luis Valdez's *actos*. I studied the organizing strategies employed by the United Farm Workers leaders that incorporated the cultural activism of the Teatro, and watched documentaries that captured farmworkers taking on the almighty growers, challenging their power. While I appreciated my education in the canonical works of playwrights like William Shakespeare, Anton Chekhov, and Eugene O'Neill, these works didn't inspire me to want to make a change in the world. They didn't move me to action—not like the actos.

It was these small theatrical skits that embodied resistance and hope among farmworkers that inspired me. It was their ability to wield art as a weapon that introduced me to the power of performance. The archived images of campesinos stepping onto makeshift stages, in an effort to galvanize a labor movement and educate fellow workers, compellingly capture the possibilities offered by performance in service of community.[15]

These acts of resistance reverberated through the picket line and into the larger community. The publishing of the actos and the subsequent scholarship they fostered helped inspire future generations of activists and artists.[16]

The actos, however, also offer a cautionary tale about the danger of single-identity-focused activism. As the work of scholars like Yolanda Broyles-González has illustrated, Chicana activists and Teatro Campesino company members were marginalized and subject to the hetero-patriarchal structure of the movement.[17] Similar to other civil rights movements, the Chicano movement replicated leadership structures that positioned women at the bottom of the hierarchy—working for the movement but having their leadership and impact ignored. Like the movement it was supporting, Teatro Campesino focused on upholding the narrative of the charismatic male leader at the expense of the women helping make the movement possible. The sidelining of Chicana activists and members of Teatro Campesino reminds us that even within our social justice movements, we practice politics of exclusion based on established hierarchies that have become naturalized in our communities. If we do not look beyond the masculinist framing of our social justice histories—including artistic activism—we miss the contributions of a large part of our community. The existence of the published actos, along with the archives of the Teatro and the documented stories of the community, provide a fuller picture of the importance and impact of the performances while also offering us a history from which to learn.

While most of us were unable to witness the performance of the various actos during the United Farm Workers strike, we can read them and learn about the moment and spirit in which they were created. The published scripts are part of Teatro Campesino's legacy and document a history of performance and activism that goes beyond the agricultural fields of California. In spaces of learning, the published scripts of theatrical works offer the opportunity to teach and to learn from performance. It might not be possible to take my students to the theatrical productions we study, but we can still be inspired by the words on the page and moved by the visions they foster in our imagination. These scripts also make it possible for schools, community theaters, and other theater practitioners to put on their own embodied interpretations of the text. As an educator, I am drawn to the pedagogical potential of theatrical scripts and what they can teach us about the creation of art, subjugated histories, and performance of resistance. Scripts and the documentation of performance allow us to understand the impact of works long after the moment of their enactment, and they offer a base on which to continue building.

Beyond the Moment

As a teacher, I am interested in interrogating how performance goes beyond the moment of embodiment. While the ephemeral quality of a performance makes it exciting and unique, it also limits the work's impact if it is situated as simply ending when the curtain falls.[18] I might have watched *St. Jude* only one time, but the memory of the experience continues to stay with me, aided by the mementos that ground me in that recollection. While the reliance on the embodiment of the words differentiates how we read theater from how we read traditional literary prose, we can find value and inspiration in both formats. Reading a performance script might not have the excitement and vibrancy of watching an actual performance, but the documented text does offer possibilities for inspiration, education, and joy. The publication of performance scripts, the archiving of processes, and the documenting of strategies provide readers the opportunity to engage with the text outside of the moment of enactment, exponentially expanding the scope of a text's audience and the circle of its influence.

The performances I focus on in this book are dynamic texts that demonstrate how art teaches us about history, activism, and change. Each performance is brilliant in its delivery but offers so much more than a simple embodied act. The scripts and accompanying materials function as a repository of resistance that can be activated by future performers and activists. I show how the intentional use of various mediums in the organizing structures of these texts offers audiences a rich and complex understanding not only of the art but also of the creative processes behind the activist nature of the texts. I argue that through their active documenting of the processes behind the performances, these creators are helping to train future artists. They are offering a model of artistic production grounded in an informed critique of structures of power and, in the process, gesturing toward the possibilities for creating visions of a different world. The texts present a history that is often ignored—or violently erased—in the nation's narrative of itself, while also providing readers and audiences a blueprint for activist art, or what creators like Favianna Rodriguez embrace as "artivism."[19] I read the documenting of the creators' processes, in both written and digital spaces, as the creators' contributions to a repository that goes beyond merely recording individual actions or venerating the art of the performance. The repositories being created around the texts featured in the following pages offer an example of the relational process of organizing and artistic creation—a process that is working to create community where change is possible.

The type of documentation project I am invested in drawing attention to rejects the hierarchy of knowledge that is often replicated in traditional archiving practices. In employing the word "archiving" to describe the process of preserving the history, development, and creation of the performances, I am not conflating the traditional understanding of archives with the action of archiving. As Derrida makes clear, "Nothing is thus more troubled and more troubling today than the concept archived in this word 'archive'" (57). The word itself invokes images of dark and dusty shelves, old academics in tweed jackets bent over delicate pages, and the revered texts of history. Alongside these images, the word carries with it the weight of a history of exclusion and the reproduction of hierarchies of knowledge. Ultimately, archives are about power: the power to record, the power to decide what is worth recording, and the power to decide who can access what is recorded.[20] Thus, the archivist holds the power over curating the archive and the subsequent meaning created through that curatorial practice.

The creators of the texts at the center of this study do not leave the mediation of their history and performance to anyone else: They take on the process of archiving and documenting their own version of becoming. They are disrupting the traditional documentation of the present in an effort to go beyond the moment of the performance.[21] As Derrida reminds us, "The question of the archive is . . . a question of the past. . . . It is a question of the future, the question of the future itself, the question of a response, of a promise and of a responsibility for tomorrow" (27). The creators featured in this study are invoking the power of archiving to produce performance texts that offer expressions of resistance for their potential future engagement. They are wresting archiving power away from traditional archive makers to disrupt future erasures and misinterpretations of their actions and performances. They are, in effect, actively ensuring the preservation of their art and the histories of their community. In their texts, archiving becomes a ritual for remembering.

Analyzing these performances beyond the moment of embodiment—and focusing on the archiving project at play—acknowledges the centrality of seeing a text as much more than just the performance and its script. Instead, it frames these texts as a set of tools for theater practitioners and activists to use art and performance as part of a larger strategy of organizing. What makes these projects different from textbooks on performance, dramaturgical casebooks, or guidebooks on skill building is the privileging of stories and experiences as sites of knowledge.[22] The embodiment of these narratives becomes central to documenting oppression and efforts to challenge and resist. On their own, the performances teach us about intersectional oppression, but the behind-the-scenes writings, videos, and supplementary materials offer organizing guidance and models for future creative action. These materials interweave the personal narratives of the creators, allowing for a more intimate view of their artistic development and demystifying the process for a wider audience. Alongside incorporations of the personal, I read the archiving of methods and processes as a source of learning, further validating their authority as pedagogical tools.

Textual Mentoring

Although artistically inspiring, these texts also function as a form of "textual mentoring," if you will, that encapsulates the larger impact of the creators' works. Historically, mentoring has been understood as a practice between two individuals: one who has knowledge to share and one who learns from that knowledge. While these types of hierarchical mentoring relationships can be useful, we must look beyond the individual structure of mentoring in order to understand how the practice of textual mentoring can function outside of traditional constructions of support.[23] For many artists, activists, academics, and creators, lack of mentorship can be an overwhelming obstacle. If we think about the possibility of performance being created in part to help mentor the next generation of artists, activists, and scholars, we expand the parameters of how we define mentoring and organizing. Performance in service of community takes on a greater significance as it goes beyond the aesthetics of the work and expands access to strategies of resistance.

By thinking about mentoring outside of formal structures implemented by our organizations and institutions—or the more informal mentoring connections we make with friends and colleagues—we can increase the scope and impact of mentoring as a process that goes beyond simply sharing knowledge on individual success based on institutional goals. Instead, we can think about the process of mentoring as a form of navigational storytelling that offers those with less power and information a path through various systems and structures. This kind of textual mentoring is common in institutional realms like academia. For example, recently published works on the challenges faced by BIPOC faculty—including the scholarship in the edited volume *Presumed Incompetent II* (Flores Niemann et al.) and the research data offered in Ruth Zambrana's *Toxic Ivory Towers*—do not simply document oppressive work environments. They offer examples of how individuals share their personal stories in an effort to resist unjust treatment based on membership in marginalized groups. These stories document unfair labor practices and educate their readers on ways to navigate oppressive networks of power. For BIPOC scholars who lack mentorship on their own campuses, the texts become a source of mentoring as they navigate the structures in academia that disempower BIPOC faculty.

Most recently, Latinx feminist scholar Lorgia García Peña's book *Community as Rebellion* models for readers the ability to use a written text to help mentor and inspire. Through her own narrative of struggle and hardship, García Peña offers a roadmap for a liberatory education praxis that centers mentoring and teaching as a site for transformation—even within the hallowed halls of the nation's oldest heteropatriarchal academic institution. Her deliberate use of the word "syllabus" transforms the tool for organizing an ordinary course curriculum into an instrument for use outside of the traditional classroom. What makes this text especially inspiring for my conceptualization of mentoring is the emphasis García Peña places on lessons of rebellion originating outside of academia. She writes that she was "nurtured into rebellion" by the women who raised her and that it was "their *community* that made [her] rebellion possible" (xiv). Just as Audre Lorde reminded us that "survival is not an academic skill" (112), García Peña reminds us that our rebellion, our resistance, our visions for a more just future are rooted in our communities' teachings. We take those lessons into the classroom and transform our pedagogy, just as activists learn from our histories and transform our movements. For García Peña, her book "is an altar of words, onto which to lay collective hopes for the possibility of radical dreams, for redress, restitution, reparation, and triumph" (xiv). *Community as Rebellion* serves as an inspiration in thinking through how the practice of mentoring can be expanded to include written texts, especially in the absence of individual mentors. I read the archiving of processes, the insistence on being, and the documenting of embodied resistance as a form of rebellion—a way of mentoring opposition movements through the creation of performance.

The texts analyzed in this study center the stories of the marginalized in their performances, rooting personal narrative as the source of analysis in the evaluation of discrimination and oppression. The privileging of community stories in the history and performance reminds us that the personal is political, and it becomes part of an intersectional woman of color feminist praxis of creation. Such a praxis relies on learning from past social justice movements to create more inclusive visions of change and performances of resistance. I read the performance texts as sources of textual mentoring for future artivists and creators, providing guidance through their discussions of process, active archiving, and performance. In this way, we can use the texts to fill in the gaps in our own experiences and education. For many who lack the support of a mentoring relationship, the texts offer a roadmap of what is possible when combining art and activism.

While we can always learn from creative works, what sets these texts apart is the intentional sharing of information and strategy inherent in the performance of resistance. Creating a performance that incorporates pedagogical elements within it expands the project of learning from art to encompass a more active process of teaching through art. Through their teaching, the texts help guide an audience looking for ways of using art to advance change and to resist unjust structures of inequality. Viewed in such a way, these texts become a means of supplementing more traditional mentoring networks for creators and students of art and performance. Beyond simply providing a performance script, these texts are creating a repository of resistance that is actively working to inform, to inspire, and to advocate for social change.

Performing Resistance

In the following chapters, I analyze each creative text and the various processes that informed its creation. My framing and analysis of the texts follow the model they set forth of incorporating strategies of the past—models of previous resistance—to assemble a different way of reading performance and activism in the Latinx community. These texts illustrate how we can learn from histories of resistance, study strategies of organizing in the past, and use tools that have been used against us to better serve the needs of our communities.

Chapter 1 engages with the legacy of white feminism and the co-optation of that feminism by the military-industrial complex. Using Coco Fusco's dynamic *A Field Guide for Female Interrogators* as a site of analysis, I seek to unravel Fusco's complex engagement with an essentialist feminism that refuses to acknowledge the power that women wield when acting as agents for patriarchal structures—in this case, the military. Fusco, a Latina performance artist, scholar, and theorist, has long used her work to critique the use of BIPOC people to uphold white supremacist ideologies within structures of power. By focusing on *A Field Guide*'s fictionalized treatment of the torture of detainees at the hands of US military personnel, I situate the performance of the character Sergeant Fusco as a commentary on women's ability to carry out state violence upon others. The text—a combination of script, illustrations, and essays—epitomizes the possibilities of using performance to critique structures of power in the present but also to engage with previous moments of activism. By invoking Virginia Woolf in the essay and script, the text reminds us that a feminism that is simply devoted to issues of gender equality fails to account for intersecting nodes of oppression and can replicate other forms of prejudice and bias. By mimicking the genre of an instruction manual, *A Field Guide* also offers a brilliant co-optation of the format to leave the audience with a strategic tool in making state violence tangible. Fusco's text invites her audience to think about their own complicity in state violence and the ease with which the state can co-opt previous movements of resistance for its own use.

Chapter 2 situates Virginia Grise and Irma Mayorga's *The Panza Monologues*, both the text and the recording of its 2009 Los Angeles performance, as the embodiment of a resistance to the use of BIPOC women's bodies and stories of struggle for consumption. In direct conversation with V's (formerly Eve Ensler's) well-known and controversial *The Vagina Monologues*, *The Panza Monologues* decenters the vagina as the site of womanhood and instead focuses on the *panza*—the belly—the area of our bodies where so much of the everyday structural oppression we face gets processed. Through their emphasis on the body, the incorporation of Chicana stories, and the rejection of Western medical authority to define health, Grise and Mayorga call into question the legitimacy of single-identity-focused activism around violence against women and environmental racism. The power of *The Panza Monologues* lies not only in its script but also in the context, history, and resources the text offers, including writing exercises and a how-to guide. Grise and Mayorga's structuring of the text provides the audience with a script for the performance, but, as important, it explains the context for the creative work, including the structural oppression the community experiences. The creators focus their time and attention on discussing the women whose stories make up the script, ensuring that the personal narratives performed are moored in the women who themselves tell their stories. The number of resources the larger text offers provide a clear and helpful roadmap for inserting the stories of our own bodies into the larger conversation around gender, race, violence, and health.

Chapter 3 does not focus on a specific performance published in a text but instead centers the organized action and subsequent digital archive of the 2012 No Papers, No Fear Ride for Justice to study the role that performance plays in helping activists advocate for social change. I take the Ride as a case study that offers a powerful example of how activists and community members invoke performances of resistance from the past to create a new script of opposition for the present. Using digitally archived videos, blog entries, press releases, and news stories, I trace the Ride's movement from Phoenix, Arizona, to Charlotte, North Carolina, to explore the various performance strategies employed by the Riders and organizers in advocating for comprehensive immigration reform. The strategies used during the Ride were a combination of past movement scripts—including those of the civil rights and gay liberation movements—and current understandings of intersectional oppression, resulting in a performance of resistance that incorporates complex constructions of immigrant subjectivity. From the invocation of lowrider art culture to the works created by artists like Julio Salgado, Favianna Rodriguez, and César Maxit, the visual imagery of resistance played a vital role in the Ride's strategy to create a message of resistance rooted in community and love. By reading the Ride as a performance and its Riders as performers, I argue for the importance of recognizing how cultural producers are an integral part of activism and how activism inspires the creation of art that matters.

My reading of the works in *Beyond the Moment* might seem utopic and too hopeful, given how insurmountable the current structures of oppression might feel. But I find hope to be a form of resistance worth cultivating—a hope that is shaped by understandings of history, facts, and experience. This hope is grounded and not simply a form of excessively optimistic thinking or the product of a naïve understanding of systems of inequality. My visions of a hopeful future are deeply inspired by the work of José Esteban Muñoz, especially *Cruising Utopia*. Muñoz's conceptualization of queerness as a forward-dawning futurity and performative practice is integral to my understanding of resistance and community. My analysis expands Muñoz's notion of queer futurity, which, as he writes, "is not yet here" but represents a mode of imagining "new and better pleasures, other ways of being in the world, and ultimately new worlds" (1). This perspective allows me to frame Latinx performance as not only an enactment of resistance but also a site for imagining alternative temporal and spatial possibilities. Furthermore, Muñoz's assertion that "the present is not enough" provides a critical lens through which I examine the urgency and necessity of these performances in relation to their sociopolitical contexts (27). I draw on Muñoz's theorization of utopia as a "flight plan for a collective political becoming" to argue that the performative acts I analyze serve as blueprints for imagining and enacting a "fuller, vaster, more sensual, and brighter" future (189), while remaining attentive to the complexities and contradictions inherent in these acts of resistance.

The texts I write about in the following chapters illustrate the power that performance continues to hold in inspiring change and opposition. They range from a single authored script to a collaboration between artists and activists. Although different, each of the three texts focuses its attention on a specific issue that represents larger systems of oppression and violence. The texts create a repository of resistance that can act as a blueprint for future activists and creators working toward social justice. They model activist art informed by an intersectional analysis of inequality that rejects the single-identity-focused organizing of the past and makes clear that it is possible to incorporate all of our identities into our movements. By making their art available and their creative processes apparent, the creators are able to inspire and influence us beyond the moment of performance. They leave behind a documented history of enacting resistance, a rich archiving of knowledge, and a strategy for others to follow. They gesture toward the power and potential of creating art in the service of community. These performances are cruising utopia: learning from the past to organize in the present to work for a better future. They offer us a glimpse of what is possible when performance makes visible the structures that uphold inequity in order to help us topple them.

ONE

Performing Violence

Coco Fusco's Guide to Resistance

On a typical Wednesday evening in 2004, viewers tuned in to watch the CBS news program *60 Minutes II* and witnessed the breaking story that would generate an international scandal and challenge, yet again, the nation's credibility as a champion of democracy. The news segment, "Abuse at Abu Ghraib," documented the torture of detainees at the hands of US military personnel and set off a crisis for the military, the intelligence community, and the George W. Bush administration.[1] While rumors and stories about abuse of detainees had been circulating, the April 28 story provided visual proof to support these claims and focused worldwide attention on the cruelty taking place in the Iraq prison known as Abu Ghraib.[2] The photos included images of detainees being held in humiliating sexual poses, of guard dogs threatening attack, of a hooded figure standing on a box with electrical wires attached to his body. Alongside these detainees were military personnel, grinning and seemingly entertained by their abusive behavior. A few days later, *The New Yorker* posted an investigative piece by the journalist Seymour Hersh on its website that further supported the *60 Minutes II* segment on the abuse at Abu Ghraib and documented information from the military's own inquiries into the accusations of violence (Hersh, "Torture").

The allegations and photographs stunned the world and were especially difficult to fathom by those who continued to trust in the constructed narrative of the United States, and its military, as the force spreading democracy worldwide. In a 2016 interview, *60 Minutes II* executive producer Jeff Fager discussed his initial reaction to the pictures: "It was really hard to believe at first . . . because there hadn't been a lot of US involvement in a full-scale war, I think, shocking really, [that] Americans would do this to people who were prisoners. You like to think that the world is going to think more of America because they are going to meet our wonderful soldiers, you know, and so naïve . . . I was really shocked. We all were" (Fager). Fager's naïveté echoed the disbelief many expressed at the level of violence captured in those images. While previous allegations of abuse at the hands of intelligence officers and military officials had remained mostly hidden from public view, the visibility of Abu Ghraib made it impossible to simply sweep away the allegations.[3] The photographs gestured toward a level of cruelty that could not be justified, even by the staunchest supporters of the war effort, and led to calls for investigations and demands for justice.

The story of abuse and torture in Abu Ghraib posed a crisis for the Bush administration that had to be tactically addressed in a manner that allowed for the continued support of the war and the occupation of Iraq. Along with claims of ignorance and deniability, top military and intelligence officials scrambled to find a narrative to exculpate the administration. The Bush White House and top military leaders quickly distanced themselves from the violence, and the blame was placed squarely on the service personnel captured in the photographs. These individuals were seen as bad apples who had dishonored the military and the nation: individuals who went rogue and disobeyed standard operating procedures. They became the face of the scandal, and the media attention focused on them helped support the Bush administration's discursive strategy of deflection. The photographs and stories of abuse, however, would not be simply subsumed under the official narrative of deflection and negation.

Among the varied public responses to the Abu Ghraib story was surprise that women had been involved.[4] The traditional gender construction of women as weaker and more passive than men—more often the victims of violence—did not fit the image of Sabrina Harman and Lynndie England, the two female soldiers caught on film. The attention of the media quickly focused on these women, and speculation ran rampant on the role of Harman and England in the scandal. What had led to their involvement? Were they also victims, simply following orders of their male supervisors? Or were they as depraved as their fellow male soldiers? Harman and England's participation added a whole level of complexity that the media did not necessarily know how to address, and the public ignored, minimized, or fetishized the women's role in the torture of detainees. These women became the most visible of the bad apples, and discussions of their gender helped draw the focus further away from the larger military and intelligence structures that had permitted the torture to take place.

In the midst of the sensationalist coverage of the Abu Ghraib story, voices of resistance began to emerge. Artists, scholars, students, and activists refused to consume the narrative of the violence being the result of a few bad apples. Instead, they focused their words and creative energies on resisting the narrative that excused the administration of responsibility and on challenging the official account of the violence being an isolated incident outside of the parameters of standard operating procedures. They translated the findings of investigative journalists and scholars into creative works for the public that critiqued the governmental and military structures that had created the conditions under which torture not only was acceptable but became a form of entertainment. As in previous antiwar movements, art and performance became a tool for crafting oppositional narratives that centered the victims of the violence and rejected the xenophobia that framed the military's rationalization of its interrogation tactics. The artivism that emerged from this moment challenged the imperialist logic of the state—a logic that framed Iraq as a lawless land full of dangerous insurgents and religious fanatics—and refused to shift the responsibility for the violence from the US government and its agents.

This chapter focuses on one of the most powerful creative critiques of this moment, Coco Fusco's complex multimedia performance text *A Field Guide for Female Interrogators*—a work directly inspired by the photographs of Abu Ghraib, images "both real and imagined," that haunted Fusco (*Field Guide* 21). An award-winning and critically acclaimed Latina artist, scholar, and educator, Fusco is known for provocative and destabilizing interdisciplinary art that questions colonial legacies of power. Originally published in 2008—four years after the story of Abu Ghraib aired on *60 Minutes II*—*A Field Guide* is a rich work that includes several essays, a script of a performance recorded and available online, and an illustrated manual. Read as a whole, the text offers a brilliant critique of the abuse of power and the co-optation of feminism in the so-called war on terror. In the process of critiquing the actions of the US military and intelligence communities, the performance rejects the military's linguistic strategy of obfuscating the practice of torture under the guise of "interrogation." What makes Fusco's text especially relevant to my discussion of performance is its engagement with feminist activism of the past and the cache of military and government reports and documents on the US government's use of violent interrogation practices. Fusco repurposes repressive ideological tools to create a counterperformance that subverts structures of power. Her extensive research, documented throughout the piece, is translated into a creative performance of resistance that I situate as an archive of opposition to sanctioned state violence. I read this repository as part of a legacy of oppositional storytelling through performance and as a form of textual mentoring—a type of mentoring that offers guidance through discussions of process and active archiving and thus a roadmap for resistance—for future generations of readers and activists creating art in service of marginalized communities.

While the events of Abu Ghraib may have faded from our national consciousness—like most atrocities carried out in the name of the nation—their legacy remains with us, offering a lesson in the corruption of power and the complicity of human beings in the oppression of others. Fusco's text documents this history and provides an alternative interpretation of that legacy. *A Field Guide* becomes part of a longer Chicanx/Latinx tradition of using art in service of antiwar campaigns to draw connections between the oppression experienced by communities of color in the United States, who continue to live with the imperialist legacy of the nation, and the oppression experienced by communities of color abroad, who are being affected by modern forms of US imperialism.[5] I also read *A Field Guide* as a cautionary tale of the dangers of believing that gender and racial equality is possible under a system of power that continues to uphold white supremacy and heteropatriarchy. This reading rejects simplistic ideas of equality and instead offers a powerful example of how our movements for change can be co-opted and used against us and other marginalized communities. Positioned as an intervention in the violent erasure of injustice and historical amnesia that surrounds US imperialist projects, Fusco's guide becomes a blueprint for creating art that challenges our conceptions of gender, power, and violence. In archiving her creative process and translating official discourse into narratives of resistance, Fusco's performance goes beyond the moment and offers a model to study and learn from in creating future works of resistance and refusal. In thinking about the power of performance to educate and inspire, *A Field Guide* becomes another tool for creators and future artists to use in crafting their own works of resistance.

The Theater of War: Setting the Stage

The photographs of the Abu Ghraib prison torture offer one small part of a much larger picture of abuse at the hands of the US government and its agents. While the photographs were at the center of the national conversation on Abu Ghraib, Fusco's text pulls back from them to show her audience—both in her live performance and in her text—a much more complicated landscape of state-sanctioned violence and the role that gender plays in orchestrating that violence. *A Field Guide* focuses instead on making visible the connections between multiple structures of power and the actions of the so-called bad apples. The richness of the text's multimedia format offers the audience an opportunity to deeply engage with the topics Fusco unravels. The structure of *A Field Guide* is an especially important aspect of how the message of the text is delivered to its audience. The work is divided into four sections, in the following order: a series of three essays written in the form of a letter to Virginia Woolf, titled "Invasion of Space by a Female"; a copy of an FBI memo; a script of *Our Feminist Future*; and the illustrated field guide that shares its title with the larger text. While each section is compelling on its own, read as a whole they offer a powerful and disturbing critique of women's role in the ever-expanding project of war and the perpetuation of violence against communities seen as inferior based on race, religion, and other markers of difference. In my analysis of *A Field Guide*, I read each segment of Fusco's text and its specific interventions separately, beginning with the performance script. Such a reading allows for an analysis of the text both as a performance and as a pedagogical tool for organizing artistic resistance.

The 2008 published version of the performance text is a culmination of several years of work that Fusco began shortly after the Abu Ghraib photographs were made public. The performance included in *A Field Guide*, *Our Feminist Future*, is a version of Fusco's earlier work *A Room of One's Own: Women and Power in the New America*, first presented in June 2006 at the Victoria and Albert Museum in London and performed in various venues from 2006 to 2008.[6] *Our Feminist Future* is the script of the performance delivered at a Museum of Modern Art symposium, The Feminist Future. The performance is structured to mimic the format of a military briefing and is based on Fusco's extensive research. Part of her research included participation in a July 2005 course on interrogation run by Team Delta, a group of retired military interrogators.[7] Her experience with Team Delta deeply influenced her understanding of how torture is constructed by interrogators and the role that performance plays in the practice of information gathering.

For Fusco, an understanding of the relationship between interrogation and performance provides insight into the strategies of the interrogator and helps expose the abuses that take place in the performance of interrogation. In explaining her methodology, Fusco makes clear the connection between performance and torture: "What I learned is that every interrogator assumes a fictional persona when working" (*Field Guide* 28). She writes that "for many human rights activists who seek to condemn the use of torture by the US military, considering interrogation as a form of performance and as a kind of political theater might seem like a distraction or even a perverse avoidance of the 'real' issue" (*Field Guide* 68). Although Fusco acknowledges this concern, she argues that looking at torture and interrogation as a form of performance is a powerful tool in recognizing the organizing logic of the practice. As is the case with the construction and performance of identity, understanding the artificial enactment of interrogation allows for a deeper analysis of the actions of the interrogator and the ideologies directing those actions.

Fusco's creative use of a framework that positions torture as dependent on performance is essential to her work's impact and significance, as it allows her to replicate the performance of interrogation practices. She reasons that "torture is indeed painfully real, but theater and performance are crucial to make it work. The tortured person is made to believe that things may happen through illusions created by the combined effects of stress and suggestion. Theatrical devices are put to the service of coercion. Soldiers learn to disassociate emotionally and psychologically from the violence they perpetrate by developing interrogator characters in the same way that actors shape their personae" (*Field Guide* 68–69). Fusco is not the only theater scholar to make such a connection. Her methodology aligns with Diana Taylor's argument that "the recognition of the performance qualities of terrorism and torture does not reduce them to performance acts; on the contrary, it allows for their demystification" ("Theater and Terrorism" 166). While

Taylor is specifically referencing Griselda Gambaro's staging of the state-perpetrated political violence that occurred during Argentina's "Dirty War," Taylor's analysis of state violence through the lens of performance is useful in further understanding how interrogation and torture rely on presentation to instill fear and ensure compliance.

In discussing Fusco's disruption and appropriation of terminology and her insistence on using performance as a lens of analysis, it is also worth noting the reference to the word "theater" and its employment by the military. While the word is most often used to indicate a play or dramatic performance, the space in which such performance takes place, and a tiered seating room (including lecture halls and cinemas), it is also used by the military to describe a space of engagement, the theater of operations. The War Department's 1943 *Field Service Regulations, Administration* manual defined a theater of operations as the portion of "land, sea, and air areas . . . necessary for military operations, either offensive or defensive, pursuant to an assigned mission, and for the administration incident to such military operations" (7). The War Department's guide organizes the theater of operations into the combat zone, where the active operations take place, and the communications zone, where the administration of the action is performed.[8] While the connection between the performance of interrogation and the theater of operations might not seem important, such a connection allows for an analysis of the role performance plays in shaping our perception of military campaigns and strategies of war. Interrogation is also dependent on two different zones. In this case, the combat zone is the room where the active abuse takes place, while the communications zone is where the actions of the interrogator are directed. When Fusco discusses the performativity inherent in torture, an understanding of the military stage on which torture is located allows for a more informed analysis of what is taking place in the interrogation room.

Looking at how these forms of state violence are reliant on performance and theatricality pulls back the curtain and identifies the actors who carry out such violence, providing an opportunity to look beyond the performance to focus on the histories and structures that direct such brutality. *A Field Guide* contributes to a larger discussion on structures of violence by embodying the performance of interrogation itself. Fusco's occupation of the role of interrogator destabilizes and denaturalizes the performance. As José Esteban Muñoz points out, "Fusco infiltrates rather than attacks" (Fusco and Muñoz 137). Her infiltration is essential to subverting the state's power to shape the narrative around torture and interrogation practices.

Our Feminist Future
Sergeant Fusco Takes the Stage

In *Our Feminist Future*, the third section of *A Field Guide*, Fusco expands her critical analysis of the military to include the art world, showing how both institutions have manipulated feminist discourse to appropriate and negate its power. The script is introduced with a brief paragraph that sets up the context for Fusco's performance at the January 2007 symposium at MoMA. In *Our Feminist Future*, Fusco alters her original 2006 performance of *A Room of One's Own: Women and Power in the New America* to draw connections between performances of gender inclusivity by both the military and the art world.[9] While her critique of the art world isn't the central focus of my analysis, Fusco's decision to publish this specific revised version of the performance is important, especially as she references the original version in her opening essay. I limit my discussion of the MoMA performance in favor of focusing attention on the script provided in the text. It is the script included in the book and is therefore in conversation with the previous two sections of the text. Reading the assimilation of feminist discourse occurring in both the military and the museum demonstrates the ease with which the goals of past movements of resistance can be twisted and turned into a discourse of advancement that does nothing to change structures of inequality: It only creates a performance of progress to obfuscate the continued oppression of marginalized groups. I read *Our Feminist Future* not only as Fusco's critique of the art world's and the military's use of feminism but also as a performance of resistance through her infiltration of space and appropriation of tools used by these two powerful institutions.

In the introduction to the script, Fusco strongly critiques the public discourse around feminist art that the symposium created, including the question of whether feminist art and feminist art history have been mainstreamed. For Fusco, the discussion seemed a misguided one, based on her own experiences as a feminist artist. For her, "the art world continues to be hostile to all practices that politicize aesthetic values and ruling tastes . . . [and] neither MoMA nor MOCA were committing to acquire feminist art works." She informs the audience that she "decided to use my fifteen minutes on a MoMA podium to perform as a visitor from the US Army who had arrived to congratulate my peers in the art world for their strategic containment of feminism and their effective use of women" (*Field Guide* 93). Her presentation underscores the performative nature of the event: merely token gestures toward inclusion that don't invest in the fostering and supporting of feminist art making. The strategies of repression practiced in the art world and in the military converge in the performance through Fusco's embodied resistance to the symposium's empty celebration of feminist art. Naming this section of the text *Our Feminist Future* reworks the title of the symposium, The Feminist Future, and expands the conversation around feminism and the future beyond the realm of the art world.

The introductory paragraph is followed by a two-page photograph, credited to Kambui Olujimi, from Fusco's 2006 performance of *A Room of One's Own: Women and Power in the New America* (*Field Guide* 94–95). On one side of the spread, Fusco's face dominates the page. She is dressed in army fatigues, and we can see the stars of the American flag behind her. On the opposite page, we see a blurry image of smoke billowing from the Twin Towers. The image of the attack on the towers is situated in the upper left and fills almost three-quarters of the page. The darkness that surrounds the towers makes the black-and-white image more visually striking. Fusco's face is framed between the two symbols—the American flag and the burning towers—and is turned slightly right. The photograph captures her in the middle of speaking, and while her gaze is not directed immediately toward the audience, we can sense her sadness. The image positions her feminist body—even in its performative drag—at the center of a larger discussion of patriotism, terrorism, and military violence. The inclusion of the burning towers is significant, as it contextualizes the so-called war on terror and the role that torture has played since the fall of the towers. The powerful image of the towers has become a vital tool in the propaganda that follows the justification of torture and the obfuscation of the unethical nature of the practice.

Fusco's short introduction and two-page image precede the script of *Our Feminist Future*, which she performed as part of the panel "Activism, Race, and Geopolitics." The panel included Fusco (as Sergeant Fusco) and two artists from the Guerrilla Girls, Frida Kahlo and Käthe Kollwitz, along with art historians Carrie Lambert-Beatty and Richard Meyer. The performance recording, available on MoMA's website, offers the opportunity to witness how the character of Sergeant Fusco comes to embody Fusco's critique of structures of power ("Feminist Future"). While the majority of my analysis of *Our Feminist Future* is focused on the published script, I briefly discuss the taped version to illustrate how Fusco's performance unfolds on the stage—in this case, during the symposium at MoMA. The recorded performance begins with David Little, the museum's director of adult and academic programs, who, after announcing that a cocktail party will follow the panel discussion, introduces the artist: "We will start off with Sergeant Fusco. She will begin by disciplining us"—a subtle but titillating nod to BDSM that causes the audience to laugh and clap ("Feminist Future").[10] Little's sexual innuendo is reminiscent of the eroticized discourse that was often used when describing Harman and England.

During Little's welcoming remarks, Fusco is the only one onstage, sitting at the far left of the frame. She sits with her head down, looking up occasionally. As Little leaves the stage, Sergeant Fusco rises and walks to the podium. At this point, the audience can see her full body, dressed in military fatigues, with a cap on her head and glasses on her face. As she stands at the podium, her back straight and in a commanding pose intended to express authority, she looks out at the audience, speaking to them in a clear and decisive monotone voice. Occasionally, she looks down at her paper and to the side, toward her slides. Her presentation style, dry and informative, mimics the more formal type of presentation one would expect in a military briefing. She adjusts her glasses at various moments, and at one point she breaks from her script to acknowledge that she has fallen behind in her slide presentation—"Oh boy, I'm behind here" ("Feminist Future"). While her delivery is very straitlaced and matter-of-fact, there are moments when she emphasizes specific words by slightly raising her volume and uses strategic pauses to make a point, but she never breaks character.

Initially, it might be unclear to the audience why Fusco has chosen to perform this role at what is supposed to be an event celebrating the accomplishments of feminists in the art world. The uncomfortable and hesitant laughter scattered throughout Sergeant Fusco's presentation documents the audience's discomfort with the performance and their possible confusion.[11] Fusco uses her time on the panel to critique the US military's interrogation practices while making the uncomfortable connection between the military's and the art world's appropriation of feminism. As Sergeant Fusco continues, the performance makes the uncomfortable connections visible, and its critique of both institutions becomes clear. In a conversation on the reasons women join the military, scholar-activist Setsu Shigematsu argues that "the compartmentalized approach taken by many feminists and civilians is that they believe themselves to be outside and above the military system; and therefore don't interrogate enough the complementary function of these institutions, and how the education system and the military work together" (99). As creatives and supporters of the arts, the audience at MoMA would not have seen themselves as connected to the ideological underpinnings of the military, but as Shigematsu points out and Sergeant Fusco illustrates, the two institutions' co-optation of feminism for the purpose of upholding structures of power is based on similar sociopolitical constructions of gender and power.[12] Beyond their similar approaches to what Fusco has called the "effective use of women," both the military and the museum industry are rooted in the same colonial education system—a system based on white supremacy and violence.

In the case of the MoMA audience, their understanding of the critiques being made would have been dependent on individual knowledge of Abu Ghraib and the violence of interrogation. While watching the MoMA performance live must have been electrifying, it is possible that many in the audience would have been unable to recognize, or unwilling to acknowledge, the critique Fusco was making in the performance. In contrast, the essays and memo that precede the published script offer the audience of the written version a more complex critique of structures of power. The published script highlights the potential for a performance to live beyond the moment of embodiment and, in this case, the possibilities of creating a multimedia performance text that can expand the scope of the conversation. Given that the majority of the focus of *A Field Guide* is on the military's acculturation of feminism and its weaponization of femininity, I concentrate my analysis on this part of Fusco's performance script.

Sergeant Fusco on the Page

The script of *Our Feminist Future* begins with Sergeant Fusco addressing the audience and invoking the religiously patriotic rhetoric of the phrase "God bless America." Sergeant Fusco sets the stage for the performance, speaking the military's language and telling her audience that she has been "briefing the civilian community on the subject of female interrogators and their use of sexual innuendo as a crucial weapon in the fight against global terrorism" (*Field Guide* 97). By setting up *Our Feminist Future* as a military briefing, Fusco integrates the audience into her performance, making us part of the act.[13] Sergeant Fusco explains that these civilian briefings are aimed at making it "more widely known that the War on Terror offers women an unprecedented opportunity to demonstrate our strength and charm by providing us with an enemy for whom sexuality is a key weak point" (97). The language is important, as it innocuously refers to female interrogators' use of sexual innuendo as a weapon that can be wielded in service of the nation's fight against terrorism. Fusco alludes to a connection between women's strength and their charm, a gendered generalization that illustrates the limited discourse of a femininity constructed purely in terms of sexuality. It also positions the ability to demonstrate this "strength" as being contingent on an enemy that is deliberately framed as "weak," replicating the sexist practice of defining women only by their relationship to men. Sergeant Fusco continues, "As female interrogators we can take advantage of the fact that the male populations of traditional societies cannot conceive of us as powerful or violent, much less as highly trained military officers. Thus, we use the tried and true B&B tactic, posing as 'bimbos and babes' to extract actionable intelligence without them knowing what is happening to them" (98).[14] By naming the strategy "bimbos and babes," Sergeant Fusco uses humor to make light of the tactic, but the audience knows that the two terms carry strong sexist connotations. While the terms might be funny, the underlying message that reduces women's worth to their sexuality is not.[15]

Given that the military is an institution founded on masculinity and violence, it shouldn't come as a surprise that female soldiers are expected to perform the gender stereotypes upheld by this heteropatriarchal organization. Fusco's audience is aware of the masculinist structure of the military, and some might even be aware of the struggles female soldiers have faced when trying to integrate into this bastion of maleness. Fusco's script turns its focus to the military's strategies for incorporating women into its ranks. Sergeant Fusco offers a brief history on the need to recruit women following the end of the draft and the "expanding theater of operations in the age of global warfare" (100). She points out that it was necessary that the incorporation of more women into the military not be seen as a form of weakness or as a capitulation to the feminist movement's demands for gender equality. Thus, the military's challenge became one of getting the most out of female ambition while also "severing the attraction to power from the desire for change" (101): in other words, attract women with the promise of empowerment but ensure that it is based on assimilation into the structures of power in place and divorced from any attempts to use power to change the system.

Fusco's character tells her audience that the military "had to train our recruits to embrace the golden rule that in order to be good soldiers they have to stop thinking about being women" (101). Her words gesture to an understanding of how the discourse of assimilation serves the military's incorporation of women into its ranks.[16] Our social movements are littered with strategies of assimilation—strategies aimed at becoming part of the system and not dismantling the system itself. Given the military's insistence on uniformity and unquestioned obedience, such an assimilationist strategy would seem to work well, but, ironically, the military did not forget that these recruits were women. What the story of Abu Ghraib and the subsequent information made public have proven is that those in power instead found ways of exploiting female recruits' femininity—an exploitation based on their own sexism and misogyny. In Fusco's earlier discussion on women's current incorporation into the military, she writes that "key to all these deployments of female sexuality as a weapon is that they are planned. To me they are indicative of the state's instrumentalist attitude toward gender, sexuality and cultural difference. In other words, if the military is going to incorporate women, it is also going to capitalize on their particular assets and take advantage of permissive societal attitudes regarding sexual exhibitionism" (*Field Guide* 47). The character's invoking of assimilationist politics in the performance draws on Fusco's larger critique of how exploiting gender has become just one more strategy in larger colonial projects currently being carried out by the military.

The military is nothing if not opportunistic in how it has incorporated women into the armed forces without eroding the heteropatriarchal power of the institution. Sergeant Fusco tells her audience that "the sexual freedom women gained in the course of the twentieth century has turned out to be a highly effective means of disarming our enemies" (*Field Guide* 97). That sexual freedom has been used not only in the abusive interrogation tactics but also in framing our military interventions. As Fusco argues, "Women's presence also creates the impression that American institutions engaging in domination are actually democratic, since they appear to practice gender equity" (*Field Guide* 41). This critique aligns with Zillah Eisenstein's argument that "imperial democracy uses racial diversity and gender fluidity to disguise itself—and females and people of color become its decoys. . . . Imperial democracy mainstreams women's rights discourse into foreign policy and militarizes women for imperial goals" (27).[17] In this way, the US armed forces become the harbingers of democracy and the liberators of oppressed women in the Global South.[18]

The use of white women in imperial projects is not a new occurrence. In fact, it is an old strategy that has served colonial powers well. For the past three centuries, "empires . . . found that if they could devise ways to hold up their own women as models of civilization and purity, while at the same time demoting the men of the conquered territories as either hypermasculinized savages or feminized Others, then empire-building became easier" (Enloe 37).[19] The US military has revised these colonial strategies to move away from notions of feminine purity in favor of embracing the sexual liberation of American female soldiers as part of so-called civilizing and modernizing projects. Writer and organizer Huibin Amelia Chew implicates feminists in this process, pointing out that "burqas and veils have come to embody the ultimate in gendered persecution. Bikinis equal freedom; sex is emancipation. In this way, imperial feminist attitudes help to render our own patriarchy invisible" (82–83). Fusco's performance echoes these critiques, illustrating how adept the US military has become at exploiting the femininity and sexuality of its female service members while ensuring that heteropatriarchal structures remain intact.

Fusco uses her character to further critique the unquestioned incorporation of women into the military and the individualistic discourse used to enfold women into the homogeneity of the armed forces. Sergeant Fusco explains how the political conservatism of the 1980s has made the tenets of the feminist movement undesirable to new recruits, and that for them "the personal is profitable as long as the political is inimical to it" (*Field Guide* 102). Sergeant Fusco claims that although most women who join the military have successfully stayed away from "the feminist dinosaurs that continue to walk the earth and talk up a storm," the military has created a plan to contend "with potential disruption, or even better, form preemptive strikes against the return of radicalism" (102). She offers the audience recommendations of strategies the military has employed, including finding ways "to make women's achievement seem antithetical to feminist politics. Make sure to show that lots of attractive and appealing women already cooperate in, if not lead, this process" (102–103). Her words make clear the performative politics of gender and the importance that the visual plays in creating an image of female empowerment that continues to work in service of the existing power structure. It isn't enough to have women visibly in power. The women paraded as examples of success must not only support the structure that rewards their complicity but also continue to uphold patriarchal standards of nonthreatening femininity to offer desirable images of achievement.

Sergeant Fusco's ironic celebration of the opportunistic co-optation of feminism by the military echoes the critiques that many radical feminists have made about women's ascendance into the higher echelons of power. As Shigematsu points out, "Now we have a select category of women in the US who have risen into the ranks of powerful white men, whether that is in the military, government, corporations or the academy. The way in which women in the US become 'empowered' often involves a process of assimilation, incorporation and domestication by the values and practices of established institutions" (99). Fusco's character, her version of Shakespeare's sister, embodies the assimilation necessary to become part of the power structure—in this case, the military. Through Sergeant Fusco's performance, we come to see how easy it is for the military to use female soldiers' desire for success in service of the institution. Power is seductive, and Sergeant Fusco exposes the strategies used to incorporate women into the military while ensuring they do not question the structure in place.

The military, however, is merely following an established pattern of behavior. As Shigematsu argues, the assimilation and domestication of women may be found in all institutions of power, including the museum industry that Fusco also critiques in the performance. The danger in seeing individual advancement as a representation of progress lies in the unquestioned perpetuation of structural oppression and violence. In her critique of the co-optation of feminism, Chew writes that "'feminism' is becoming a power-CEO or Secretary of State Condoleezza Rice. This shallow vision of gender justice has so permeated even progressive circles that our very definition of sexism is circumscribed. Too often, sexism is merely seen as a set of cultural behaviors or personal biases; challenging sexism is simply seen as breaking these gender expectations. But sexism is an institutionalized system, with historical, political, and economic dimensions" (88).[20] Separating feminism from other forms of structural oppression allows for its co-optation and incorporation into the institutions that feminism is supposed to be working to transform or dismantle. While she might be a fictional character, Sergeant Fusco is a reminder of the real and problematic incorporation of women into structures of power. In her discussion of former Brigadier General Janis Karpinski's memoir, and Karpinski's belief in herself "as part of a generation that led a feminist revolution within the military," Fusco asks, "How could feminism be reconciled with the goals of an authoritarian and patriarchal structure like the military?" (*Field Guide* 61). The text encourages its audience to question their ideas of power and to resist the discourse invoked by Sergeant Fusco's performance of militarized femininity.

The Scripting of Race

In studying Sergeant Fusco's embodiment of assimilated femininity, it is also important to discuss how race functions in the co-optation of women's sexuality by the military. Fusco does not use the word "race" in the script, instead replicating the linguistic practice of using the racially coded language central to the intelligence community's weaponization of sexuality. Such coded language attempts to circumvent charges of racism by relying on the discourse of cultural difference to explain constructions of nonwhite communities. Sergeant Fusco's parroting of broad generalizations about Muslim men—for example, as being vulnerable because of their views of sexuality—plays into the practice of othering that is at the center of the linguistic strategy invoked when discussing global terrorism. This rhetorical construction of the Islamic world is predicated on Orientalist legacies and Islamophobic misconceptions to further vilify Muslim men.[21] The strategy described by Sergeant Fusco relies on the stereotype of "traditional societies"—in this case, Middle Eastern societies—being less modern because their antiquated notions of gender do not recognize women's power. The irony of her words lies in the subtle way in which the strategy also applies to the US military's own sexist view of female soldiers, which positions them as merely "bimbos and babes" whose talents in intelligence gathering are based solely on the objectification of their bodies. Fusco's performance text illustrates that to exploit the sexuality of its female service members, the military must rely on its own sexist and racist ideologies of gender and not necessarily on an informed understanding of non-Western cultures.[22]

Fusco strategically employs an intersectional framework in crafting her character's dialogue. Although she does not specifically discuss Abu Ghraib in the performance, the letter to Virginia Woolf and the FBI memo that precede the script in the text ensure that her broader audience will be aware of the prison and the abuses that took place at the hands of US military personnel.[23] She doesn't refer to the racial difference of the detainees, instead relying on the coded language of racism when using words like "traditional" and gesturing to racial difference through the language of cultural and religious difference. While the euphemisms might work to obfuscate the racist and colonialist legacies inherent in these military strategies, the visual evidence in the Abu Ghraib photographs makes clear that race is only possible to ignore when one refuses to look closely. In "When Is Prisoner Abuse Racial Violence?" feminist scholar Sherene Razack writes, "My stomach contracts and I feel a deep chill in every pore of my Brown skin when I see the prisoner abuse photos. I know that this is about racism." She wonders, "So why are so many publicly reluctant to say so? Or is it that we can't get our words in print?" Razack's powerful words of recognition intervene in the mainstream silence around the race of Muslim detainees. The proof of racism is present in the discourse and images that surround military and intelligence campaigns in the Middle East and Central Asia. Abu Ghraib becomes an embodiment of this racism. As transnational feminist Isis Nusair has argued, "Militarized and masculine presumptions about the oriental other were at the heart of the acts of sexual domination at Abu Ghraib. These were not singular or pathological events, but systematic oppressive acts integral to power relations and complex productions and significations of gender, race and sexuality" (182). Sergeant Fusco's dialogue gestures to the convoluted and complex power relations that facilitated the torture of detainees at Abu Ghraib.

The representation of race in *Our Feminist Future* is a complicated one, in part because of Sergeant Fusco's role as an agent of the state. In today's current political climate, the military would be much more cautious in vocalizing the racist ideologies that underpin their understanding of Muslim communities. Thus, Sergeant Fusco is limited in her ability to openly discuss race, which limits the performance's critique of the racism present in the violence perpetrated on Muslim detainees. Unlike her character, Fusco, the interdisciplinary artist and scholar, has built her reputation as one of the most important radical voices in the art world. For those in attendance at the MoMA symposium, Fusco's racialized body and her status as a woman of color artist would have provided some context for the performance and the critique being made.[24] As members of the art world, it is likely the audience would have known about Fusco's critique of the racist and imperialist logic of colonial institutions, including the museum. After all, this is the artist whose 1992 performance of an Indigenous woman in *Two Undiscovered Amerindians Visit the West*, in collaboration with Guillermo Gómez-Peña, garnered international attention.[25] For an audience unaware of Fusco's long history of intersectional art making and scholarship, Sergeant Fusco's roundabout way of critiquing racist ideologies in the military would be harder to recognize.

Fusco's identity as a woman of color and Sergeant Fusco's nonwhite presence further complicate the performance's representation of race. If the role of state agent is being played by a woman of color, what does it say about the absorption of communities of color into the service of the nation?[26] How would the predominantly white audience at MoMA read Sergeant Fusco's race and its relationship to power? While it would be easy to read the performance as an illustration of the assimilation of women and people of color into the military, Fusco's ironic use of the military briefing and the biting critique of mainstream feminism in her earlier essays add complexity to this analysis. I want to read Fusco's sardonic performance as a form of resistance to the shift from oppositional to hegemonic that B. V. Olguín traces in his analysis of Latina/o writings spanning the war on terror. Olguín identifies a growing number of cultural texts by Chicanx/Latinx people and Latin American immigrants that embrace the capitalist and imperialist ideologies of the United States and its military, especially after 9/11.[27] *A Field Guide* stands in opposition to this disturbing shift. While Fusco's text does not directly address race, her critique of women in the military is predicated on an intersectional analysis that recognizes the hegemonic shift in the militarization of feminism and communities of color. As a Latina, Sergeant Fusco's character implicates communities of color in the service of imperial US projects, and women of color are not exempt from this critique. An especially useful lens for reading the text's intersectional feminist framing is Muñoz's argument that "by considering the ways in which US womanhood becomes militarized, Fusco's audiences understand how women 'over here' and 'over there' are part of globalization's oppressive script" (Fusco and Muñoz 139). Sergeant Fusco embodies the colonial logic of women "over here" who are actively working against the interests of marginalized women in Iraq, Afghanistan, and other nations in the Global South. The audience is left with the knowledge that Sergeant Fusco's racial identity does not exempt her from absorption into the nation's imperial war machine. The character embodies the white Western feminism that transnational feminists of color have been criticizing for decades. As Melanie Richter-Montpetit points out, we can make sense of the role of female-identified soldiers in the violence "if we understand 'Operation Iraqi Hope' as a colonial endeavor, the racialized encounter between prison guards and detainees as a colonial one and the torturing of detainees as acts of colonial violence rooted in the desire to enact 'Whiteness'" (45).

The performance and script of *Our Feminist Future* make a powerful intervention in the mainstream constructions of gender and power and put forth an alternative analysis of what happens in a practice of interrogation based on colonial histories of racial and gender violence. It is a practice that involves torture, no matter how strongly the US government denies it or tries to frame it. Fusco writes that "for those in proximity to the practice, torture is experienced as a real life political drama that ritualizes the violence of occupation through excruciating compulsory performances of mental and body submission. We, on the other hand, are experiencing torture . . . as a spectacle from a faraway place" (*Field Guide* 35). With her script and the MoMA performance, Fusco brings the spectacle to us—the audience at MoMA, the reader of her script, the viewer of the recording. She is again making the connection between performance and drama and implicating us in our roles as spectators. In her letter to Woolf, Fusco writes, "I knew I couldn't bring an end to women's involvement in torture by writing or making art about it, but at least I could make an effort to understand it through a dialogue that would help me and other civilians to look more closely at what soldiers do" (*Field Guide* 64–65). The script and its performance at MoMA are part of this larger project of fostering discussions on gender, violence, and power and acknowledging our own complicity as subjects of the nation. The translating of research into performance further offers Fusco's audience a model for creating art in opposition.

The Players Behind the Curtain

In order to comprehend Fusco's intervention in the official narrative of torture and state violence, it is important to understand the context under which Fusco created *A Field Guide* and performed *Our Feminist*

Future. When the torture of detainees at Abu Ghraib prison became public, the Bush administration spun into crisis resolution mode and called for multiple investigations into the abuse. The most prevalent narrative in the official reports that followed the military investigations blamed the torture of Abu Ghraib detainees on a handful of individuals and absolved the US military of responsibility. After Specialist Joseph Darby delivered physical evidence of the abuse to the army's Criminal Investigation Division, the military ordered multiple investigations into the treatment of detainees at the prison and at other military installations. The findings of these investigations were conveyed to military officials in various reports, including the March 2004 Taguba Report (investigation led by Major General Antonio M. Taguba), the August 2004 Schlesinger Report (led by former Secretary of Defense James R. Schlesinger), the August 2004 Fay-Jones Report (led by Major General George R. Fay and Lieutenant General Anthony R. Jones), the March 2005 Church Report (led by Vice Admiral Albert T. Church III), the April 2005 Green Report (led by Lieutenant General Stanley E. Green), and the April 2005 Schmidt-Furlow Report (led by Lieutenant General Randall M. Schmidt and Brigadier General John T. Furlow). The Taguba, Schlesinger, and Fay-Jones investigations were specifically focused on the events that had occurred at Abu Ghraib, the system in place that had allowed for the abuses to take place, the leadership structure, and the overall operations of the prison.[28]

All three of the army investigations—those led by Taguba, Schlesinger, and Fay and Jones—offer hundreds of pages of documentation regarding the events of Abu Ghraib. The executive summary of the Fay-Jones Report summarized the investigators' findings that "the chain of command directly above the 205th MI Brigade was not directly involved in the abuses at Abu Ghraib. However, policy memoranda promulgated by the CJTF-7 Commander led indirectly to some of the non-violent and non-sexual abuses" (Fay and Jones 4).[29] In its executive summary, the Schlesinger Report claimed that the images of the abuse represent "deviant behavior and a failure of military leadership and discipline" (Schlesinger 5).[30] Taguba's findings, published in the report most critical of the abuse, acknowledged the level of cruelty but also focused a great deal of attention on the lack of leadership and mistakes made in the chain of command (Taguba 16).[31] While the Taguba Report indicated that the abuse was more widespread than initially recognized, it placed most of the blame on the individuals who were captured on camera performing the violent acts and on those in direct command, specifically former Brigadier General Janis Karpinski.[32] All three of the reports focus their attention on the bad behavior of the few and excuse it as possible only because of the extenuating circumstances present at Abu Ghraib prison: the absence of enough trained personnel, the overcrowding of the prison, the unclear directives from leadership, the ambiguous command structure, and the confusion over approved interrogation practices. The reports are also quick to emphasize the notion that these bad apples did not represent the majority of those who served in the military.[33] The strategy of casting abusive personnel as outliers works as a smoke screen to divert attention from the systemic abuse of detained individuals that is part and parcel of the theater of war. The lack of training, resources, and personnel at Abu Ghraib may have made for horrible working conditions, but these conditions cannot be used to rationalize the human rights violations of detainees.

The restrictive focus of each investigation assured the creation and perpetuation of a coherent set of narratives that placed the blame for the abuse on the seven individuals charged and on the lack of leadership offered under Karpinski's command, rather than on the structure under which the abuse was possible. As Mark Danner points out, "With no fear of a full, top-to-bottom investigation from a Congress that is firmly in Republican hands, administration officials, and particularly those at the Department of Defense, have managed to orchestrate a slowly unfolding series of inquiries, almost all of them carried out within the military by officers who by definition can only direct their gaze down the chain of command, not up it" (40).[34] Where the reports clearly succeeded was in limiting the focus of the investigations and covering up the widespread abuse found within the military's structure of detainment and interrogation. While the storyline in the various military reports echoes the account promoted by the White House and the mainstream media, there is ample evidence that the decision to interrogate detainees with more extreme interrogation techniques was not limited to the individuals caught up in the Abu Ghraib case.[35]

Scripting Torture

The abuses at Abu Ghraib did not happen in a military bubble or in isolation from national policies. They are part of a long history of imperial violence perpetrated by the military and the intelligence community on the nation's so-called enemies—a violence that has only increased since 9/11. These abuses were also in line with the sanctioned practices of torture known as "enhanced interrogation techniques," which ignored the protections for prisoners set in place by the Geneva Conventions. Multiple memoranda written by the US Justice Department's Office of Legal Counsel indicate a larger conversation on the use of enhanced interrogation taking place before the abuse at Abu Ghraib was documented.[36] While the early 2000s memos do not directly link to Abu Ghraib, they do offer a glimpse into the type of conversations around torture that the military, the CIA, and the White House were having before the events occurred—conversations that help shape Fusco's performance.[37] Even though the memoranda, now known as the "torture memos," have been withdrawn, repudiated, and widely condemned, they remain an important reminder of how easy it is to manipulate discourse and meaning when those in positions of authority choose to exercise their power to promote their own agendas.[38] While much has been written on the torture memos, their importance for this project lies in what they tell us about the collaboration between the Department of Justice, the White House, the Department of Defense, and the Central Intelligence Agency—a collaboration with which Fusco directly engages in her text, especially through her inclusion of an FBI memo.[39] In order to analyze that engagement, I offer a very brief summary of some of the documents that set the legal context for the use of enhanced interrogation.

The 2002 memo titled "Standards of Conduct for Interrogation Under 18 U.S.C. §§ 2340–2340A," sometimes known as the Unclassified Bybee Memo, dismissed previously accepted definitions of torture, including immediate physical and mental harm, in favor of a construction of torture that relied on ambiguous notions of long-lasting injury like organ failure or the severity of injury leading to death.[40] By limiting the definition of torture to extreme injury, the memo offered the White House, the military, and intelligence officers the legal protection to perform interrogation tactics that would have been defined as torture under previous definitions of abuse.[41] Furthermore, the Unclassified Bybee Memo argued that in order to constitute torture, the intent to injure must be established.[42] The memo granted the executive branch the power to circumvent the legal restrictions on torture by arguing that abuse of detainees does not count as torture if the intent is not to injure, giving President George W. Bush the power, without legal consequence, to approve interrogation methods previously defined as abusive.[43] In its entirety, the memo lays out a clear case for the permissibility of torture as an interrogation practice that the Bush administration could employ against detainees, circumventing both domestic statutes and international treaties against torture.

The 2002 memo "Interrogation of al Qaeda Operative," sometimes called the Classified Bybee Memo, offers an eighteen-page analysis of the physical tactics the CIA wanted to use in the interrogation of Abu Zubaydah, a high-ranking al-Qaeda leader detained by the United States. The memo stands out for its discussion of enhanced interrogation techniques and whether they constitute torture.[44] It is clear that the Office of Legal Counsel minimized and ignored common medical knowledge about the effects of certain practices like sleep deprivation.[45] The memo offered the CIA the legal protection necessary to undertake these techniques under the pretext that enhanced interrogation was not torture and was necessary when interrogating high-value detainees like Zubaydah.[46] While the Classified Bybee Memo was not made public until 2009, a year after the publication of *A Field Guide*, it provides context for the larger conversation around the use of torture taking place before Abu Ghraib entered the public's consciousness.[47]

The rise in nationalism and Islamophobia after 9/11 allowed the White House, the intelligence community, and the US military to control the narrative around the use of torture in the interrogation of detainees.[48] Most US citizens only got a glimpse of what was actually happening at Abu Ghraib and other military detention sites.[49] Mainstream media often parroted the official accounts circulated by the Bush administration, choosing to focus on the more scandalous stories around the so-called bad apples, especially the women. The broader story about widespread cruelty at the hands of military and intelligence officers became a story of individuals acting badly and not an indictment of the misuse of power or the orchestrated efforts to obfuscate that violence. *A Field Guide* engages with this history of disavowal and offers a critique of the military and intelligence communities' violence based on a strong understanding of the complex system that allowed the violence to occur. Unlike the work of investigative journalists and nonfiction authors, Fusco's performance text addresses the use of torture in interrogations creatively and pedagogically. Fusco translates the plethora of information, both official and unofficial, for her audience in an example of what Muñoz refers to as the "performance of research/research of performance" (Fusco and Muñoz, 138–139). She documents her engagement with official state narratives in order to undermine their authority and destabilize their framing of violence. Her work offers an opportunity to learn about the abuse of detainees in a creative way that does not simply uncover the misuse of power at play or preach to its audience. Through the structure of the performance text, Fusco archives her process of creation and translation, producing not just a brilliant piece of performance art but also a form of textual mentoring—an actual guide for radical theater making—that can be of use for those who seek to invoke the power of performance to refuse complicity in oppression. By invoking the question of gender, she also challenges mainstream feminism's framing of women in the military.

"Invasion of Space by a Female"
Invoking a Feminist Legacy

In carrying out her critique of single-issue-focused feminism, Fusco opens the first section of *A Field Guide* with the salutation "Dear Virginia," and in doing so begins a conversation with one of the most lauded feminist thinkers of the twentieth century, Virginia Woolf (*Field Guide* 8). Woolf is most widely known for her stream of consciousness novels and nonfiction writings advocating for the rights of English women. By addressing Woolf personally, as if in a direct exchange, Fusco is not only engaging with Woolf's work but also modeling her dialogue on the structure Woolf employed in one of her feminist texts, *Three Guineas* (1938), which took the form of a series of letters addressing the rise of fascism, war, and feminism. In employing the structure of a letter, Fusco constructs her performance as a dialogue between the two women and creates a level of intimacy with her audience that invites them into the conversation. This first section of the text, "Invasion of Space by a Female," is broken up into three smaller sections that together constitute one long letter to Woolf. I read Fusco's use of the letter as a form of navigational storytelling that leads the reader through the narrative but also archives her personal process of discovery and creativity.

The three parts of the letter are organized around connected themes that offer context for Fusco's creative process. The first section, "Torture: The Feminine Touch," discusses how women's access to power has changed since Woolf's time, pointing out that "the more access American women have to the exercise of political power and the use of deadly force in war, the more apparent it becomes that we aren't using it very differently from men" (*Field Guide* 18). Fusco discusses how the military has weaponized women's femininity in carrying out violence while simultaneously using the femininity of the women caught up in the Abu Ghraib scandal to divert attention from the larger practice of torture in detainment centers and military prisons. The second section, "Now You See It, Now You Don't," continues the process of upending the understanding of sexual aggression when it is performed by women, arguing that "when male interrogators perform sex acts on non-consenting subjects it is understood as sexual assault, but when women do it, it can be authorized as invasion of space" (33). The final section, "Interrogating Interrogation," further calls into question the government's framing of torture as simply interrogation based on a lack of visible physical harm and challenges feminist discourse that refuses to acknowledge the abuse of power by women. For Fusco, "It is high time that we recognize that it is nothing short of a lie to frame American women's experience exclusively in terms of powerlessness. . . . If we persist in viewing female aggression as stemming exclusively from our own victimization or psychosis, we have no way to address serious and real ethical and political questions emerging from women's involvement in systems and structures of dominance. If we refuse to address the ways that women embrace power then we deny ourselves the means of understanding how conservative forces exploit identity politics" (81). The letter provides the audience with the information necessary to question assumptions about women's connection to power and helps inform the larger critique Fusco is making in her work. Given Fusco's creative decision to position Woolf as her interlocutor, and Woolf's reputation as one of the most influential feminist thinkers of the twentieth century, a brief understanding of Woolf's work is in order.

The primary text Fusco most directly references is Woolf's popular work *A Room of One's Own* (1929), an essay based on two papers Woolf read at the Arts Society at Newnham College and the ODTAA Society at Girton College, respectively, in October 1928.[50] In the essay, Woolf critiques gender inequality and women's lack of access to economic independence and education. She advocates for the right of women to have the time and space to create in order to rectify their absence in history and literature, and to write their way into being more than just subservient to men. In her musings, she laments the lack of women writers and ponders the question, "What would have happened had Shakespeare had a wonderfully gifted sister, called Judith" (*Room* 46). After much contemplation, Woolf concludes that Judith would have ended up pregnant and would have taken her life after being denied the opportunity to act and write like her brother, for "any woman born with a great gift in the sixteenth century would certainly have gone crazed, shot herself, or ended her days in some lonely cottage outside the village, half witch, half wizard, feared and mocked at" (49). Woolf's grim answer to her question reveals much about the limitations women of her time faced in England.

Given her occupation as a writer, it is understandable that Woolf centers her analysis of gender discrimination in the academic and literary realm. For Woolf, intellectual freedom—the freedom to write what one thinks—is best represented by the ability to write poetry, an art form that Woolf believes takes more time and energy than prose.[51] In her argument, writing offers an avenue through which to write women into history and, therefore, the nation. She envisions the inclusion of women into these structures as a way of deconstructing the patriarchy that limits women's potential as leaders. The name of the essay comes from Woolf's claim that what a woman needs to be an active participant in the world is money and a room of her own.

In *Three Guineas*, the work echoed by Fusco's text, Woolf extends her critique of the abuse of power by men to argue that it is the patriarchal structure of governance that has led to the projects of war—which men fight—and the violence that affects everyone else. While not as well known or well received as Woolf's previous works, *Three Guineas* played an important role in Woolf's development as a writer and feminist thinker and is part of a feminist legacy embraced by multiple generations of activists, writers, and scholars. Naomi Black opens the first chapter of her book-length study of Woolf with the writer's powerful assertion that "I have already said all I have to say in my book *Three Guineas*," a work Woolf considered her "credo" (Black 1). As in *A Room of One's Own*, the speaker in *Three Guineas* addresses a specific audience, and the text includes responses to three letters requesting funds—hence the title—and six photographs.[52]

Understanding Woolf's preoccupation with the limits placed on women of her own class, it is not surprising that she spends a great deal of time discussing women's role within the construction of patriotism and resistance to war. She articulates the exclusion of women from the project of patriotism: "But the educated man's sister—what does 'patriotism' mean to her? Has she the same reasons for being proud of England, for loving England, for defending England?" (*Three Guineas* 9).

The questions raised by Woolf's narrator illustrate the different stakes in projects of nationalism and who benefits from pride in the nation. Woolf is not arguing for the participation of women in the war project—just the opposite. She believes women can prevent war. Using the fictional character of a member of the Outsiders' Society—a group made up of the daughters of educated men—Woolf writes that the outsider would have no inclination to ask for men to protect the nation in her name, since the nation has never belonged to her: "'Our country,' she will say, 'throughout the greater part of its history has treated me as a slave; it has denied me education or any share in its possessions. . . . In fact, as a woman, I have no country. As a woman I want no country. As a woman my country is the whole world'" (108–109).

While the discourse Woolf employs in trying to explain the subjugation of English women is highly problematic—especially as she invokes the language of slavery—her words offer a critique of how the discourse of protecting women and the nation is employed to justify war and violence.[53] The outsider's claim that because she is a woman she has no country reveals the exclusionary politics inherent in patriotism and the marginalization of women within the construction of the nation. The passage makes visible the notion that fighting in wars is a "sex instinct" found in men and not shared by those female members of the Outsiders' Society. Instead, the outsider vocalizes Woolf's argument that the daughters of educated men, as a group, belong to the "weakest of all the classes in the state. We have no weapon with which to enforce our will" (13). Such a barring from governing structures, however, allows for the possibility to resist the alluring rhetoric of patriotism and honor through war. Woolf sees women's marginalization as a location from which to defy the gendered system of domination, fight against the legitimacy of war, and ultimately transform the nation. Again, it's important to acknowledge the limitations of Woolf's arguments—especially as they are limited to the experience of middle-class, white Englishwomen—while simultaneously recognizing that her writings have firmly established her as an important voice in feminist and antiwar literature.

Although Woolf was writing almost eight decades before the Abu Ghraib scandal, her idea of infiltrating structures of power and changing them from within remains a popular one in the contemporary United States. The problem with such an optimistic strategy lies in its inability to see the danger of the structure itself, especially when hierarchies of violence are inherently a part of those structures. While women, queer people, and trans people have fought for their right to be included in the nation's armed forces, such a fight does not undermine or challenge the violence perpetrated in the name of the nation.[54] Conformist inclusivity only helps to add to the number of servicepeople who carry out the agenda of military powers and those who dictate our foreign policy. It is this critique of assimilationist ideas stretching back to Woolf that Fusco's audience is forced to grapple with, even as we are made uncomfortable and pushed to acknowledge our own complicity as subjects of the nation.

Fusco uses the letter and its three performative essays to engage her audience in a larger debate around questions of power, gender, and violence that are often ignored or dismissed in mainstream conversations on women and the military. In her conversation with Woolf, she acknowledges, "I'm sure there was part of me that believed for most of my life that women were not really responsible for the battles that destroyed so many lives because we didn't fight in them" (*Field Guide* 10). The fact that women have traditionally been excluded from combat has made it easy to view women in the military as inhabiting supporting roles in war, not acting as engineers or orchestrators of the violence of war.[55] Even as someone who grew up distrusting the military, Fusco hadn't necessarily considered the role of women in waging war. Like so many observers, she found that the abuses documented at Abu Ghraib prison forced a recognition of her own gaps in understanding. She writes that she finds herself "transfixed by the women who are waging war in my name, sensing that their presence compels me to scrutinize my own misgivings and misconceptions about femininity and power" (10). The text invites her audience to go on this journey of inquiry and to challenge misunderstandings of what happened at Abu Ghraib and the role women played in perpetrating violence and upholding structures of power.

Dear Virginia: Writing Back

So much has changed since Woolf published her writings, so why would Fusco choose to reference Woolf so heavily in her text? After all, unless one studies feminist scholarship or British literature, Woolf's works might be studied as a literature of the past, as texts that capture a now antiquated way of thinking about gender and power. Framing Woolf's ideas as belonging in the past not only minimizes the impact of her work on the literary and feminist canons but also ignores the power her work holds in imagining constructions of gender.[56] Fusco is aware that Woolf, as a well-known pacifist who wrote passionately against war, remains influential in vocalizing dissent: "Many feminists have turned to you to refine their thoughts on war and its effects on those who do not fight" (*Field Guide* 8).

Among the rush of op-eds and think pieces published in the wake of the Abu Ghraib scandal, one of the most widely discussed was the feminist writer Barbara Ehrenreich's 2004 essay "Feminism's Assumptions Upended," originally published in the *Los Angeles Times* and reprinted as the foreword to the edited collection *One of the Guys: Women as Aggressors and Torturers* (2007). This essay is especially worth noting because Ehrenreich vocalizes the widely held essentialist belief that women are inherently less violent than men. She recounts how the photographs of the abuse in Abu Ghraib broke her heart and writes, "I had no illusions about the US mission in Iraq—whatever exactly it is—but it turns out that I did have some illusions about women" (1). Her essay reads as a lament, a loss of innocence for an idea of women that no longer exists: "A certain kind of feminism, or perhaps I should say a certain kind of feminist naiveté, died in Abu Ghraib. It was a feminism that saw men as the perpetual perpetrators, women as the perpetual victims, and male sexual violence against women as the root of all injustice" (2). Like many, Ehrenreich held onto the belief that somehow women were above the warring of men, choosing to see women through a gendered lens as the caring and civilizing members of the nation.[57] Unfortunately, Ehrenreich's essay not only ignores the capacity of women to carry out violence but also makes invisible the important role white women have played in colonial projects of racial violence.[58]

The white feminist musings captured in Woolf's writings, and reiterated in Ehrenreich's essay decades later, function as the background against which Fusco launches her performance. The name of the essay with which Fusco opens the text, "Invasion of Space by a Female," is especially significant, as it is the same name given to the information-gathering strategy used by military and intelligence community interrogators. This connection is indicated in the book's description, which makes clear that the essay "takes its title from the term for the authorized military tactic" (*Field Guide*, back cover). Fusco further explains that such a strategy specifically uses women in military interrogations in order "to provoke male anxiety" (*Field Guide* 41). At first glance, generating anxiety might not seem as violent as physical torture, but the more Fusco's audience learns about the type of anxiety being provoked and how it is incited, the more we understand about the nature of this type of interrogation practice and the deep psychological damage it creates.

The use of the "invasion of space by a female" strategy by US government personnel became public in June 2005, when *Time* magazine leaked an eighty-four-page interrogation log of detainee Mohammed al-Qahtani, which details numerous instances of disturbing abuse at the hands of various personnel at the Guantanamo Bay detention camp.[59] Included in these documented cases of abuse were reports of the use of tactics based specifically on sexual assault and harassment: among them, "Pride and Ego down, Fear Up Harsh, and Invasion of Space by a Female" ("Interrogation Log" 25). The log records multiple instances when al-Qahtani was in distress while being questioned by a female interrogator, but it doesn't make clear the reason for his distress. A declaration submitted by al-Qahtani's lawyer, Gitanjali S. Gutierrez, documents the female interrogator's use of sexually explicit touch to invoke fear and to cause distress in her client.[60] The unwanted physical touching might not look like the traditional torture we've seen represented in movies and television shows, but beatings and waterboarding are not the only ways to abuse an individual.[61]

By naming this part of the text after the intelligence-gathering strategy and directly invoking Woolf's feminist writings, Fusco draws a connection between the colonial white supremacy at the heart of the military and intelligence communities and a form of feminism that ignores or refuses to acknowledge how white women willingly serve the interests of that supremacist structure. Fusco uses the US military's own language to critique the use of women in the torture of individuals like al-Qahtani and to argue that "the existence of this standardized term is testimony in itself of the state's rationalization of its exploitation of femininity" (*Field Guide* 41). Fusco also, importantly, expands the parameters of the discussion beyond the events at Abu Ghraib. By invoking the strategy publicly known to have been employed at Guantanamo, Fusco draws connections between the torture cases at Abu Ghraib, the lesser-known cases of abuse at Guantanamo, and the practices of exploiting female soldiers' sexuality for the purpose of breaking down detainees that most outside of the military and intelligence communities would be unaware existed. The title "Invasion of Space by a Female" is boldly printed in large black letters against the stark white page, making it impossible for the reader to miss. It is a powerful introduction to the text and ushers the audience into the first section, subtitled "Torture: The Feminine Touch." Fusco doesn't mince words. From the initial page turn, the reader is plunged into the work without apology.

Fusco's opening salutation to Woolf invites the reader into a performative monologue that simulates a conversation between Woolf and herself—invoking the structure of Woolf's *Three Guineas*—while simultaneously engaging with a feminine history of letter writing.[62] At first it might seem like a one-sided exchange, as we hear only Fusco's voice, but Woolf's published works provide the source with which Fusco engages.[63] Fusco explains that she feels "a little guilty about turning your best known title inside out by using it for my own performance about the dark side of advancing women's rights through warfare"; in a footnote, she explains that she is referencing her 2006 performance *A Room of One's Own: Women and Power in the New America* (*Field Guide* 8, 83n2). This guilt, however, does not stop Fusco from ripping off the veil of gentility as she writes, "Your atelier becomes my torture chamber" (8). For Fusco, Woolf's call for a room from which to create and become independent has transformed into yet another space where the power of heteropatriarchy rules supreme. Fusco writes that the deliberate use of the title and the comparison between texts "was intended to shock anyone who clings to outdated ideas about women's relationship to power" (8). Beyond the project of shocking her audience, the statement is a strong one that also gestures to a critique of a type of feminism steeped in the privilege of white supremacy—a feminism embodied by Woolf, Ehrenreich, and other well-intentioned feminists who ignore or refuse to acknowledge the protections their racial identity affords them. Reading Fusco's treatment of gender inequality through an intersectional framework illustrates the limitations of a feminist movement that centers single-identity-focused activism. Such a singularly focused movement ignores intersecting structures of oppression, rendering invisible the power that women in the atelier and the interrogation room hold, even as they lack the access to power that white men continue to enjoy.

Like Woolf, Fusco employs the form of the letter to personalize her critique of structures of power. But Fusco expands on her role as letter writer and becomes our educator and guide through a plethora of materials on interrogation. She writes that her goal was "to create a character—an implacable female interrogator who could speak about the issues and events that had unnerved" her (27). She invokes Woolf's *A*

Room of One's Own when she writes that this character is "a bit like your version of Shakespeare's sister, but she actually gets the chance to show her stuff" (27). Fusco's fictional character, Sergeant Fusco, becomes the embodiment of the access to power that Woolf's Judith Shakespeare could only imagine. Judith's tragic life ends after having been denied access to develop her talent, while Sergeant Fusco's skills are developed and employed by the military in the service of the nation. Sergeant Fusco becomes a twisted version of the empowered woman that Woolf dreamed would someday be a reality. While we are not introduced to Sergeant Fusco in the letter, Fusco does explain her methodology and walks us through the process that led to the creation of Sergeant Fusco and her performance texts. In referencing the character, Fusco writes that she "is a fiction but the things that she talks about are excruciatingly real" (28). The reality Sergeant Fusco invokes in her performance is based on a process of knowledge gathering, an investigation of government policies around interrogation, and a critical analysis of military and intelligence community practices—a process Fusco documents throughout *A Field Guide.*

Fusco's discussion of her methodology becomes a vital part of the intervention performed by her text. Unlike the secrecy behind government accounts of interrogation practices, Fusco is transparent about the sources she used in the creation of the work. She recounts that while she "found very few public documents that deal specifically with female interrogators, when it comes to interrogation, there is plenty to work with" (28). She recalls, "I poured over detainee testimonies and human rights reports, devoured soldier memoirs, and interviewed military personnel. I read CIA manuals and Justice Department memos. In short, I tried to learn their language" (29). The multiple avenues of investigation allow Fusco to shape her creative work through a position informed by the many fabrications and negations circulated within the official narrative, which leads to the formation of a work that engages with this history and makes important interventions. In attempting to learn the language used by those in power to negate the abuse taking place in interrogations, and to understand women's involvement in these practices, Fusco immerses herself in the process itself. She tells Woolf, "I took a group of young women with me to study with retired Army interrogators who offer courses on interrogation and prisoner of war resistance tactics to civilians" (29). Later in the letter, Fusco expands on her immersion and explains that she decided to "pose as a student" and take a course on interrogation led by Team Delta, a group of "retired US Army interrogators who were in active duty in the 1990s and have since parlayed their skills in the private sector" (67). It was through her training with Team Delta that Fusco learned how theories of successful interrogation tactics become praxis.

Fusco's research archive becomes a resource for her audience, a repository of knowledge to inform their own opinion. While some information on the abuses at Abu Ghraib and interrogation practices might have been public knowledge, the information Fusco gathered in her investigation would have been unknown to most. Fusco translates the data assembled through her interdisciplinary methodology into a creative set of texts that allows her to engage her audience in complicated discussions without having to go into a long explanation of the research. The creative text "shows" not "tells," while Fusco's exposition performs the role of a guide through which to enter her performance. The audience is encouraged to engage pedagogically with the performance in order to form a more informed opinion—one that has the power to destabilize the carefully curated narrative of the state. In addition to exposing the audience to a wealth of information on the state's abuses of power, *A Field Guide* focuses attention on specific aspects of gender and violence that are obfuscated in the mainstream narrative. Women are no longer simply victims of violence but become perpetrators themselves, all in the service of the nation. The focus on gender forces Fusco's audience to question their own assumptions about the nature of violence and the capacity of women to abuse power. Her footnoting of sources also adds a level of credibility to the text and establishes her authority as an informed narrator. The work becomes a powerful intervention in constructions of gender and power that ignore how state violence can be carried out by individuals upholding the goals of white supremacy, regardless of one's identity and subject position.

By positioning the letter's essays as a guide to reading the memo, script, and illustrations, Fusco further employs a popular instrument of instruction: the guidebook. The name of the book, *A Field Guide for Female Interrogators*, clearly makes the connection for the audience between Fusco's performance text and the practice of using guidebooks to direct and train. Fusco again takes a well-known category of writing, in this case military and intelligence manuals, and uses it to train her audience to see through official narratives that discount the abuse of power at the hands of female interrogators. In mimicking the official field guides that train military and intelligence operatives, the text undermines the authority of these texts and helps intervene in a discourse that seeks to ignore or minimize the harm of current intelligence-gathering strategies. Fusco studies and learns the language used in human intelligence, the gathering of intelligence from human sources, and transforms military and CIA instructional manuals into a guide of opposition. Beyond being the writer of the essays, Fusco becomes our interlocutor, helping us navigate the multiple discourses and narratives on power, gender, and the state. She guides us through the piles of misinformation and obfuscating documentation, into a performance that forces us to confront the realities of war. She reminds us that "wars don't just happen on the ground; they take place in our minds, coercing us to believe in the necessity of what we might otherwise reject as excessive" (*Field Guide* 10).

Fusco is providing a primer on the role of women in US government-sanctioned interrogation methods and pointing out the excessiveness of their actions. Given the misinformation around the military and intelligence communities' use of force in questioning detainees, it would be easy for an audience to misread or to dismiss Fusco's creative critique of the US government and its various agents. In the letter to Woolf, Fusco educates while offering a powerful critique, offering her audience an opportunity to read the performance from a specifically informed position and stabilizing its meaning.[64] Reading the letter as a project of education helps expand the influence of Fusco's embodied interpretation of the structures of power at play in the use of women by the military. In this way, her collating and translating of information helps educate the audience about the violent structure in place that made the events at Abu Ghraib possible and the complicity of women in upholding this structure. Furthermore, publishing the essays in print documents Fusco's creative critique and her methodology, offering a new archive for future creators and activists to look to for inspiration and guidance. Positioning the first section of the text as an actual guide transforms the text into a blueprint for creating artistic work that challenges accepted beliefs that uphold and re-create ideologies of power.

The FBI Memo: More Than a Few Bad Apples

Sandwiched between the essays and the script is a copy of a redacted FBI memo, "Suspected Mistreatment of Detainees." While the full memo takes up only three pages in the text and is introduced with a short informational paragraph, the importance of its inclusion cannot be overlooked. Fusco informs the reader that Guantanamo began holding captured detainees in January 2002 and that these detainees were having to endure coercive interrogation methods authorized by Defense Secretary Donald Rumsfeld. She writes that the memo "contains a description of an interrogation that an agent observed in late 2002 involving a female interrogator who made sexual advances as part of her approach to a prisoner" (*Field Guide* 87). Fusco provides only a brief context for the document and allows the memo to stand alone, giving her audience the opportunity to understand its significance. The document, with its redacted names and stamped SECRET at the top and bottom of the pages, is printed on official FBI letterhead and offers credibility and legitimacy to the story the memo tells.

The memo, "Suspected Mistreatment of Detainees," alludes to the messy and complicated history of interrogation practices, official justifications for torture, and widespread abuses I have briefly outlined in this chapter. Dated July 14, 2004, and addressed to Major General Donald J. Ryder, the memo was written by T. J. Harrington, then deputy assistant director of the FBI's Counterterrorism Division. While the memo was initially classified, it was released as part of a cache of documents obtained by the ACLU through a Freedom of Information Act lawsuit.[65] The intended audience of the memo, General Ryder, had performed his own investigation in October and November of 2003 into allegations of abuse in detention and corrections operations in Iraq, which he summarized in a November 2003 report (Taguba 7). While the Ryder Report, as it is known, remains classified, we do know of Ryder's conclusion that "there were no military police units purposely applying inappropriate confinement practices" (qtd. in Taguba 9). This finding is suspect, given that the Taguba Report concluded that "many of the abuses suffered by detainees occurred during, or near to, the time of [Ryder's] assessment" (Taguba 12). Taguba's rejection of Ryder's findings challenges the conclusion of the 2003 investigation and casts doubt on Ryder's ability to perform an objective inquiry into the army, a military system under which he also served. Ryder was not ignorant of allegations of abuse against detainees, and Harrington's concerns would have been just one more instance of individuals voicing objections to the treatment of detained individuals.

The memo, printed in full in *A Field Guide*, begins with mention of a previous meeting between Ryder and Harrington and specifies the purpose of the memo being "part of a follow up on our discussion on detainee treatment" (qtd. in Fusco, *Field Guide* 89). Harrington then lays out three specific instances when FBI agents were observed using what he refers to as "highly aggressive interrogation techniques" in Guantanamo in September and October of 2002 (89). The first case Harrington documents involves the interrogation tactics of a female marine; the second incident mentions the behavior of a civilian contractor; and the third situation refers to a traumatized detainee who had been subjected to intimidation by a canine, prolonged isolation, and sleep deprivation using intensive light. After laying out the three cases, Harrington goes on to write that the situations "were referenced in a May 30, 2003 electronic communication (EC) from the Behavioral Analysis Unit of the FBI to FBI headquarters" and that the communication had included a "draft Memorandum for the Record dated 15 January 2003" that made specific reference to two of the situations discussed in the memo (90). Harrington's words make it very clear that the concerns around the interrogation practices at Guantanamo had been raised at least one year before Ryder concluded his investigation into Abu Ghraib's detention operations.[66] Harrington's description of the three incidents and subsequent discussions prove that the abuse of detainees went beyond a few bad apples at Abu Ghraib and that the abuse there had not occurred in isolation. The memo offers a brief but powerful summary of Harrington's discussions with Ryder and reveals the chain of communication that existed around the abuse happening at Guantanamo. For an audience that might not be aware of the complicated history leading up to the events at Abu Ghraib, the memo offers a glimpse into this history and collusion and undermines the official narrative offered by the Bush administration.

Of the three incidents Harrington discusses, the first situation receives three times the amount of attention as the other two. The account centers on an FBI special agent's observation of an interrogation of an unknown detainee by a female marine. The agent reports that the interrogator "complained that curtain movement at the observation window was distracting the detainee," and she "directed a marine to duct tape a curtain over the two-way mirror between the interrogation room and the observation room" (qtd. in Fusco, *Field Guide* 89). The agent notes that "no movement of the curtain had occurred" and further characterizes the interrogator's actions "as an attempt to prohibit those in the observation room from witnessing her interaction with the detainee" (89). While a surveillance camera in the interrogation room should have allowed those in the observation room to view her actions, the interrogator positioned herself "between the detainee and the surveillance camera," further obscuring her behavior from the FBI agent (89). The interrogator's blatant attempts to hide her actions make clear her knowledge that the behavior she was engaging in was, in one way or another, wrong. The ease with which she ordered the taping over of the observation window and her knowledge of exactly where to stand to block the camera gesture toward her familiarity with these practices. What was she hiding from the FBI special agent?

Harrington's memo documents, in a handful of sentences, the kind of distress experienced by detainees. The special agent observed the interrogator "apparently whispering in the detainee's ear, and caressing and applying lotion to his arms," and explains the significance of this type of touch by pointing out that "this was during Ramadan when physical contact with a woman would have been particularly offensive to a Moslem [*sic*] male" (89). The prisoner was shackled, and his hands were cuffed, making it impossible for him to move away from her unwanted touches. We don't know what she was whispering in his ear, but given the sexual way in which she was touching him, it is highly probable that her language was also aimed at invoking a physical and psychological reaction.

The assumption that touches by a woman would be unwelcome based on religious practices rejects the bodily autonomy of the detainee. In a section of her letter to Woolf titled "Now You See It, Now You Don't," Fusco points out how "outdated anthropological arguments become the basis for the development of tactics that manifest themselves in the roles interrogators assume for themselves and impose on their sources" (*Field Guide* 32). Even if the detainee did not find the assault more harmful based on religious and cultural beliefs, the female interrogator believes that his faith is what makes her actions so objectionable. She uses her simplistic understanding of Islamic practices to devise a way to torture the detainee based on the exploitation of her femininity. In disputing the argument that using women in interrogations is solely a way of exploiting the cultural beliefs of Muslim detainees, Fusco argues that "it is equally likely that the decision to use women in this way is also informed by American perceptions of women." She notes that "the roles women are asked to play in order to harass the prisoners correspond to sexist characterizations that are leveled at them by male soldiers in other contexts as a form of denigration" (44). Women in the interrogation room are asked to play roles they are already presumed to play based on Western sexism and gender stereotyping.

Based on her behavior, the interrogator was aware that she was hurting the detainee and that this harm might be less than accepted by the FBI agent. Why else would she go to such lengths to hide her actions? Unfortunately, her physical assault continued, and the female interrogator's touching only grew more aggressive. Although her hands were often obscured, the special agent witnessed them "moving towards the detainee's lap" (qtd. in Fusco, *Field Guide* 89). He also observed the detainee express physical pain and attempt to pull away from the interrogator. When the agent questioned why the detainee had grimaced in pain, one of the marines who had been in the interrogation room admitted that the interrogator had "grabbed the detainee's thumbs and bent them backwards and indicated that she also grabbed his genitals" (90). While some might dismiss the touching as not causing serious harm because it doesn't leave physical marks, the act of touching his genitalia is a clear violation of his physical autonomy and a form of sexual assault. The idea that women cannot sexually assault men under their control implies that women do not have power in those spaces.

In the letter to Woolf, Fusco observes that "male interrogators tend to degrade male prisoners by forcing them to perform homoerotic acts presumed to be humiliating, threatening and insulting them, but stop short of performing these acts themselves. On the other hand, women interrogators use sexual insults, force them to engage in humiliating acts, and also perform sexually for them" (*Field Guide* 32–33). Fusco further argues, "Apparently, when male interrogators perform sex acts on non-consenting subjects it is understood as sexual assault, but when women do it, it can be authorized as an invasion of space" (33). The female interrogator is, in effect, performing the invasion of space strategy and taking advantage of her gender to introduce a type of aggression that would be seen differently at the hands of a male interrogator. The concept of the invasion of space further reaffirms the idea that war and torture are the domains of men and that women's participation is still exceptional. When women are deployed in the carrying out of torture, it is to use their sexuality to "invade" the spaces of men.

Fusco's decision to incorporate this specific memo into the larger performance text underscores her words in the letter to Woolf. She writes,

> Since the 1970s, feminists have tried to undermine the repressive moralistic language by arguing that female sexual assertiveness should be understood as a form of freedom of expression. While I don't disagree with that position, the sexual torture dilemma is making its limitations glaringly apparent. Flaunting one's sexuality may indeed be a form of self-realization, but it doesn't happen in a vacuum, nor is the only context for its appearance democratic. The absence of consent from the recipient turns the display into an act of violence. And when this imposition has been rationalized as part of an interrogation strategy, the act ceases to be strictly a matter of personal responsibility. (50)

Fusco's rejection of the construction of female sexual assertiveness as a simple form of freedom highlights the limitations of binary thinking: that sexual assertiveness is freedom, while sexual repression is oppressive. Fusco's critique of sexual assertiveness takes into consideration power, conditions, and the subject position of actors. The expression of female sexuality and its consequences are much more complicated, and Fusco's intersectional analysis of sexual power encourages her audience to question how that assertiveness can be employed and abused. In this case, assertiveness goes from individual empowerment to sexual assault used in the service of the nation and its imperial logics. The discussion of women's abuse of sexuality in the text challenges the audience to view the female marine's actions as more than just interrogation: They are abusive acts that use female sexuality to torture the detainee into acquiescing to the interrogator's demands. When we scrutinize the actions of female interrogators through an intersectional critique of power, the sexual assault experienced by the detainee in the name of intelligence gathering becomes just one more example of the type of violent tactics used by the military and intelligence officers in their never-ending quest for information.[67]

The placement of the FBI memo right after Fusco's letter to Woolf transitions the text from Fusco's more intimate voice to the impersonal diction of an official government document. The brief introduction to the memo offers the audience the opportunity to critically analyze the document without Fusco directly imposing her own reading. She uses the memo as confirmation of the collusion happening behind the scenes but leaves room for the damning information in Harrington's memo to speak for itself. I read the "Suspected Mistreatment of Detainees" memo as a powerful primary text that acts as a witness statement, offering proof for any reader who might be questioning Fusco's analysis. While it lacks Fusco's creative writing skills, the memo does offer a model of how documents can be creatively incorporated into a performance and used to support resistant interpretations of state actions. The starkness of the printed memo, with its redacted sections, stands in contrast to the rest of the text, making the distinction between the work of the creator and the author of the memo clear. By including the memo in the performance text, however, it becomes part of the performance itself. In this way, Harrington and Ryder—agents of the state—become actors on the stage Fusco has set.

"A Field Guide for Female Interrogators"
The Art of Performing Violence

The last section of Fusco's performance text features "A Field Guide for Female Interrogators," the handbook that shares its name with the larger performance text. The thirty-six-page illustrated manual presents various interrogation tactics employed by female interrogators under the supervision and approval of the military and intelligence communities. As with Sergeant Fusco's performance of a military briefing, the satirical guide incorporates the culture and methods of those communities. I read the guide as a textual performance of sanctioned state violence and another example of Fusco's creative representation of research. Her co-optation of the instruction manual format subverts the authority of the state's official narrative, and her performative use of illustrations denaturalizes the gendered and racialized violence that operates behind the closed doors of the interrogation room. The guide offers readers another example of how performance can be engaged to resist the erasure of state violence in contemporary imperial projects.

Fusco opens the guide with a brief paragraph that gives context for the use of military and CIA training manuals on authorized methods. She informs the reader that "these types of detailed manuals are now available online but they don't make specific mention of the use of sexual aggression by interrogators and military police even though they have been addressed in investigations" (*Field Guide* 107). Fusco's manual combines large, bold text with illustrations by Dan Turner. Turner based the sixteen illustrations on "the testimony of detainees and eyewitnesses"—a visual representation of words into images that capture the disturbing reality of the sexual tactics employed by female interrogators (107). The manual illustrates the strategies discussed in the FBI memo introduced earlier in the text.[68] Fusco's graphic intervention makes visually explicit the official techniques developed under the "invasion of space by a female" practice of interrogation.

An introduction, written from the perspective of military and intelligence authorities, lays out the purpose of the manual. It starts with a short disclaimer that the manual seeks "to present basic information about coercive techniques available for use by female interrogators of CENTCOM," but that "it is vital that this data not be misconstrued as constituting authorization for the use of coercion at field discretion. There is no such blanket authorization" (109). The satirical use of the disclaimer, offering information about techniques available but not actually authorizing them, gestures toward the disconnect between ambiguously written policies on interrogation and the actual practices of coercion and abuse. It also reiterates the few bad apples defense while exonerating those higher up in command. The use of technical discourse attempts to add credibility to the psychological aspect of this warfare. The introduction also invokes the Islamophobia that undergirds the cultural biases of interrogation practices and the military's employment of gender stereotypes of women as sexual objects or maternal caretakers—issues that Fusco discussed in detail in earlier sections of the text. Fusco's linguistic mimicry demonstrates how language is used to camouflage the reality of violence and torture through the discourse of interrogative practices.

The introduction sets the context for "Coercive Techniques," the section of the manual that gives the reader a visual representation of the weaponizing of female sexuality in coercive interrogation practices. With the exception of the two-page photograph of Sergeant Fusco that precedes the script of *Our Feminist Future*, the illustrations in "Coercive Techniques" are the only visuals in the entire text. Given the importance of the visual evidence in the Abu Ghraib case, Fusco's decision to not use photographs from the leak is a significant one. Her work has been engaging with the role of the visual in the creation of meaning for decades. Fusco is also aware of the power that photography has played in colonial projects and in shaping the constructed identity of the nation. In her accompanying essay for the International Center of Photography's exhibition *Only Skin Deep: Changing Visions of the American Self*, which she cocurated, Fusco argues that "the photographic image plays a central role in American culture. Americans are avid producers and consumers of photographs and as our culture shifts from being predominantly print-based to image-based, we grow increasingly reliant on photographs for information about histories and realities that we do not experience directly" ("Racial Time" 13).[69] For the majority of Americans, the leaked Abu Ghraib photographs informed their (mis)understanding of the use of torture in interrogation practices. The photographs themselves became the center of the story, while the focus on the women in the photos evolved into a strategy of distracting attention from the violence. Thus, the photos moved from documenting violence to containing the discussion around interrogation abuse by US government personnel.[70] Fusco's decision to illustrate the manual without photos is a deliberate one that allows her to shape the narrative outside of the preconceived ideas an audience might hold. The deliberate avoidance of circulating the photographs in this context disrupts the audience's understanding of the violence of the interrogation room and forces us to confront the image of women as abusers.

Although its format is simple, "Coercive Techniques" is one of the most disturbing sections in Fusco's text. The illustrations are not overly detailed and the text is sparse. What makes the handbook so disconcerting is that the illustrations are all based on actual testimony of detainees and on eyewitness accounts, including the FBI memo, a fact made clear in Fusco's introduction to the guide. "Coercive Techniques" includes sixteen methods employed in the interrogation room: direct questioning, establish your identity, dietary manipulation, use of loud music, silence, sleep management, Mutt and Jeff, exploiting cultural phobias no. 1, we know all, mild non-injurious physical contact, pride and ego up, pride and ego down, stress position, exploiting cultural phobias no. 2, fear up mild, and fear up harsh. Each technique includes a brief description or explanation for how the technique is intended to function, along with a drawing of the technique being carried out. All of the illustrations feature a brown-skinned Muslim detainee and a blonde, white female interrogator, with the exception of the Mutt and Jeff technique, which features an additional brunette, white female interrogator. The coloring of the illustrations makes the racial difference between the detainee and the female interrogators very clear, unlike the more ambiguous reference to race in Sergeant Fusco's performance. The combination of sardonic description with the disturbing drawings creates a troubling visual narrative of violence and power. While all of the illustrations are unsettling and clearly represent abuses of power, I focus my analysis on six of the most blatant examples of weaponized female sexuality.

The techniques at the center of my analysis all include forms of sexual harassment and assault at the hands of the white female interrogator. While the illustrations might lack the realism of the Abu Ghraib photographs, their representation of violence is much more focused and defined. The Mutt and Jeff technique—the first in the guide to mention the use of female sexuality—takes its name from the first daily comic strip, created by the cartoonist Bud Fisher, and connects the illustration to a specific legacy of drawing for the public.[71] The guide informs us that the technique is "one of the oldest tricks in the book, but it works like a charm. Basically, he's gotta go for one of you" (Fusco, *Field Guide* 124). The two white female interrogators look like they are yelling at the detainee. They take up most of the space on the page, looming over him; we only see his back and partial side. The brunette interrogator standing in front of him poses with one hand on her hip and the other pointing at him. The blonde interrogator bends over him as she holds the back of his neck in a grip with her left hand. Her right hand is blocked by his body, and we can't tell what it is doing. Her blonde hair is loose around her face and body, and she is no longer wearing her fatigues shirt. Instead, we see only her black bra, which stands out against the lightness of her skin and her very blonde hair. Unlike the drawing of male nudity in the establish your identity technique, which suggests weakness, the semi-dressed state of the interrogator is intimidating and threatening.[72] The revealing image of the blonde interrogator, combined with the description of the technique, emphasizes how the sexuality of the two women is being utilized.

The technique called mild non-injurious physical contact further lays out the use of sexual contact as a form of interrogation. The guide describes the technique as "'a little bit of smacky face'": "Unlike other forms of contact that lead to physical injury, sexual contact is unlikely to leave scars and is more likely to induce guilt that can be taken advantage of by a good interrogator" (130). Here Fusco uses humor to obfuscate and negate the violence of the interrogation process (i.e., "forms of contact"). The name of the strategy, and the assertion that sexual contact doesn't leave scars, connects the technique to the text's previous juridical discussions on what constitutes torture. The effect of the sexual contact is reduced to a simple inducement of guilt, dismissing the trauma that results from sexual assault and harassment. In the accompanying illustration, the detainee is again sitting on a chair, with his eyes closed and his head leaning back. The scene is drawn from above, slightly looking down on the action, as the interrogator—wearing her blonde hair down around her shoulders and her top open to reveal a black bra—holds out pink underwear, putting it in the detainee's face. Her expression is one of disdain, with her mouth in an open smile and her brow furrowed. The prisoner's hand is on his lap, illustrating his inability to swat the underwear away; he can only close his eyes and try to move his head back. The pink color of the underwear draws attention to the femininity of the interrogator and, combined with her exposed chest, gestures to the sexual nature of the abuse.

The pride and ego down technique bolsters the strategy of using sexual contact that avoids scars while also alluding to the psychological damage, as such a technique "is more likely to induce guilt that can be taken advantage of by a good interrogator" (134). The interrogator is drawn shirtless, with her plunging black bra on display. Her blonde hair is down, and her lips are darkly drawn, with her mouth slightly open. This image has the detainee positioned standing and facing forward. His upper body is leaning away from her, and he is nude, covering his genitalia with his hands while looking worried or afraid. She is positioned at his side, slightly behind him, leaning up on him, and rubbing her breasts on his arm. Her legs are spread slightly open, and her arms are on her waist in a position of power, while her torso leans to bring her chest into contact with the detainee. The juxtaposition between his brown skin and her whiteness is stark. Although the illustration makes evident the size difference between the smaller interrogator and the larger detainee, the female interrogator's power is clearly displayed.

The strategy of stress position introduces the religious difference between the two individuals in the interrogation room: "Direct sexual advances from a white Christian female generate anxiety in devout Muslim males by forcing them to confront their desire to break cultural taboos" (136). The stress position is an already established torture technique, but instead of putting physical stress on the body, Fusco's position is stressing the bounds of religious devotion and exploiting cultural differences. The strategy again makes reference to the stereotypes of Muslim men and their desires but also includes specific reference to the interrogator's identity as a white Christian, aligning Americanness with Christianity and whiteness. The illustration features the detained man sitting on a chair, his head leaning slightly back, away from the interrogator, and his right hand at his side, holding the chair. The white female interrogator is almost sitting on his lap, simulating a lap dance, leaning back into him. Her blonde hair is down, she is again shirtless, wearing only a black bra, and her pants are unbuttoned. Her left hand is posed behind her head, while her right hand is suggestively placed between her legs. It is clear from the expression on the detainee's face that this sexual contact with the interrogator is unwanted.

The last two strategies discussed in "Coercive Techniques" center the language of fear and allude to the infliction of psychological damage. The technique called fear up mild again references stereotypes around Muslim beliefs as a point of weakness to exploit: "While most sexually explicit gestures may induce guilt, the ones that violate religious doctrine are most likely to push your source to the crisis point where he will either confess, collapse, or both" (140). The illustration has the detainee kneeling on the floor, partially resting on his haunches, drawn in a three-quarter profile. His shoulders are bent forward and his face is in his hands. The interrogator is bent over him, in a position of power, shoving her breasts toward his face. Her hands are on her black bra, pushing her breasts together, and her pants are undone, revealing her pink underwear. Her blonde hair is down, and her expression is one of disdain. The technique frames the detainee's religious doctrine as a weakness that can be exploited.

The last technique of the guide, fear up harsh, is the most incendiary. In fact, the text states that "this tactic is so inflammatory that it should be reserved for only the most resistant sources. There is no way to resume a normal exchange after the severe emotional crisis that it is likely to generate" (142). The description clearly gestures toward the long-term psychological harm created by the strategy, but Fusco's language comes across as clinical and detached. In the illustration, the detainee kneels in front of the interrogator, resting on his haunches. His hands are tied behind his back, and we see three red stripes of blood on his face. We see only half of his face, but his anguish is captured in his tightly shut eyes and open mouth, as if he is screaming. The female interrogator is in the same state of undress, with black bra and unzipped pants. She leans her torso back and pushes her groin forward, toward the prisoner. Her hand is in her underwear, and we can see blood there. Her other hand spreads menstrual blood on the side of his face that is turned away from us. Her expression is one of anger and rage. It is with this unsettling image of abuse and sexual assault that Fusco ends *A Field Guide*.

Fusco's decision to use drawings in the manual works to focus our attention on the sexual tactics of female interrogators and the military and intelligence communities' use of gender—a focus that was lost in the mainstream discussions of torture. Instead, the women involved in the Abu Ghraib case were strategically employed to take the blame for the abuse and to distract from the larger conversation of interrogation tactics.[73] Sabrina Harman and Lynndie England's personal lives became part of the story, and the public narrative created around them relied on tired gender stereotypes that positioned the women as victims themselves or reduced them to sexual objects.[74] While Harman and England were clearly used as scapegoats, the length to which their defenders went to excuse their actions was telling of a racial privilege that prioritized the women's experience as white women over the violence perpetrated on their victims. The emphasis on their low status within the military, their lack of power in carrying out orders, and their femininity became the focus of the story. It is not surprising that Harman's defense attorney invoked her gender when trying to make the case that Harman "actually cared about inmates and tried to help inmates . . . [and] went to limits to see that they got proper care, safeguard[ing], and medical treatment" (Frank Spinner qtd. in Caldwell 26).[75] In their quest to theorize the role of Harman and England, well-known white feminists also prioritized the women's identity as victims of patriarchy. Lucinda Marshall argued that "the vilification of Private First Class Lynndie England is perhaps the most deliberate and misplaced attempt to blame women. . . . That England has a history of mental incapacity and learning disabilities and was ordered by Charles Graner, her lover and superior officer, to pose was simply not deemed relevant" (52–53). Ehrenreich positioned the women as victims of their circumstances, simply going along with what they were told: "In all likelihood, [Megan] Ambuhl, England, and Harman are not congenitally evil people. They are working-class women who wanted an education and knew that the military could be a stepping-stone in that direction. Once they had joined, they wanted to fit in" (2). V (formerly Eve Ensler) also supported this analysis: "My bet is that at some point she was sexually abused or hurt in a fundamental way. . . . I think Lynndie England felt she had to prove herself. Still, it's just hard to believe. It's hard to imagine that women's hearts have been so hurt and numbed, that women's ability to empathize has been so tragically damaged that we are capable of torture" (Ensler, "Leash" 18). V went further, explaining the torture as a form of revenge: "I also think that Lynndie England and other women like her perpetrate abuse on others as an outlet for abuse they once may have experienced—you know, an outlet for the rage that results from being violated. . . . Their positions at Abu Ghraib gave them circumstances where they could act out on what some man has done to them" (19). While these feminist thinkers acknowledge the abuse at the hands of Harman and England, they overlook the impact of that violence on their victims. Through their single-identity-focused analysis, they reduce Harman and England to their roles as victims of patriarchy. It is important to acknowledge the ways these women were used by the military, but not at the expense of ignoring the violence they helped carry out or the men who were on the receiving end of that violence.

The problem with the linguistic strategies employed to explain, or excuse, the actions of Harman and England lies in the erasure of white women's role in perpetuating systems of violence. Oppressed communities are well aware of the danger of women who wield the institutional power of whiteness.[76] This is not a practice of the past, but rather part of a colonial legacy of white supremacy.[77] I situate Fusco's illustrations as an intervention within this ongoing obfuscation of women's capacity for racial violence. The actions of the interrogators captured in the images leave little room for an interpretation that seeks to diminish or dismiss the violence of their activities. The pairing of text and drawings in "Coercive Techniques" becomes visual evidence of the violence of the white female interrogator in the interrogation room—a room she has made her own. The female interrogators illustrated in Fusco's guide, like the interrogators observed by FBI agents, are not victims, and their actions are drawn as deliberate and state sanctioned. Reading reports of sexual coercion and abuse is troubling, but seeing the actions in an illustrated form gives the audience a much more concrete and alarming understanding of what has taken place in the interrogation room. Fusco's co-optation of military and intelligence manuals for this intervention challenges the power of the original texts and subverts their authority by deconstructing and mimicking their form in the service of refusal. I see Fusco employing an intersectional ethics of care that centers the humanity of detainees and refuses to see them as inferior. "Coercive Techniques" develops a form of textual performance that offers readers another tool in the formation of creative resistance. Fusco takes all of the information she has gathered in her research and translates it into an understandable performance text that does not allow the reader to ignore the realities of the US government's use of torture and the role women play in supporting state violence.

Attempted Conversion

The illustrations of the female interrogators take us back to the beginning of the performance text and to Fusco's discussion with Virginia Woolf on women's ability to abuse power. Fusco's embodied critique of gender and power culminates with the disturbing combination of her writing and Turner's images. In concluding the performance text with the manual, Fusco rejects the official narrative and the mainstream discourse around interrogation and leaves her audience with a profoundly unsettling image of women as abusers who actively carry out state violence. The growing number of women and people of color in the military is of concern to those who worry about the use of violence against transnational communities of color in the name of the nation, and works of resistance like *A Field Guide* help convey a cautionary message.[78] The text's intervention offers a model of using performance to embody resistance. Fusco's documentation of her process and the transparency with which she presents her research provides future creators with a blueprint for creating oppositional texts.

The introduction to "Coercive Techniques" identifies the final step in the interrogation practice as "attempted conversion." The manual urges the interrogator not to simply gather information from the subject. The introduction notes that "interrogatees should not be squeezed and forgotten," again alluding to the dehumanizing process of interrogation practices, a process further emphasized by the ending words of the introduction: "A successful conversion can lead to the creation of an enduring asset" (*Field Guide* 110). The humanity of the detainee is further stripped away in the process of creating just another object for use by the military and the government. Fusco's text employs a similar strategy of conversion, attempting to shift the perspective of its audience through the use of performance and the appropriation of military language, practices, and textual forms. With her use of these powerful tactics, Fusco reminds her audience of the humanity of detainees and interrogatees and is particularly effective in prompting a critical political reflection that rejects the narrative of the US government. It is also a reminder of how creators can appropriate tools of oppression to subvert the power of hegemonic structures. In a way, I too am attempting to convert my audience, hoping that they will see Fusco's text as a powerful performance and a form of textual mentoring that centers resistance and leads us to question our own relationships to power. *A Field Guide for Female Interrogators* is an example of the possibilities of creating performance in the service of opposition and refusal.

TWO

Topographies of Resistance

On Monologues and Embracing the Panza

In August of 2009, a small group of creators came together to put on a one-day performance of a powerful set of monologues that told the story of Chicanas' bodies and their struggles with various forms of oppression. Set in the city of San Antonio, Texas, *The Panza Monologues* is a collection of narratives compiled and dramatized by theater scholar and practitioner Irma Mayorga and playwright and performer Virginia Grise. The August 2009 event took place at the Plaza de la Raza's Margo Albert Theatre in Los Angeles, California, for an overflowing audience of over two hundred. The only performer featured was Grise, who took the stage in a simple all-black ensemble against the backdrop of a colorful raised altar. The one-day event was professionally filmed, and the recording offers a contemporary audience the opportunity to watch the performance of the monologues. The recording captures the joy and enthusiasm of the audience, as we hear their cheers, laughter, and other sounds of engagement. The footage offers a snapshot of a moment in time when community came together to bear witness to the embodied stories of Chicana lives as told through Grise's performance.

Several years before the performance of *The Panza Monologues*, a very different set of monologues was being performed to an audience that could not have been more dissimilar. On February 10, 2001, eighteen thousand individuals showed up to watch a star-studded performance of *The Vagina Monologues*, the play by V (formerly Eve Ensler) that had taken the world by storm. The production had come a long way from its first off-off-Broadway performance in 1996, when V was the only actor onstage. Five years later, the monologues were being performed by award-winning actors like Jane Fonda, Rosie Perez, Glenn Close, and Queen Latifah at a gala benefit. This sold-out Madison Square Garden production featured Oprah Winfrey's performance of the script's newest monologue, "Under the Burqa," a tribute to Afghan women living under the Taliban ("Eve Ensler's Tribute"). The Saturday evening gala benefit, which raised more than $1 million, was part of a fundraising campaign for V's V-Day organization ("V's 'The Vagina Monologues'"). While the performance's fundraising effort was promoted as benefiting women all over the world, the organizers focused special attention on the women of Afghanistan ("February 10th"). Oprah's monologue proved to be a major draw, and many audience members "wore burqa swatches as a symbol of remembrance for Afghan women and girls" and signed petitions calling for an end to gender apartheid in Afghanistan ("Eve Ensler's Tribute").[1]

The success of the gala was strongly predicated on its message of empowerment and its ability to connect the performance of the monologues to the issue of global violence against women. The audience watched celebrities perform narratives about vaginas, pleasure, empowerment, and violence onstage. The evening provided the audience with the opportunity to be moved by the performances while also feeling good about their ability to support the fundraising efforts through their patronage and consumption of artifacts, like the burqa swatches. The funds raised through the event were part of what has become a long-term fundraising strategy that has helped the V-Day foundation raise more than $120 million for antiviolence efforts ("About V-Day").

At first glance, the two productions seem very similar: At their center is the impetus to tell the stories of women and women's relationships to their bodies. Both sets of monologues began as performances and continued their evolution as texts through their publication, expanding their audiences and the scope of their influence. *The Vagina Monologues* was initially performed in 1996, in New York City, with the publication of the first version of the script occurring in 1998. The original script for *The Panza Monologues* was published in 2004, the same year the production premiered in Austin, Texas, after being performed as a series of staged readings in 2003. What is different about the productions is the process of storytelling, the focus of the performance, the archiving of the narratives, and the centering of the women whose stories are told. Analyzing the role that positionality and intersectionality play in the creation of *The Panza Monologues*, I focus my analysis on Grise and Mayorga's deliberate deviations from V's model of monologue construction.

While an earlier version of *The Panza Monologues* was published in 2004, my analysis focuses on the second edition of the script, published in 2014 by the University of Texas Press. The latter edition is a rich volume that incorporates the script alongside primary and secondary texts that help enrich the audience's understanding of the play and the creative processes of the creators. I read the book as a coherent whole; this combination of script and additional materials allows the reader to understand the text beyond the limitations of analyzing the script in isolation. As with Coco Fusco's *A Field Guide for Female Interrogators*, the materials produced and compiled in the published version of the performance text offer an opportunity to read the script within the context of its formation and to engage in a textual conversation with the work's creators. Through the melding of nonfiction and fiction, *The Panza Monologues* offers a rich and complex story of performance in service of community and provides a model of textual mentoring through an archiving of a creative process for future artists to learn from in generating their own art.

In this chapter, I read *The Panza Monologues* as an example of a performance that challenges essentialist ideas of identity to create a more complex text that centers intersectionality in a story of community and its quest for justice. The text embodies the possibilities that radical theater making holds for envisioning a more just future. The evocation of feminist texts of the past to inspire and create contemporary performances that more accurately engage with complex issues of difference and identity is a strategy that both relies on those scripts of resistance and challenges universalizing experiences. It relies on audience recognition and allows for creators to build on previous work, not having to reinvent the wheel. Similar to how Virginia Woolf's work inspired *A Field Guide*, I position *The Vagina Monologues* as an influential precursor for *The Panza Monologues*. Like *A Field Guide*, *The Panza Monologues* takes the structure of a previous feminist text and builds on a foundation that centers gender equity. While Fusco is more interested in situating her performance as an intellectual project of resistance, Grise and Mayorga position their performance as a project of radical community building. In the process of creating a more intersectional performance, *The Panza Monologues* also highlights the limitations of single-identity-focused activism demonstrated by *The Vagina Monologues*. Although Grise and Mayorga might not be as directly engaged with V as Fusco is with Woolf, their work is clearly engaging with the politics of representation and storytelling at the center of V's monologues. While V includes stories from women all over the world, Grise and Mayorga choose to focus on the stories of women in their geographical community. By choosing to write the stories of women in their own hometown of San Antonio, Texas, Grise and Mayorga privilege local knowledge in constructing their monologues. They don't need to travel beyond their home to find stories worth documenting, sharing, and situating as repositories of knowledge from which the audience can learn. Although their work is locally focused, Mayorga and Grise expand the scope of analysis through an insightful discussion of body politics rooted in a critique of structural oppression. They move beyond a critique of *The Vagina Monologues* to offer a body of work that gestures toward a radical vision of theater making and textual mentoring.

Monologues: Listening and Creating Meaning

The importance of the monologue in a performance text cannot be underestimated. A badly delivered monologue can take the audience out of the world being built by the performance, while a well-delivered monologue can help the audience feel connected to the character, feel what the actor's words are trying to convey. The use of multiple monologues in a production offers a creator the opportunity to weave the narratives of various individuals into a coherent whole that tells a unique and cohesive story. When those monologues are fictional creations, there is freedom to build the different characters that shape the story. When the monologues are rooted in the experiences of real individuals, the process becomes complicated by the weight of responsibility present in accurately representing the individuals' stories. The documentary-style type of theater that relies on the format of the monologue to create meaning is both powerful and inspiring but also is made difficult by its reliance on reality. The reliance on the monologue by both *The Vagina Monologues* and *The Panza Monologues* affords us an opportunity to explore the feminist practice of emphasizing the personal within a discussion of the political represented in a performance, while also allowing for the interrogation of the role that positionality plays in the process of delivering someone else's story. Both texts rely on the various stories of their interviewees to craft their monologues but do so in ways that are markedly different, illustrating two distinct approaches to using source materials and the intricacies inherent in the practice of incorporating diverse voices into one singular performance.

Given that both *The Vagina Monologues* and *The Panza Monologues* are structured as a set of interrelated monologues, it is important to begin an analysis of *The Panza Monologues* with an understanding of the positionality of its creators and of the individuals whose stories play out onstage. From the very beginning, Mayorga and Grise locate themselves within the text and make clear their positionality. The front cover features an adorable photo of a five-year-old Grise, sporting two ponytails and sitting on a swing. The cover text offers the typical information normally found on a book—title, author, edition—but also informs us that the work has been "written, compiled, and collected" by Grise and Mayorga. The purposeful use of the words "compiled" and "collected" allows the creators to emphasize the archiving project taking place and their role as curators of the project. Inside the book, adjacent to the main title page, a prominent acknowledgment reads, "*The Panza Monologues* script also features stories contributed by Bárbara Renaud González, Petra A. Mata, and María R. Salazar." By crediting these three contributors, the creators recognize the importance of their stories in the project and reject the anonymity of collecting multiple individual stories into one totalizing narrative. The placement of the acknowledgment is significant, as it is a highly visible companion to the main title.[2] From the very beginning, the audience is made aware of the collective aspect of the play and knows the names of Grise and Mayorga's contributors.

The script itself is only fifty pages, but the text is over two hundred pages long. The book is separated into the front matter and five chapters. The first pages include an academic foreword by theater scholar Tiffany Ana López that helps contextualize the work within a theoretical framework that recognizes the impact of the play on the fields of theater studies and Chicanx/Latinx studies. The front matter also includes the creators' acknowledgments, "*Muchas* Many Thank-Yous to All Our *Panza* Allies," in which Mayorga and Grise specifically thank "María Berriozabal, Petra A. Mata, Bárbara Renaud González, Cindy Rodríguez, and María R. Salazar," who answered their "plea for stories about their *panzas*. Each of these women has generously allowed us to perform a moment from her life experiences. We always strive to honor their stories. The gifts of their words and insights make *The Panza Monologues* sing with a deeper truth" (Grise and Mayorga xix). Like the credits listed in the previous pages, the gratitude expressed in this section acknowledges the collaborative role that the women who shared their stories played in the creation of *The Panza Monologues.* The contributors are again mentioned a few pages later, in Grise and Mayorga's introduction to the second edition, where the writers assert their commitment to a feminist theater practice by acknowledging that "our work has been conceived by, written in part by, and compiled by the two of us with important contributions culled from writing and life stories offered by [Renaud González, Mata, and Salazar]" (xxviii). The visibility and positioning of these acknowledgments is significant, as the section is placed at the beginning of the text, before the reader encounters the script. From the beginning, it is clear that *The Panza Monologues* is the work of more than just Mayorga and Grise.

The in-depth description of the creators' collaborative process and the repeated naming of their collaborators stand in contrast to V's recollection of her writing process, as outlined in her short introduction to the script for *The Vagina Monologues.*[3] V writes that "some of the monologues are close to verbatim interviews, some are composite interviews, and with some I just began with the seed of an interview and had a good time" (Ensler, *Vagina* 7). There is a sense of freeness and fluidity in V's description that comes through in her words. Later in the introduction she recounts, "I asked all the women I interviewed the same questions and then I picked my favorite answers" (13). Her ability to pick and choose what stories to tell and how to tell them is described as an enjoyable process, a "good time." While the freedom to express oneself is an important aspect of the creative process, it is complicated when dealing with stories that are not one's own. The lack of specificity used in describing the women behind the monologues offers V the ability to pick and choose and create without being accountable to the original source interview. The overall lack of naming offers V the opportunity to claim complete creative license over the stories of the women.[4] V's description of her process raises important questions about the ownership of these stories and the representation of the women whose lives are supposed to be captured in these monologues. Which monologues are verbatim? Which are composites? Which are her sole creations? The importance of these questions lies in how the narratives become stand-ins for the women they are supposed to represent, and the possibility of misrepresentation inherent in the process.

V herself admits that her curatorial practice is flawed, even as she attempts to dismiss these flaws. I focus briefly on V's described process because it gestures to the difficulties present in attempting to capture someone's personal story without fully understanding the context of their oppression, and it raises questions about how the story is used and for what purpose. In the introduction to one of the monologues, V writes,

> After I finished "The Woman Who Likes to Make Vaginas Happy," I read it to the woman on whose interview I'd based it. She didn't feel it really had anything to do with her. She loved the piece, mind you, but she didn't see herself in it. She felt that I had somehow avoided talking about vaginas, that I was still somehow objectifying them. Even the moans were a way of objectifying the vagina, cutting it off from the rest of the vagina, the rest of the woman. There was a real difference in the way lesbians saw vaginas. I hadn't yet captured it. So I interviewed her again. (Ensler, *Vagina* 113–114)

While the sharing of the monologue with the unnamed woman with whom it originated gestures toward a more collaborative process, it also makes clear that V sees her inability to capture the woman's narrative as a failure of understanding based on differences in sexuality. She isn't just objectifying the vagina, she is diminishing lesbian sexuality and situating it as a curiosity, an object of study—not as part of someone's identity. There is no conscious understanding that the process of translating the woman's story into the monologue is a process rooted in a difference in power. V has the power to decide how to tell the woman's story, but also the power to dismiss her informant's concerns simply because V isn't a lesbian and therefore cannot understand her point of view. The essentialism with which V addresses the critique further marginalizes queerness in her text and reinforces heterosexist ideologies that diminish the power of the monologue. It is an example of the pitfalls present when treating gender as a totalizing frame of reference in isolation from other identity formations.

While gender remains an important lens through which to analyze structures of oppression, analyzing gender oppression separately from other forms of oppression upholds certain systems of power—in this case, V's privilege as a white, heterosexual, cisgender woman. Did the interviewee like the revised monologue? Were the changes significant enough to help the nameless woman see herself in the monologue? Was V able to decenter herself from the monologue to understand her interviewee? As readers, we don't know, since V doesn't tell us. As a result, the introduction to "The Woman Who Likes to Make Vaginas Happy" ends up illustrating the dangers inherent in trying to speak for someone else without interrogating one's own subject position. The monologue, which should be a celebration of a queer woman's pleasure, instead becomes a warped representation of queer desire predicated on V's ignorance of sexual difference.

V's use of monologues acts as a cautionary tale of the dangers of totalizing narratives based on a Western feminist framework, even when well intentioned. Her process raises serious questions about the lack of accountability to storytellers and the cannibalizing of stories into her narrative performance. It is no easy feat to put on a coherent series of monologues that centers the experiences of women and to turn it into a cultural phenomenon that leads to the creation of a powerful nonprofit organization aimed at eradicating gender-based violence. There is no denying the impact that V's performance monologues have had in reframing how we discuss gendered bodies and gender-based violence, and in the creation of the V-Day foundation. It has become an influential model for the blending of performance and activism.[5] While we can acknowledge the good that has come out of *The Vagina Monologues*, it is also important to challenge the problematic aspects of a text based on a limited understanding of difference that celebrates a discourse of feminism rooted in a reductive white perspective. Scholars and theater practitioners have pointed out the issues inherent in trying to create a piece of theater that attempts to offer a universal experience. In order to make *The Vagina Monologues* successful, the performance had to appeal to as wide an audience as possible. That success, however, comes with a price: the loss of specificity that further marginalizes underrepresented groups.

While inspired by V's documentary theater practice, there is a marked difference in how the creators of *The Panza Monologues* approached their production and the collection of women's stories. There is something quite striking in how Mayorga and Grise discuss the process of compiling the stories they translate into the monologues. For Mayorga, the work "became an assemblage of women's writing and voices," but unlike V's script, there is a transparency present in the description of this assemblage that goes beyond naming the women whose voices are represented in the monologues. Mayorga writes that all submitted pieces "were performed in at least one phase of the play's development before [the cocreators] arrived at the final sequence of the script" (Grise and Mayorga 16). The fact that all of the pieces were performed shows a deep level of respect for the women who shared their stories, an acknowledgment that all the submitted stories were worth telling, that each one had value and deserved to be performed and witnessed. These submissions might not have made it into the final published script, but they did not simply vanish. The voices of those women were heard by an audience, even if only once.

Through Mayorga's recollections, we learn about the relationship between the creators and their contributors. We read about Bárbara Renaud González, who served as a "storytelling instigator" and who, along with Grise, engaged in "riff after riff on *panzas* as well as insights, self-deprecation, and smart-aleck wisecracks. In this cacophony, some of the first one-lines that would later be developed as monologues for our play were articulated" (Grise and Mayorga 11–12). Mayorga recounts her own role as a contributor during these exchanges, but "more important I also listened hard, took it all in, and wrote it all down" (12). In addition to crediting Renaud González, this section of the text also illustrates the organic roots of *The Panza Monologues,* whose origins lie directly in conversations with other women, in community. Mayorga describes conversations among girlfriends and coworkers, full of joy and laughter. The pleasure captured in the description of the storytelling practice of the women in their community gestures toward a sharing of personal narratives within a feminist ethos of reciprocity and care. Mayorga documents these stories in the context in which they are told, adding a layer of understanding that can only come from being in community with those sharing the stories.

By documenting the influence of the contributors' stories on the text, Mayorga also highlights the diversity of experience that exists within the group, a diversity that is reflected in their narratives and backgrounds. Even within this group of Tejana women, the distinctions between them are recognized and honored. For example, Renaud González's role as "storytelling instigator" is not the same as the role of the other collaborators. In describing the various writing experiences represented in the submitted works, Mayorga discusses María Salazar's "Inside the *Panza*," a poem Salazar had previously workshopped with Xicana writer, scholar, and activist Cherríe Moraga. Salazar's ability to translate her stories of the panza into skillfully crafted poetry led to her invitation to submit three new monologues, "Sucking It In," "Panza to Panza," and "Praying"

(Grise and Mayorga 16). Although Salazar had developed her skills as a writer, the collaboration includes the stories of women who don't identify as writers, including Petra Mata. Through Mayorga, we learn that Mata is a workers' rights activist whose interview with Grise was shaped into the monologue "A Hunger for Justice" (Grise and Mayorga 16). Mayorga writes that when they first asked Mata to share her story, she responded hesitantly with, "I'm not sure what to say" (Grise and Mayorga 17). Grise was adept at navigating Mata's uncertainty, and it was her understanding of Mata's reticence and her ability to listen that generated a two-hour conversation. Mata's capacity for sharing her story of family, love, and justice was predicated on her ability to trust the person with whom she was sharing such intimate parts of her life—in this case, Grise. While the account of Mata's participation is short, it is extremely significant because it demonstrates the strong link between the cocreators of *The Panza Monologues* and their contributors—a link based on mutual trust and respect. Mayorga and Grise had to establish genuine relationships with their contributors to gather the personal narratives that make up their monologues. These women shared their stories with creators from their community who valued their experiences and their words. Relationality is necessary in the process of a feminist theater-making methodology that credits contributors and holds in reverence the life stories of community.

Understanding the differences found in collecting, curating, and creating performances based on monologues helps identify the politics of representation at play. When a project involves representing the stories of marginalized groups by a creator with the privilege to tell those stories, it is imperative that we understand how those stories are shaped and presented. Recognizing the power the playwright has in crafting monologues allows for an interrogation of that power and its role in creating meaning for an audience. Such an examination demystifies the positionality of the writer in shaping the story of an individual's life and experience. Understanding the process of monologue creation helps explain how Grise and Mayorga's employment of the monologue structure differs from V's use of the format. The documentation offered by the creators of *The Panza Monologues* presents a process of storytelling rooted in collaboration and in community. The monologues become more than simple stories: They become a rich site of analysis for exploring the power of collecting the narratives of marginalized communities for a theatrical audience. They also gesture to the potential of crafting monologues as a form of archiving community narratives of opposition that can serve as models for future forms of resistance.

Locating the Panza

> IN THE BEGINNING . . . CUZ EVERY PEOPLE NEEDS A STORY THAT STARTS THAT WAY.
>
> **"HISTORIA,"** ***THE PANZA MONOLOGUES***

When examining the importance of monologue construction, a monologue's framing within the text becomes an important site of analysis. The presentation of the monologues helps locate the creator within the process of creation and offers the audience a lens through which to engage with the stories being told. From the moment one opens the texts, the difference between *The Vagina Monologues* and *The Panza Monologues* is clear. V begins her text with a loving dedication to her partner, Ariel, "who rocks my vagina and explodes my heart" (Ensler, *Vagina* vii).[6] Grise and Mayorga begin with a dedication to community, "to all the PANZAS in the world for which there is hunger, pain, or sorrow . . . you inspire us to work harder" (v). V's intimate words to her partner are a sexy acknowledgment of their relationship and highlight the role he has played in her life and her work. It is a sweet and cheeky statement. The sentiment felt in Grise and Mayorga's dedication is a more collective one that acknowledges the role their audience plays in motivating their work and recognizes the "hunger, pain, or sorrow" they might be feeling. V's personal dedication reflects the more individually focused storytelling process of *The Vagina Monologues,* while Grise and Mayorga's dedication gestures toward the collectively centered practice characteristic of their creative methodology in *The Panza Monologues.* They are building on the practice of using monologues to generate a creative project that employs an intersectional feminist framework to embrace the distinct voices represented by the monologues. In their introduction, they make it clear that their creation stems from a "feminist ethos that believes a collection of voices does in fact paint a more detailed picture about the complexity of social issues, historical circumstances, and the individual plights of women" (Grise and Mayorga xxvii). The spirit of their sentiment is present in their dedication and echoes throughout the text.

Unlike most creators, who might include a short description of the production history, a casebook, and a brief discussion of process, Grise and Mayorga devote an entire chapter to a discussion of their process. In "*The Panza Monologues*: From Cuentos to DVD," a chapter written by Mayorga, we learn not only about the development of their text but also about the amount of work—both individual and collective—that was required to take the production from idea, to script, to performance, to publication. The chapter provides an in-depth and personal glimpse into Grise and Mayorga's work as artists and community activists, their struggles with working with a cultural center, their relationship with food, and the friendships and collaborations that have made their work possible. We read about the 2003 *Texas Monthly* article "30 Texas Women," which included only three Hispanic women on a list of the most important women in the state's history (Grise and Mayorga 15). The *Texas Monthly* article inspired Mayorga to crowdsource the names of historically important Tejanas to draft a response to the magazine. In the course of challenging the exclusionary and imagined history put forth in the article, Mayorga discovered the willingness of women to share their stories.

The enthusiasm with which community members impart their stories helped Mayorga and Grise create the methodology for collecting the narratives that would become the monologues. This methodology blended the specificity of their community's experience with what they had learned from other creators. Mayorga writes that they "drew on strategies from the traditions of documentary theater, notably contemporary techniques practiced in the work of women playwright/solo performers such as Anna Deavere Smith and Eve Ensler" (Grise and Mayorga 15). The openness with which they share the origin of their project, and their inspirations, offers readers the opportunity to understand the organic growth of the script. There is no grand narrative of the genius artist toiling away in isolation, creating brilliant works to inspire the masses. Instead, we get a narrative of a creative process rooted in community and collaboration—a narrative that builds on the work of other feminist playwrights to produce new works that demonstrate the power of intersectional feminist theater making.

Mayorga and Grise's work also situates the experiences of women with their panzas within an intersectional analysis of oppression that cannot be subsumed under a simple critique of gender. Mayorga recounts the learning that occurred through their work with the monologues: "When people of both sexes and a wide variety of genders talked to us about their *panzas*, they inevitably created linkages that exposed the interconnections of race, culture, socioeconomic history, material and political realities and adaptations, and their bodies." The creators "began to realize that we had struck on something much bigger than our locale, our *chistes*, and ourselves" (Grise and Mayorga 16). In this way, Grise and Mayorga engage with the lived realities of members of their community to create monologues in relation with, and from within, their community for a wider audience.

Mayorga and Grise's ability to create such an intimate and personal set of monologues is based on their insistence on specificity, geographic location, and positionality. While V's mission to compile stories from women throughout the world is an admirable one, it is impossible to responsibly represent the diverse voices of many when filtered through the universalizing voice of one, especially when dealing with such complicated histories of violence and constructions of identity. While many have celebrated the accomplishments of *The Vagina Monologues* and the impact that V-Day has had on other organizations, it is important to recognize how V's use of women's stories differentiates the two monologue projects. V has been roundly criticized for her practice of collecting narratives without an acknowledgment of her position of power or the power of those who perform those narratives. In her reflections on *The Vagina Monologues*, anthropologist Sealing Cheng argues that "the appeal of universality is also what makes 'global vaginahood' so palatable—especially for those who would consume this culturally specific text and mode of feminist activism as universals" (21). In her insightful reading of *The Vagina Monologues*, the performance's use of the burqa, and what she calls the ventriloquial nature of the text, anthropologist and gender studies scholar Srimati Basu argues that the "performers project, render experiences, and speak 'for' women assumed to be invisible and silent, thereby foregrounding the cultural assumptions and political imperatives of the writers' and performers' locations" (32). In part, the criticism levied against V and her project highlights the dangers of attempting to capture the experiences of individuals who don't share similar cultural backgrounds and histories. What we are left with is an incomplete act of translation that privileges the misinterpretation of the storyteller—in this case, V.

As theater professionals and cultural critics, Grise and Mayorga would have been aware of the conversations fostered by V's monologues. In fact, in recognizing the influence of *The Vagina Monologues* on their work, Mayorga acknowledges the limitations of V's methodology, writing, "We, of course, were both familiar with Ensler's solo performance success with *The Vagina Monologues*, but unlike Ensler's wider ethnographic reach, we wanted our work to be culturally specific. We didn't want to look outward for our stories but rather inward, to the *historia* held on the tongues of San Antonio Chicanas—something we believed was not in the public sphere" (Grise and Mayorga 15). The impetus for focusing their work on the specific stories of women in their community is significant, as it highlights the importance of specificity within representations of difference. Mayorga and Grise's awareness of the limitations of V's text allows for an analysis of *The Panza Monologues* that goes beyond a simple critique of V's work. Instead, *The Panza Monologues* offers an example of what Chandra Talpade Mohanty terms a "politics of engagement" that moves away from the popular "politics of transcendence" practiced by Western feminists (122). Mohanty argues that the latter mode of "universal sisterhood, defined as the transcendence of the 'male' world, thus ends up being a middle-class, psychologized notion that effectively erases material and ideological power differences within and among groups of women" (116). Mohanty turns instead to Bernice Johnson Reagon's text on coalition politics to point out that "the experience of being woman can create an illusory unity, for it is not the experience of being woman, but the meanings attached to gender, race, class, and age at various historical moments that is of strategic importance" (Mohanty 118).

By practicing a politics of engagement, through directly speaking with community members in discussions of the panza, Mayorga and Grise learn about the issues that are most pressing in their community. The knowledge they gain through their conversations helps shape the focus of the monologues to center the experiences of their interlocutors, privileging the local but situating it within the global—an artistic form of thinking locally but acting globally. In centering the local stories of the panza, Grise and Mayorga ensure that the most pressing concerns in their community are centered through a framing that allows a non–San Antonio audience to recognize and connect with the issues being represented. Through its focus on specificity, the text rejects the move to universalize the experiences of women and their panzas and instead relies on the audience's ability to follow the connections the monologues make for them—connections that allow for an engagement with the storytelling. The audience can relate to a monologue's focus, seeing a reflection of their own struggles with the panza, and, at the same time, they can recognize and respect important differences.

In locating themselves and their community at the center of their monologues, Grise and Mayorga embrace a process of writing from the margins. Instead of simply replicating existing models of creative engagement like *The Vagina Monologues*, Grise and Mayorga choose to root their writing practice within the San Antonio community whose contributions to the city and to Texas history remain unacknowledged. While existing in the margins can be a site of disadvantage, it can also be a site of possibility. In her brilliant essay "Choosing the Margin as a Space of Radical Openness," bell hooks writes, "I am located in the margin. I make a definite distinction between that marginality which is imposed by oppressive structures and that marginality one chooses as a site of resistance—as location of radical openness and possibility" (23). Instead of seeing their place of existence as merely a site of exclusion, Mayorga and Grise embrace their community and their stories, understanding the strength and resilience of the people who reside within the margins. It is their positionality within this marginal space that grants them the ability to recognize the gestures of resistance in the stories of their contributors. It affects how they collect their monologues, how they represent the women whose lives are performed, and how those lives are framed for the audience.[7]

When thinking about the practice of creating art in the service of community, *The Panza Monologues* offers a model of how to use a position from the margins to create radical work that doesn't insist on assimilating into the center. As hooks reminds us, the space of "radical openness is a margin—a profound edge. Locating oneself there is difficult yet necessary. It is not a 'safe' place. One is always at risk. One needs a community of resistance" (19). In discussing the origins of their collaboration, Grise and Mayorga reveal the struggles they face as activists in their community and how those struggles gave birth to the idea that would become *The Panza Monologues*. The story of the play is a story of resilience in the face of multiple forms of oppression, including economic and racial inequality. The first chapter of the text provides the context necessary for the audience to understand the challenges encountered by the cocreators in their journey from idea to performance while also demonstrating the strength of the creators' connection to the San Antonio community. It is their work as community organizers that helps them foster the community of resistance necessary to successfully create from the margins. It is what motivates their artistic production but also allows them to push beyond the limitations imposed by their marginalization.

This commitment to community is what led to the book project. Grise and Mayorga tell the reader, "We didn't start off our playmaking journey by imagining an end point that consisted of our play as a published text. . . . Over time it became clear to us that creating a testimony through print . . . was part of a necessary material politics that could not only address the transitory quality of live theater's appearance and disappearance but could also amplify the cultural role theater has to play in publicly articulating and circulating facets of Latinas' agency, their/our *self-described* subjectivity" (xxix). The reference to "their/our" and the very specific italicizing of "self-described" in the description of their process are worth noting, as the phrasing is a discursive strategy that reinforces their positionality as members of the community they are representing. Their words also gesture to how the larger project of publishing the monologues and sharing their process—what they refer to as "testimony through print"—becomes an example of a repository of resistance whose captured knowledge can be activated by future creators.

The publication of the script along with the additional materials becomes a project of ensuring the continued life of the text beyond the moment of performance. Grise and Mayorga express that their "desire to have our play in print not only acknowledges requests from our audiences and allies but also seeks to interject a Chicana feminist worldview into the conversation held through U.S. American theater. Self-representations, such as this book, forsake our silence not only in theater's discussions but also in those held in our city, in our Latina/o communities, in our nation" (xxix). The creators position the publication of their text as part of a larger archiving project that disrupts the invisibility of their community in multiple locations. Through the published version of *The Panza Monologues*, the impact of the production extends beyond the stage. In acknowledging why publishing the script and its supplementary materials is important, Grise and Mayorga demonstrate to their community of readers why representation matters. By presenting stories of a community marginalized—both geographically in their city and artistically in the theater world—they challenge the structures in place that disregard or ignore its existence. Readers are invited into the performance through the story of the production and the community in which it was created. Making the script the second chapter of the book encourages a reading of the context that helps educate the audience about the community before they enter the world of the panza. The placing of the background materials before the script also functions as a kind of show-and-tell, divulging the process that led to the script, while allowing the script to show the results of that process.

Reading the Panza

SO IT WAS WRITTEN ON THE BODIES OF WOMEN.

"HISTORIA," *THE PANZA MONOLOGUES*

By the time the reader gets to the performance script of *The Panza Monologues*, the panza as a site of history and knowledge has been firmly established. The heart of the text, the script itself, is only fifty pages long, but it is filled with the stories of a vibrant community full of love, laughter, pain, and resistance. I use the word "heart" to describe the script because the stories encapsulated within it beat with life, giving the larger text a vibrancy that captures the essence of the dynamic community it represents. Having the script follow the first expository chapter allows the reader to enter the creative text with an understanding of the site-specific and community-oriented aspect of the performance. The script is a rich compilation of local knowledge and narratives, made up of fifteen monologues, ten of which tell individual stories of the panza. The performance opens with a prologue, includes a *Noticias* (news) section in the middle, and ends with "Panza Girl Manifesto." Each of the monologues offers the audience a distinct way of looking at the panza that illustrates the complexity of the body and the identity written upon it. All of the monologues are worth studying, but I limit my discussion to the prologue and five monologues that most closely fit the parameters of my analysis: "A Hunger for Justice," "My Sister's Panza," "Noticias," "Praying," and "Panza to Panza." These sections of the script engage with larger conversations about social justice, structural oppression, and resistance. They illustrate the power of performance to invoke storytelling in service of community.

Grise and Mayorga's decision to begin the performance with a prologue establishes the context for the monologues that follow. The prologue contains the basic information an audience would expect, including descriptions of the set, the projection screen behind it, props used throughout the performance, and stage directions. The primary structure onstage is an altar, a sacred site of ritual and remembrance. The importance of the altar is evidenced by the paragraph devoted to describing the items placed upon it: from family photographs, to pieces of clothing, to food, and to objects used as props. Among these items, according to the stage description, are "*piles of books by women of color feminist writers such as Cherríe Moraga, Gloria Anzaldúa, June Jordan, Audre Lorde, and Sharon Bridgforth and others as well as plays that serve as inspiration*" (Grise and Mayorga 39). From the beginning, Mayorga and Grise name the writers who have influenced their work and make clear the intellectual feminist of color legacy with which their text engages. They credit the plays and women of color writers that have played a role in their creative process, ensuring that their impact on the work will be visible. By placing these influential works on the stage, and on the altar specifically, the production cues the audience to the positioning of the performance within a community of feminist of color thinkers and creators. The description of the altar, and its focal point on the stage, ensures that the audience will understand the intentionality behind the personal and political objects that create the backdrop of the performance.

While playwrights will often provide introductions to their scripts, Grise performs the background needed to understand the production in the prologue.[8] Similar to Coco Fusco's summoning of Virginia Woolf's foundational feminist work in *A Field Guide for Female Interrogators*, Grise and Mayorga open the dialogue of their text with a direct reference to V's *The Vagina Monologues*: "There once was this play. This really quite interesting play. It was this play about women. . . . It described all these women from different places, different groups, different races, different ages. . . . And it told stories. Stories about these women that united them through one particular thing. The play was about *(beat)* their vaginas" (40). Given the popularity of V's text, it is fair to state that many readers and audience members would have at least heard of *The Vagina Monologues*. The creators' feminist politics of citation are again evidenced in the work. Furthermore, the reference to so many different women being united through their stories' emphasis on the vagina illustrates Grise and Mayorga's understanding of the universalizing strategy of V's text.

The script credits *The Vagina Monologues* with expanding the conversation on the war being waged over the bodies of women. Grise and

Mayorga write that "what this woman's play said once again—as so many great women have said over and over—is that we are in a war. A war for our own bodies" (41). Grise and Mayorga not only acknowledge V's text but also make clear that its discussion of the struggle for women's bodily autonomy is part of a larger conversation—that V's work does not exist in isolation. By openly referencing *The Vagina Monologues,* Grise and Mayorga acknowledge the importance of their text's precursor, and they place *The Panza Monologues* within a broader legacy of women resisting gender violence. While the recognition of V's text is important, it is also significant that they do not name V, which stands in stark contrast to the naming of the feminist of color writers included in the earlier description of the altar. The strategy might seem dismissive, but it offers Mayorga and Grise the opportunity to recognize the precursor text's importance without necessarily centering its creator and, in the process, to reject the positioning of their own text as simply a copy of V's work. Instead, *The Vagina Monologues* becomes just one small part of a larger legacy of feminist texts that Grise and Mayorga engage with in developing their intersectional performance text.

In their creative treatment of oppression and the gendered body, Grise and Mayorga choose to shift the focus from the vagina—or what they refer to as the *chocha*—to the panza. Grise tells the audience, "In the war of our bodies, it became clear that before you can get to the battle of the *chocha,* we have another score to settle, another place on our beautiful bodies to baptize, actualize, a place that had been demonized, sterilized, starved, stuffed, covered over" (41). Grise and Mayorga don't dismiss the importance of the chocha, but they shift the audience's attention to the panza, the repository of the body's story of joy and struggle. They write that the panza "knows, about us, about you. But the *panza* also knows that it ain't alone there in the middle of us. That it needs the legs to walk, the arms to carry it, the mouth to feed it, and the heart to excite it" (42). For Grise and Mayorga, the panza is part of the whole: It doesn't exist in isolation from the rest of the body, or from the material conditions within which it lives. In the glossary that immediately follows the script, they define "panza" as "(1) The core. (2) Center of the body. (3) Center of life." (91).[9] It is important to note that they do not define "panza" as simply "belly." The three definitions expand the meaning of the word, growing from the core, to the center of the body, to the all-encompassing center of life. Their defining of the word beyond the borders of the physical mirrors the larger project of the text, as it invites us to learn about our bodies and their condition within the context of our social location.

Furthermore, among the members of Mayorga and Grise's community, the panza is the site that nourishes the story of their lives. While experiences with the vagina inspired the disclosure of stories in *The Vagina Monologues,* Grise tells us that "when I talked to my homegirls, they weren't all spilling over stories about their *chocha.* There we would be—with big plates of *fideo,* or *pan dulce,* or *menudo,* or *tripas* . . . and we'd all be telling the stories of our *panzas*" (42). The fact that these stories were being communicated while consuming culturally specific meals that nourish the panza is significant, as it illustrates the importance of food both to the panza and to the communal process of storytelling the script is trying to capture. It is also a decolonial practice of reclaiming the culturally specific food traditions that assimilation and colonial logics have tried to erase. The practice of breaking bread and sharing one's story is an integral part of being in community, and the script documents the creators' rooting of their monologues within this cultural tradition. It is these community-based conversations with the women in their lives that shape the focus of the script. The script doesn't dismiss stories about the vagina, but it does insist on centering the stories of the community that helped bring the project into being—stories that revolve around the panza.

The prologue's discussion of the stories of the panza is vital to understanding Mayorga and Grise's process of compiling the monologues that make up the script. Grise tells the audience, "And I thought, we gots to hear the story of the *panza.* And so I listened, with my heart in my hands. I listened as women told me about the life of their *panzas. Panzas* were crying out everywhere: 'Tell my story!'" (42). Grise and Mayorga's description of listening—openly and with a loving heart—makes it clear that these stories are significant and worth witnessing. The panza is represented as having agency, the power to tell its own stories and to demand that others hear it. The panza is not silent; we just don't listen. By laying out their approach to gathering the stories of women in their community, they ensure that the audience understands their feminist methodology of documentary playwriting.

For Grise and Mayorga, the discussion of women's bodies has to be rooted in an act of storytelling that values the narrative and honors the storyteller. They compellingly write, "Now someone's *panza* story is a sacred story, and to share it with someone else is to tell them about the conditions of your life" (42). The deliberate use of the word "sacred" gestures to the importance that the stories of the panza hold for the performance's creators. These aren't simply stories; they are meaningful narratives worthy of veneration, and they represent the complexities of women's lives. The positioning of someone's story of their panza as sacred is a powerful strategy of resignification: It rejects the historical dismissal of the narratives of women of color and recognizes the power of these stories to inspire and teach us. After all, "when you listen to the *panzas* of all the *mujeres* out there, you can hear the world according to women. That's the power of a *panza* story" (Grise and Mayorga 42). It is empowering to situate the body of women of color as the site of knowledge, and the panza as being able to tell the story of the world from a perspective that refuses the white supremacist logic of male-centered history.

In their centering of their community's panza stories, Grise and Mayorga also gesture to some of the problematic practices involved in the compiling of individual narratives for creative projects. Grise vocalizes this critique in the prologue: "Well, *that* woman, she called *her* play *The Vagina Monologues.* And for her play, she sat on a stool, kind of like this, like me here. She got paid to go all over the world collecting stories about the *chocha*. . . . And she spoke her stories from her stool" (42–43). Again, Mayorga and Grise don't name V, but they do make it clear that they recognize V's proprietary approach to the stories she collected for *The Vagina Monologues.* The choice to italicize "*that* woman" and "*her* play" emphasizes V's individually centered approach to storytelling, while the reference to V's funded trip to collect these stories gestures to the privilege of such a practice. The use of "her stories" in the description of V's performance is also significant because it again emphasizes her ownership of the various monologues. Mayorga and Grise's description of V's text reflects some of the critiques that have been made about *The Vagina Monologues.*[10] Mayorga and Grise resist V's practice of consuming the stories of others in an effort to popularize their work.

Grise tells the audience she can't simply sit on a stool: Her panza has to move. The stories of the panza she is telling cannot be told from a static position at the center of the stage, looking over the audience from the stool and vocalizing words we assume belong to various women. She disidentifies with V's use of the stool as the place of power from which to speak. Instead, Grise and Mayorga choose to use Grise's body to perform the stories with which they've been entrusted. They do not write about these stories as if they own them. Instead,

> in honor of all those women who let me borrow their stories, I share them with you cuz they're not just her stories
>
> *points to a woman in the audience*
>
> or her stories
>
> *points to another woman in the audience*
>
> or my stories anymore. They are us. They are our stories. (43)

Grise and Mayorga's deliberate use of the word "borrow" rejects the idea of their ownership over the narratives of the women who have shared them—a stark contrast to V's practice. The script positions the creators' sharing of the panza stories as a way of honoring the women who allowed their stories to become a part of the project. The stage directions indicate Grise pointing to members of the audience, a strategy that brings the audience into the performance and further emphasizes the centering of community in the production. The monologues performed by Grise become "our stories" of the panza—our stories of struggle, resistance, love, and joy. The centering of community becomes a practice of feminist theater making that encourages an active engagement from the audience—not a voyeuristic consumption of the stories of nameless women.[11] While Mayorga and Grise use the prologue to draw a distinction between their performance and V's well-known play, they don't allow their critique of V's process to move beyond that first monologue. They briefly, but meaningfully, engage with *The Vagina Monologues*, but they leave the topic in the prologue and move on, choosing to focus on the stories of their community.

The prologue leads the audience into the performance of the monologues that follow. Among these is the fifth monologue, "A Hunger for Justice," based on the story of Petra Mata. The previous chapter of the text introduced Mata as one of Grise and Mayorga's collaborators in the process of collecting the stories of their community. Mayorga recalls, "When originally asked to share her *panza* story, Petra responded, 'I'm not sure what to say.' She began slowly with the words, 'I have always been *pansonsita* . . .'" (Grise and Mayorga 16–17). Mata's hesitation perhaps signals a lack of confidence in her story, but the fact that she spent two hours sharing it proves her storytelling ability and establishes that she has something important to say. Their decision to incorporate Mata's story into the script demonstrates that Mayorga and Grise recognize the sacredness of her story and the importance of sharing it without rendering her invisible. They shaped the two-hour interview into "A Hunger for Justice," but it is Mata's own words that open the monologue. The choice to begin with a voice-over of Mata's original words is a powerful way of honoring her story: Grise and Mayorga are ensuring that Mata is present in the monologue, even as Grise embodies her narrative through the performance. Unlike V's monologues, which are loosely inspired by the stories V collects, Grise and Mayorga center Mata in the telling of her story, never appropriating it or claiming ownership over the narrative. Instead, we get a monologue based on the life of an extraordinary labor activist that tells us a story of community resistance and the panza.

"A Hunger for Justice" is the first monologue that makes use of the screen behind the altar. The scene description describes a video made up of various photographs and images of early twentieth-century Mexican American families in South Texas, curated from the digital photo collection of the Library of Congress. The use of photographs selected from the archives helps visually contextualize Mata's story, but it also situates her narrative within a community history of perseverance and resistance. Over the photos we hear a voice telling Mata's story, beginning with, "I have always been *pan-son-cita*" (Grise and Mayorga 55). The voice tells us the first-person story of our narrator and her life in Mexico on a rancho, and shares memories of her grandmother making tortillas from scratch. The voice describes a simple life, living in community, and being happy with what Mata's family possessed, even if it wasn't much. At this point, Grise enters the scene, carrying an ironing board, and she begins pressing a shirt while she takes over the story from the voice-over. She starts by telling the audience, "But the reality of living is getting food to your *panza*," setting the scene for a monologue that makes the connection between labor, exploitation, and the physical well-being of the body (56). The use of the ironing board as a prop is significant because it positions the narrator's body as fully engaged in labor—in this case, the gendered labor of ironing, or of garment work. This centering of labor is vital, given that the monologue focuses on Mata's experience with labor organizing after the 1990 firing of Levi Strauss factory workers.[12]

"A Hunger for Justice" is the first monologue that directly links the panza to the embodiment of oppression. The monologue tells the story of women who were callously discarded by an employer looking to maximize profits by cutting labor costs. Their story becomes one of resistance as the narrator tells the audience, "Overnight, we became organizers. We were connecting the movement, the struggle, with the economy, with the systems" (56). The script describes the growth of these women into organizers as they came to understand the complex economic conditions and the structures of oppression that facilitate them. These women are not reduced to victims whose stories of struggle are performed onstage for the consumption of the audience. Instead, the monologue gives the audience a complex narrative of struggle and agency, as told through the panza: "When the plant shut down, what experienced the majority of the pain was the *panza* because there wasn't going to be nutrition, and we had a hunger for justice. A lot of us lost weight because the suffering is reflected in all the parts of your body. So if you are suffering—so is your *panza*" (56). By describing the panza as the physical site of suffering, Grise and Mayorga ground the discussion of economic injustice on the body, moving from the abstract to a kind of specificity that acknowledges the humanity of the worker/narrator. The pain of the panza because it isn't being fed, or because it is feeling the stress of the protest movement, becomes a manifestation of the economic exploitation experienced by the workers. Rather than being a simplistic monologue that focuses solely on the violence played on women's bodies, "A Hunger for Justice" strikes a balance between describing the physical consequences of the strike on the women—the suffering felt in the body because of their economic reality—and conveying the empowerment that comes with their organizing. The hunger for nourishment becomes a stand-in for the hunger for justice—both hungers the organizers endeavor to feed.

The script's focus on the panza as the site where intersecting systems of injustice manifest allows for a complex narrative to unfold onstage. Just as the narrator's condition as a worker affects her life outside of the workplace, the knowledge she gains in organizing influences her personal life. The narrator tells the audience, "We have to pay attention and do things for our bodies. Why can we do things for our family, for the organization, but for us—when do we do for us? If we start with the *panza* that's good because the *panza* is a room where everything comes from" (56). Mayorga and Grise use the panza not only to critique the economic exploitation experienced by Mata and her fellow organizers but also to illustrate the burden of care work for family and community that falls on the shoulders of women. The exploitation of women's labor is not limited to the workplace. By positioning the panza as "a room where everything comes from," however, the script also frames the panza as the site of strength and flexibility. Like its stories, the panza is a sacred place that must be cared for: "I think our *panza* has a heart that in extension suffers—suffers from our not taking care of it. So, if the *panza* is one of the most important parts of our bodies, it's important that we think about it and tie it to everything we do. If our body breaks down, then how are we going to do all this work?" (Grise and Mayorga 57). The monologue gestures to both the personal and the political ways in which the panza is affected by economic oppression. The inability to care for one's panza—for one's body—because of the material conditions of the labor movement affects not just the individuals participating in the protests but the entire community.

The monologue's insistence on the power of the panza to tell the story of labor and resistance provides a model of storytelling that complicates simple narratives of oppression that ignore the agency of marginalized individuals. "A Hunger for Justice" illustrates the possibilities of using the stage to document resistance to economic and labor injustice. I read this monologue as part of a legacy of using performance to represent injustice and opposition by Chicanx/Latinx communities. Similar to the members of Teatro Campesino employing performance to inform, educate, and resist labor exploitation, Grise and Mayorga shape Mata's story into a monologue that documents hardship while also representing the strength of a community. By centering the experience of Chicana workers, they are also expanding Teatro Campesino's legacy of performance and activism by directly inserting Chicanas into that history of labor and resistance. While the protests might not have been successful in stopping the factory's closing, Mata and her fellow organizers created Fuerza Unida, an organization that fought for their rights as workers and continues to advocate for the well-being of their community.[13] "A Hunger for Justice" becomes a beautiful story of a marginalized group of women resisting unfair labor practices and economic exploitation, and it provides students of theater and performance an opportunity to witness how storytelling on the stage can document and celebrate the narratives of individuals like Petra Mata.

Another monologue that draws connections between an individual narrative and structures of inequality is the emotionally charged seventh monologue, "My Sister's Panza." While "A Hunger for Justice" connects the condition of the panza to economic and labor exploitation, "My Sister's Panza" takes on a discussion of how food and culture can become weaponized against a community. As the narrator of the monologue, Grise tells the story of her sister's struggle with her body, her panza, and heartbreak. The first words of the monologue—"My sister lost her *panza*, lost it because of her husband. It left because he left her," spoken as Grise sits on a stool with a book in her hand—indicate that this story will be about pain and loss (Grise and Mayorga 61). We learn that the narrator's sister met her husband through a personal ad, and that "my sister still had her *panza* then. That's what amazed her. This guy loved her, really loved her—big, beautiful *panza* and all" (61). As Grise speaks, the stage directions note, "*She pulls out a paper chain of red hearts from the book. They hang over the edges onto the floor*" (61). The fact that the sister is amazed at being loved fully for who she is—*panza* and all—is heartbreaking but also indicative of the messages that women internalize about what bodies are worth loving. The chain of hearts spilling from the book is a simple prop that gestures toward a love story—one we learn will not have a happily-ever-after ending.

The monologue traces the sister's complicated relationship with her *panza* back to childhood. The narrator recounts, "She's had that *panza* since she was seven when she was all heat and baby fat. When we would run out to greet ice cream men calling us with their bells. Seven, when she slowly became more and more thirsty each day, itching for water at every moment, and then she'd pee hot streams of burnt yellow, every thirty minutes. Until finally, *mamí* took her in to see the doctor man" (61). The description of the childhood joy of running after the ice cream truck even with her panza gestures toward a time of innocence, before she become conscious of the messaging that would alter her relationship to her body.[14] As Grise tells the audience, "The tests came back and there it was: sugar, sugar running *como* syrup in her urine, turning it golden sunset yellow, poisoning her pancreas," she pulls out a second strand of paper from the book—this time long, white, curled ribbons to symbolize the sugar coursing through the young girl's body (62).

The sister's diagnosis becomes a life-altering moment for the entire family. Although it is terrifying to learn that her child is ill, the mother questions the diagnosis of diabetes: "'What's that?'" (62). The doctor's answer, rather than focusing on the illness, becomes entangled with cultural biases. Grise tells the audience, "Our *mexicana* mother didn't know what he meant when he said we had too much of us around to love. She said, 'That's the way kids are supposed to be.' But, to save us, we had to change—everything. All of our *comidas* had to change, now, today, this minute!" (62). The doctor's strategy of describing diabetes as a result of "too much love" directly links the disease to how the mother cares for her children, and it replicates colonialist discourse that positions non-white, culturally specific foods as nutritionally inferior.[15] The urgency behind the words used to describe the meals that had to change places blame on the mother's cooking and makes value-laden judgments on the family's culturally specific foods. The narrator recounts that "worst of all, they made *mamí* go to a nutritionist to learn how to cook out her love. They were teaching her how to lose the savings of our *panza* banks. Our *panzas*, they are what told her that her kids were never 'over her dead body' gonna starve. Even if we sometimes did" (62). The painful description of a mother being taught that her expressions of love and care are wrong—that her cooking and her efforts to nourish her family are the problem—is heartbreaking. The passage alludes to the poverty and hunger the family has experienced, but instead of addressing the larger social determinants of health, the medical community focuses on the actions of the family: "Mamí was crushed, broken. What had she done to her baby's pancreas? She didn't know, but she learned to poke my sister with life-giving shots to keep her *bebita* alive" (62). Instead of attempting to understand how poverty and other structures of inequality are affecting this family, the medical experts simply blame the mother and the culture of the home. Such blame ignores the social and material conditions that affect the health of communities. As anthropologist Michael Montoya makes clear, "Type 2 diabetes . . . occurs in populations subjected to specific environmental, historical, social, and political pressures—pressures that shaped the formation of the ethnic group in the first place" (35). For the family's doctor, however, blaming the mother's cooking for her daughter's diabetes provides an easier answer for dealing with the disease.

At first glance, the monologue might seem like a simple story of a sister who struggles with illness and heartbreak. The narrative, however, offers a strong critique of the medical establishment's failure to meet the health care needs of communities of color, and it highlights the impact such approaches to treatment have on individuals and families. The blame placed on the mother for cooking with "too much love" is rooted in a white supremacist hierarchy of food that situates traditional non-Western foods as inferior. The way that traditional Mexican food is vilified by the medical establishment is part of a larger historical process of assimilation and white supremacy. The doctor's and the nutritionist's "education" efforts are reminiscent of the types of Americanization programs, popular in the first half of the twentieth century, that emphasized moving away from traditional immigrant foods toward "American" food staples in order to properly assimilate. Historian George Sánchez has traced how "food and diet management became yet another tool in a system of social control intended to construct a well-behaved, productive citizenry" (102). Mexican mothers were seen as instrumental in changing the culture of food in these communities and ensuring the health of their families.[16] Completely overlooked were the structures of inequality in place that more deeply affected the health and wellness of these Mexican and Mexican American communities. Decades later, the same biases against culturally specific foods continue to influence the discourse of illness. Instead of understanding the complex relationship between poverty and the family's diet, the doctor reduces the cause of the sister's diabetes to the mother's cooking.

We see the impact that the medical establishment's messaging about brown, working-class bodies has on the narrator's sister. After the sister finds out that her husband is leaving her for a "thin little blonde," her panza becomes the site where her heartbreak manifests itself: "I think it was that moment, that moment of fury and disgust, that her *panza* began to shrink, pulled into her by the gravity of her collapsing heart" (Grise and Mayorga 62–63). Her husband's rejection of her love and the fact that he leaves her for a "thin little blonde" reinforces the messages the sister received as a child about being fat and Mexican: She isn't good enough. The shame of being fat and of seeing her panza as something that needs to be managed and made small is a result of years of fatphobic messaging by the medical establishment and mainstream culture—messaging the sister has internalized. The pain of the dissolution of her marriage and her husband's callousness manifests in her physically shrinking size. The narrator recounts, "She stopped eating, stopped the *panza*, stopped feeding it the happiness it needed" (63). The phrase "stopped eating" is repeated four more times, culminating in the description that she "stopped eating until every roll of her *panza* was gone" (64). The mourning of her marriage is played out on her body and in her inability, or unwillingness, to feed her panza. The heartbreak transforms her once-full body into a body that more closely aligns with Western standards of beauty: "One day, she turned sideways, and you'd never know she'd even had a *panza* 'cause the sorrow of her hip bones pushed up against new, size 6 dresses she had to buy instead of 14's. And where her *panza* had been, only a hollow bowl of smooth skin" (64). The use of "sorrow" to describe the sister's new body does not allow the audience to view her weight loss as some misguided version of a makeover.[17] Instead, the narrator uses the description of her sister's transformation to help us understand how the pain of heartbreak plays out on the body, even as she mourns the emptiness left behind. Given the messaging her sister had received for all of her life, it is no surprise that the panza, the site of "too much love," again becomes a location from which to control and manage the body. The monologue, however, intervenes in the discourse that would celebrate the loss of the panza, or frame its loss as healthy, and instead focuses on the harm its absence creates.

Given the overwhelming messaging in mainstream culture that equates thinness with happiness, the sister's weight loss should have made her happy. But the monologue quickly dispels the myth of health and happiness based on thinness. We learn that even as the sister lost weight, "she measured her blood sugar to find sky-high readings of sugar, sugar, sugar" (64). Losing weight did not solve her pancreas's inability to produce enough insulin to regulate her glucose levels. The fact that her sugar levels were high even as her panza disappeared rejects the simple narrative that equates being overweight with illness and, in this case, with diabetes. The practice of defining good health based on anthropometric indicators, while relatively recent, has become normalized in both the scientific world and mainstream culture. Various methods have been used to measure bodies in an effort to determine whether someone is overweight, but the most popular is the body mass index (BMI). The use of BMI to identify ideal weight in populations was endorsed by the National Institutes of Health in 1985 and was included in the definition of obesity in a 1985 joint report of the United Nations Food and Agriculture Organization, the World Health Organization, and the United Nations University (see Flegal et al.). Although it remains popular, BMI is known to be a problematic metric in the definition of good health (see Nuttall). When seeking to understand the causes of chronic diseases like diabetes, it becomes even more important to acknowledge the limitations of BMI. In their study of the association between BMI and type 2 diabetes, S. Strings and colleagues argue that "BMI has received unwarranted focus as a prime predictor" of type 2 diabetes (29). In fact, their findings "directly contradict claims that the prevalence of obesity can explain differences in [type 2 diabetes] rates across racial and ethnic categories" (29).

Just as the sister's diabetes does not magically disappear with her weight loss, neither does her heartbreak. The narrator painfully tells the audience, "And I know as she slid the needle of her insulin shot under her skin, she wondered how much would it take to take away the *panza* pain for good?" (Grise and Mayorga 64). The monologue ends with a clear and biting critique of the medical system that instigated her sister's journey of body shame and insecurity: "I wonder if the doctor would think she'd done enough to help control the sugar sweetness of her diabetes now?" (64). The story of a sister's personal heartbreak becomes a powerful narrative about the dangerous equation between health and weight and a larger critique of how the discourse of illness is influenced by racial and cultural biases.[18] "My Sister's Panza" is a story of pain and heartbreak that illustrates how our panzas are used to diminish our self-worth and to define our health through metrics rooted in racial biases and cultural ignorance. The powerful ending phrase of the monologue helps connect the personal story of the narrator's sister to the monologue that follows and to a larger history of health inequality experienced by the San Antonio Chicanx/Latinx community.

Strategically placed after "My Sister's Panza," the monologue "Noticias" includes health statistics from the city of San Antonio. While Grise sits at the altar, the audience's attention is drawn to a solo performer in the center of the stage. Identified as Laura Cambrón in the description preceding the monologue, the dancer performs a traditional *zapateado*, a percussive dance considered the heartbeat of *son jarocho*, a musical genre from the Mexican state of Veracruz. The rhythmic pounding of Cambrón's feet on the *tarima* (wooden platform) punctuates the health statistics projected on the screen behind her. The music and her dancing add a soundtrack upon which to layer the *noticias*, or news, being shared with the audience. Grise and Mayorga's description notes that "*each slide contains a headline or health fact gathered from our hometown paper, the* San Antonio Express-News, *about the health conditions of Mexican Americans in San Antonio—named one of America's 'Fattest Cities'*" (65). The creators' phrasing situates them as part of the community the newspaper is writing about, and it identifies the assumed correlation between weight and health. The dubious distinction of being named one of the fattest cities in the nation negatively frames the residents of the city and perpetuates moralistic discourse that sees fatness as inherently bad, or as a moral failing.

"Noticias" features thirteen projected slides, each providing a fact related to the health of San Antonio's residents. The first slide cites the source for the *panza* facts being shared, ensuring that the audience understands that the information is not of Mayorga and Grise's own creation.[19] The slides tell a story of a population whose health and wellness have been reduced to alarming statistics. We learn that "the number of obese or overweight Texans has increased by 10% in the last decade," and that "the highest increase in obesity has been observed among Hispanics and African-Americans" (65, 66). The slides inform us that "among kids 12 to 19, 44% of Hispanics are overweight and 23% are obese. Nearly 40% of younger children are overweight and 24% are obese" (66). The statistics point to the issue of weight being a problem not just for adults but also for the children raised in these communities. The emphasis on the highest increase occurring in communities of color further pathologizes those communities.

As in the case of the doctor who blamed a mother's cooking for the illness of her child, using statistics to tell a story without context misidentifies the underlying problems with a community's health and places the blame, and the responsibility for a solution, solely on individuals. What is important about these slides, however, is that Grise and Mayorga interrupt the medical discourse that blames communities of color for the impact of health inequity on their bodies.

Among the information shared are facts that shift the focus from individuals to structures. We learn that "the average restaurant plate has grown from 10" to 12" in diameter," that schools in the state "generate about $54 million a year from vending machine contracts," and that "the food industry produces roughly 3,800 calories a day for every man, woman, and child in America . . . twice what they need" (65–66). The slides gesture toward the role that food industries play in normalizing the overconsumption of unhealthy foods. The statistics shared also point to the reality that there is money to be made from this overconsumption. The fact that the state's school systems generate such an exorbitant amount of money from selling students highly processed foods in vending machines should raise serious questions about the state's investment, or lack of, in the health of its children. The slides disrupt the narrative that one's health is simply a question of one's individual choices and illustrate the role that capitalist structures play in the shaping of food choices.

Grise and Mayorga further expand the audience's understanding of the living conditions experienced by residents of the state. They point to the role of geography in health outcomes, noting that "living in sprawl can increase your spread—those in compact counties weigh up to 6 pounds less"; and they draw an important connection between education and poverty with the statement that "in 2000, more than half of Texas Hispanics had less than a high school education. Less than 9% had a college degree, and the income for Hispanics . . . was two-thirds what it was for Anglos" (66). These statistics further illustrate the impact of poverty on the health outcomes of Mexican Americans in the state. As scholars like Alfonso Morales have pointed out, "low-income people and people of color, [paradoxically] are overweight yet malnourished. They face an overwhelming variety of processed foods but are unable to procure a well-balanced diet from the liquor stores and mini-marts that dominate their neighborhoods. These groups are food insecure, but furthermore, they are victims of food injustice" (149). Their food insecurity comes in part from the disinvestment of supermarkets in urban communities and the resulting difficulties in finding non–highly processed foods. It's one thing to tell working-class people to eat better; it's another to actually make it possible for community members to have access, both economic and geographic, to better-quality foods.

The slides' curation of information offers a powerful intervention in the erasure of structural inequality in the discussion of health outcomes. Grise and Mayorga situate the story of illness from "My Sister's Panza" within a discourse of health rooted in a complex understanding of how environmental factors, or the social determinants of health, affect the body. The World Health Organization defines social determinants of health as the "non-medical factors that influence health outcomes. They are the conditions in which people are born, grow, work, live, and age and the wider set of forces and systems shaping the conditions of daily life." Among these factors are education, food security, housing, discrimination, and other conditions affected by inequality and intersectionality (see López and Gadsden). Social determinants of health have a deep impact on the health and well-being of community members, but they are often overlooked in favor of simply blaming individuals for illness. While "Noticias" is specific to San Antonio and Texas, it tells us much about the overall social determinants of health experienced by working-class communities of color, including poverty, urban sprawl, and education outcomes. These connections to health are important, because "if the role of social determinants is not sufficiently addressed in chronic condition management, they will continue to be a key barrier to the improvement of population health" (Hill et al. 68). The scene also instructs us on the creative use of research in telling stories of inequity. By placing "Noticias" after the very personal and emotional story of "My Sister's Panza," Grise and Mayorga humanize the statistics they share. The sister is part of the story the slides are trying to tell, and the pairing helps the audience understand that the numbers in the slideshow represent human beings. They are not simply statistics. At only two pages, "Noticias" makes a short but powerful statement about the panza, health, and inequity.

"Praying," the narrative that follows "Noticias," recenters Grise on the stage. As she stands in front of the altar, we hear a heartbreaking story of domestic violence, told from the perspective of a child. The monologue takes place in a car, with the eight-year-old narrator sitting in the back seat, witnessing her father's abuse of her mother. As she sits, holding her little sister's hand, all she can do is pray. We hear the terror in her voice when Grise speaks the words, "If I tried to talk to him *(whispered)* / We would all be dead" (Grise and Mayorga 67). The girl's fear for her mother, for her sister, and for herself is deeply felt, as the phrase "we would all be dead" is repeated five times throughout the short monologue. We feel her powerlessness as she watches her father hit her mother's panza and she repeats, "All I could do was pray" (67–68). We watch Grise use a pillow as a prop, hitting it as she recounts, "He slugged it . . . He hit her *panza* . . . Hard" (68). The narrator "prayed and prayed . . . prayed and prayed," begging God to stop her father (68). Even after her mother slumps over, "He kept hitting her / Screaming at her / He kept hitting her *panza*" (68). The mother's panza, which we learn holds the narrator's baby brother, is the site upon which the father unleashes his rage and anger. The mother's panza becomes the location where domestic violence manifests itself—the place on the woman's body where the patriarch can focus his need for control. The fact that the mother is pregnant makes the father's explosive violence on the panza even more terrifying. The entire family is deeply affected by the brutality they cannot control. The young girl's only avenue is to pray to a god that doesn't respond to her pleading.

While the domestic violence narrated in "Praying" could easily fit within the structure of *The Vagina Monologues*, the specificity of *The Panza Monologues* allows the audience to recognize its critique of the Latinx community. The monologue focuses on the impact of domestic violence beyond the target of the violence to demonstrate how such violence affects those who love the person being abused. It expands the scope of those affected from the individual to the community. What further distinguishes "Praying" from the types of monologues included in V's performance is that the critique of the Latinx patriarchal family structure, which allows for such violence to occur, is coming from within the Latinx community. The critique from within disavows the voyeuristic impulse that comes when performing narratives that are culturally specific but are written and produced for audiences who might lack an understanding of that culture and who are not being encouraged to decenter their own positionality. While one doesn't have to identify as Latinx to be moved by the monologue, the audience does not forget that it is a monologue written by and about the experience of growing up in a violent Latinx household. Having Grise, a Chicana actor, perform the monologue helps ensure that the cultural specificity of the narrative is visible. Mayorga and Grise don't have to change that specificity to make the monologue relatable; after all, domestic violence affects families from all cultural and economic backgrounds. But it is significant that Chicanas and Latinas, whose stories of violence are often hidden behind familial silence and remain invisible in mainstream theater, feel seen and represented in the narrative of "Praying."

As readers, we know that the monologue was written by María Salazar, one of the women Grise and Mayorga recognize as contributors to *The Panza Monologues*. The acknowledgment of Salazar's creation of the monologue, both in the front matter and throughout the text, stands in contrast to V's practice of anonymizing the monologues in her performance. In addition to identifying Salazar as the writer of "Praying," Grise and Mayorga ensure that readers understand its deep impact on audience members. In their introduction to the second edition of *The Panza Monologues*, Grise and Mayorga share that women have approached them after shows to discuss their own experiences with abuse. They write that "'Praying' not only depicts the spoken terror of domestic abuse but also specifically articulates its force within the structure of a Latina/o family," which allows for Chicanas and Latinas to feel a connection to the performance that helps capture the pain of familial violence (xxx). The monologue "often serves as a catalyst for these women to speak, to find the fortitude to name, or mark their life experience in spite of the cultural values that ask only for their shame or silence" (xxx–xxxi). Salazar's ability to write her panza story into being offers the eight-year-old girl who cowered in the back seat, terrified of being heard praying, the opportunity to speak. The danger of vocalizing her fear before was too strong: The only time she speaks to her mother in the monologue is to ask, "'Mommy, are you OK?'" to which the father angrily responds by "swerv[ing] the car / 'Shut up! / *¡Cállate el hocico!*'" (69). The threat of further violence ensures the girl's silence and compliance. The last, whispered lines of the monologue, "If I talked to him / We would all be dead," painfully capture the narrator's fear of using her voice (69).

"Praying" becomes a way to talk back to the violence of the father, and in the process it gives audience members who see part of their experiences reflected onstage the courage to speak their own truth. For Grise and Mayorga, connecting with these audience members is part of the transformative power of the performance. The monologue's ability to inspire others to break their own silence "is important—for them, for us, for our culture. Their voices testify to the efficacy of staging our stories, our very Latina/o stories" (xxxi). The specificity of the monologue allows for a different type of connection with an audience hungry to see their own experiences, even of pain and violence, captured on the stage. Although it is hard to witness the cruelty and terror experienced by the young narrator, the monologue voices an important critique of the structures of oppression replicated within our own families and communities. Grise and Mayorga's critique shows respect for their community and does not reduce the Latinx experience to the problematic mainstream stereotypes of violent Latinidad.

The monologue that follows "Praying," also written by María Salazar, is a short but sweet story of queer love. "Panza to Panza" rejects the practice of seeing a survivor of violence as just a victim, instead presenting the narrator as a confident queer woman who "*enters with the swagger of a Chicana* macha. *She sits on the chair. Legs wide and attitude large*" (70). As embodied by Grise onstage, this narrator is not small and quiet, but instead takes up space and bravely speaks her love for another woman. In her story, the panza is transformed into a site of adoration and tenderness.

While the preceding three monologues expressed the violence to which panzas are often subjected, "Panza to Panza" shifts the audience's attention to the beauty of the panza and the possible joy to be found in embracing it. The first lines of the monologue proudly express the narrator's desire: "I must say / I love her *panza* / It's full and round / Perfect in all its roundness / I love kissing her *panza* / It's so perfect in all her fullness" (70). The narrator's love for her partner's panza, articulated repeatedly throughout the poem, with language of abundance and acceptance, stands in stark contrast to the messages we are given about what makes a panza beautiful: thinness. Instead of being loved for its slenderness, this panza is full and round and worthy of adoration. This panza is complete in its fullness, described lovingly as "perfect" several times in the monologue. There is no flaw to be found in this panza—just a part of the narrator's lover to kiss, embrace, and hold. The love for her lover's panza, however, is a reciprocal one based on mutual devotion.

In "Panza to Panza," the panza becomes a site of queer love—a love that rejects heteronormative and patriarchal definitions of beauty and desire. In this manifestation of love, the partner's panza "rests perfectly in the curve of my back" (70). It is the panza's roundness, its fullness, that allows for it to fit so tenderly against the narrator's back. As they lie together, her lover "holds me, whispering, / 'I got your back, girl' / Her lovely *panza* has my back" (70). In this narrative, the panza that is loved is an active participant in the relationship, protecting and loving in return. The whispering is intimate and tender, promising to support and to defend. As the story comes to a close, the narrator tells the audience that her favorite part "Is when we first go to bed / I'll face her on my side / She will face me on her side / We will chat of the day / *Panza* to *panza*." When they kiss good night, "All the while / There we are / *Panza* to *panza* // Perfect in all our roundness / Perfect in all our fullness // *Panza* to *panza*" (70–71).

"Panza to Panza" offers the audience a balm of healing. It is a beautiful and empowering narrative of love and true acceptance of the panza. Even if the audience is unaware that "Praying" and "Panza to Panza" are written by the same person, the intentional placing of the monologues back-to-back makes clear that the panza is a site of both pain and joy. With "Panza to Panza" we get a story of love that rejects the fatphobia and homophobia instilled in us by mainstream culture and our own families. The narrator loves her panza and the panza of her lover in all of their beautiful abundance. Unlike V's problematic representation of queerness in "The Woman Who Likes to Make Vaginas Happy," this representation of same-sex desire is intimate and complex. There is no shame in this expression of queer love and happiness. The panza is celebrated as a deeply loved and cherished part of the whole. With the knowledge that Salazar wrote both of these stories, we see the possibility of finding love and joy in the panza even after experiences of pain and violence. The panza is resilient, and it can grow and flourish in spectacular ways when it is nurtured and celebrated.

Like the other monologues, "Panza to Panza" illustrates the possibility of using narratives to tell complex stories that represent diverse experiences within one community. "Panza to Panza" and the other monologues remind the audience that the stories of the panza are as complex as the members of the Latinx community. The monologues offer a model of how to perform stories that are difficult to tell, without giving the audience a voyeuristic window through which to observe the pain of others, while also showing us how to celebrate those pieces of us that are often seen as unworthy of love. But the script does not end with the monologues. The pedagogy of the panza continues with an account of the production's development, offering readers further insight into the process of coming into being.

The final section of the script, following the glossary, includes a comprehensive timeline of the development of the project. In "A Chronological Production History of *The Panza Monologues*," Grise and Mayorga trace the journey they undertook in the process of developing the script from workshop to staged performance to filmed production. Unlike the in-depth description of the processes of becoming documented in the text's first chapter, this section provides a more standard timeline of the script's chronological development. For performers and dramaturgs who might lack access to resources available to established theater professionals, this section provides a brief view into the role that community can play in creating independent theater productions. Grise and Mayorga's overview of their chronology makes clear that *The Panza Monologues* is a product of their work in, and with, community. They discuss the role that friends and volunteers played in helping put on various performances, writing that they "have continuously drawn on the resources within our immediate circle of friends or close allies for help with the finer details of putting together a performance" (103). The section ends with a list of "Panza Pláticas"—gatherings that combined elements of "presentation, demonstration, and *testimonio*"—which offered them the opportunity "to experiment with how to describe the story of making *The Panza Monologues*" (104). The eight *pláticas*, which took place at various academic institutions and annual meetings, included partial screenings of the recorded performance alongside participatory discussions about the process of writing the monologues (109). Because the pláticas were primarily held at academic conferences and universities, they offered the creators an opportunity to expand the scope of the play's reach, bringing the stories of the San Antonio community into the classroom. For Grise and Mayorga, the pláticas became "increasingly important to us because they put into practice our desire to think within a theoretical and creative dialectic" (104).

While it is a common practice to include production histories in scripts and performance programs, they are most often concise and factual, briefly marking the journey of the performance to the stage. There is a marked difference in the very detailed chronology documented in Grise and Mayorga's first chapter and script. In keeping with the creators' commitment to relationality and creating in community, the chronology features the many names of those who helped with the productions, ensuring that credit is given to everyone who brought *The Panza Monologues* into being.[20] Mayorga and Grise are confident in their work and are not afraid to admit that the strength of the project lies in the collaborations that helped create it.[21] Their emphasis on naming their collaborators and crediting their community partners is a deliberate invocation of an intersectional feminist methodology that honors the community that helped create *The Panza Monologues* and the groups and individuals that welcomed the performance into their communities. The production and the subsequent text illustrate the power of working in the service of community and the reciprocal relationships that foster creativity and learning on the stage.

Learning from the Panza

...TO CLAIM THE *PANZA* IS TO BE FREE...

"POLITICAL PANZA," ***THE PANZA MONOLOGUES***

If we think about the prefatory materials and the first chapter as the foundation upon which the script is built, the chapters that follow the script continue the process of constructing *The Panza Monologues* as a project of performance, pedagogy, and mentoring. Earlier in this chapter, I discussed the importance of Grise and Mayorga's acknowledgment of their positionality as creators and caretakers of the monologues shared with them and their emphasis on geographic specificity. These priorities are certainly woven into the script, but they are even more deeply developed in the three chapters that follow it.

The text's third chapter, "Tejana Topographies," opens with a map drawn by a local San Antonio artist, Debora Kuetzpal Vasquez, which she created specifically for the text. *El Mapa de San Antonio* is a beautiful illustration that captures the richness of the city's geography. The map includes famous locations like the Alamo and the Tower of the Americas, but it also features locally important sites like Ray's Drive Inn and the lesbian bar The Boss. By beginning the chapter with Vasquez's map, Mayorga and Grise visually capture the mapping project they have undertaken in *The Panza Monologues.* They don't just tell the audience the monologues are from San Antonio; they use the chapter to help us navigate the topography of their storytelling—a topography that comprises a physical landscape, a history of oppression, and the resilience of a community. Grise and Mayorga emphasize that "as Tejana-Chicana artists, we've worked hard to locate our history, to discover the roots and origins of the material circumstances in our city and state" (114). The materials that follow the script invite their audience to follow the map that charts the journey to the creation of the monologues.

Using *El Mapa de San Antonio* as a visual aid, Grise and Mayorga invite the reader to engage with the creative practice of painting by number as they tell the layered and complex history of San Antonio: a four-hundred-year-old history of racism and segregation, educational discrimination, labor exploitation, feminization of poverty, and the adverse effects of tourism. The structuring of the section as a coloring exercise invites an engagement with the text that goes beyond simply reading statistics or learning historical facts. It becomes an exercise in analyzing space as a constituted formation based on intersectional relations to structures of power. By positioning geographical locations as more than simply markers on a map, Mayorga and Grise encourage us to see how spaces are imbued with meaning, predicated on historical processes of oppression. In a discussion of the important role of intersectionality in the field of feminist geography, Sharlene Mollett and Caroline Faria argue that "intersectionality was, at its inception, *already* a deeply spatial theoretical concept, process and epistemology," and that "the interlocking violence of racism, patriarchy, heteronormativity, and capitalism constitute a spatial formation" (566). Thinking of space and intersectionality as relationally constituted offers us the opportunity to analyze the larger project of deconstructing networks of inequality through the geographical practice of mapping. Framing the oppression of their San Antonio community through an intersectional lens allows Grise and Mayorga to expand their audience's understanding of the community and to inspire a more critical way of thinking about the relationship between history, space, and community.

The eleven-page section offers a powerful history of oppression and provides further evidence of the impact such a history continues to have on the city's population. Why would Mayorga and Grise take on such a time-intensive project of mapping their community? For them, it is part of their text's larger project: "To better understand the socioeconomic and political dynamics that *The Panza Monologues* was created within, we present written topographies each of which in its own way attempts to map the history of our city, which in turn tells the story of people's relationship to economics, food, place, and other insidious forces of oppression" (Grise and Mayorga 114). They do not simply gesture toward these issues in hopes that the audience will understand; they draw out the connections and map out the history for us. The paint-by-numbers exercise becomes its own navigation project and provides a model of how one can structure such a project. They end the section with the powerful argument that "justice begins at home. Only then can we render a self-made portrait of our city" (126). Vasquez's portrait of San Antonio becomes the visual representation of Mayorga and Grise's positioning of their community as the site of resistance and possibility. The mapping project models a practice of focusing within, on the strengths of one's community, when looking for strategies to combat oppression, instead of simply looking outside the community for answers.

As part of their textual mentoring practice, Grise and Mayorga provide readers with a guide to creating their own mapping project. Among the guided discussion topics and activities in chapter 5, "Pedagogy of the *Panza*," they offer a "cultural mapping" exercise to lead readers through their own process of mapping their community (209–210). The six steps outlined, and the important questions they raise, help readers graph a story of community based on the same plot points Mayorga and Grise highlight in their analysis of *El Mapa de San Antonio*. Readers are encouraged to identify spaces of resources and privilege (universities, museums, farmers' markets, gyms), spaces of surveillance and control (police stations, jails), and spaces that serve communities (hospitals, public parks, cultural centers). The exercise asks them to think about important issues like access to transportation, fresh fruits and vegetables, and medical care, alongside an analysis of the types of businesses found in their cities' neighborhoods. Such spatial analysis allows readers to think critically about the inequalities around them to better understand the challenges faced by their communities. The mapping exercise culminates with the creation of a personal countertopography of one's own neighborhood, a charting of the spaces that are most important to individual readers and their communities. By encouraging readers to make their maps "as personal as you can," Grise and Mayorga further advocate for a creative methodology situated in one's own history and rooted in community (210).

Chapter 3's discussion of Tejana topographies ends with "Autogeographies," a section that intimately centers Mayorga and Grise's own family histories. Readers have learned about San Antonio's spatially constructed structures of inequality, and now the text gives them the opportunity to understand how those structures very specifically affected the lives of the authors. The format of the "autogeography"—a term Grise and Mayorga use "to mean auto (self) + geography (spaces, places, cities, features of space) in order to describe our personal histories"—lends itself to the larger project of mapping identity through an analysis of space and the configurations of power that constitute it (216). The section opens with two beautiful full-page photographs of Grise's grandfather and mother and Mayorga's grandmother and mother, respectively. The photographs are artifacts from the authors' own family archives, and they visually invite the reader into their personal history. The decision to begin the section with these images helps visually frame the autogeographies that follow. The stories of Mayorga's and Grise's families are intertwined with the history of their location: Their family narratives cannot be separated from the history of the city. How often do we get to see these types of family histories documented in performance texts? The use of the creators' own autogeographies models a methodology of combining the personal with the political in ways that do not obfuscate or ignore the power of storytelling and the curating of narratives. In contrast to V's unlikely and perhaps flippant assertion that *The Vagina Monologues* is not really any of her business, and that she just "show[s] up" and tries "to stay out of the way" (Ensler, *Vagina* xxv), Grise and Mayorga understand the importance of transparency in locating themselves within the text. There is a vulnerability in the sharing of their personal stories: It creates a connection with the reader that is more personal, almost intimate. It also makes clear Mayorga and Grise's positionality as creators. As feminist geographer Sophie Tamas argues in her essay on autogeography, "*Location matters.* Humility is hard. Showing where you speak from (aka your standpoint) can minimize the potential trespass of speaking for others" (513). By inserting their own family histories into *The Panza Monologues*, Grise and Mayorga locate themselves within the community, and they resist the practice of simply speaking for those who lack access to storytelling conduits.

The autogeographies provide a deeper understanding of how Mayorga's and Grise's histories and experiences have influenced the creation of *The Panza Monologues*, and they offer a model of what it looks like to craft such a narrative. Given their commitment to pedagogy, it is not surprising that the creators also guide readers through the development of their own autogeographies. In chapter 5, Grise and Mayorga include two activities that directly connect to their autogeographies in chapter 3. The five exercises in "Writing with Personal Photographs" guide readers through a process of reflection and story development based on family artifacts (213–215). Centering the photograph as the site of history worthy of analysis reframes the importance of one's own family history within a larger community. The exercises ask readers to reflect deeply on what they see, with the intention of developing critical insights about who and what the images show. The audience—having seen the power of using photographs as tools of storytelling in the monologue "A Hunger for Justice" and in the authors' autogeographies—are now given the tools to write their own family narratives, informed by what may seem to be just a simple family snapshot. The photograph, however, not only inspires the creation of a story but also reframes how we think about these familial artifacts. These images have the potential to become part of a community's repository of resistance as they make interventions in historical gaps of place and time. Even if no one else sees these photographs or reads the stories they inspire, the exercise has the power to encourage the audience to think critically about their family histories and their connections to community, resistance, and constructions of space.

Mayorga and Grise use their text to offer tools to burgeoning writers, and to readers who might never have considered themselves writers, to tell their own stories through a process of mapping their identity. The exercise "Autogeography" guides readers through the process of creating their own stories of identity. Grise and Mayorga begin by posing the question, "How does space/place help determine your subjectivity, who you are, and how you see things?" (216). This invites readers to think critically about their own subject formation and how it is connected to their community. The set of questions and prompts guide the process of contextualizing one's own positionality in space. It gives readers the tools to undertake the project of mapping out who they are in the context of where they come from and the history that preceded them. This recognition of the constitutive connection between identity and space leads to a deeper understanding of the self, an understanding informed by complex histories of structural inequality and injustice. In this way, the text offers room for experimentation within a tradition of storytelling.

There is power in writing our own stories. In her foundational and inspiring letter to women of color, Gloria Anzaldúa explains why she writes: "By writing I put order in the world, give it a handle so I can grasp it. I write because life does not appease my appetites and hunger. I write to record what others erase when I speak, to rewrite the stories others have miswritten about me, about you. To become more intimate with myself and you. To discover myself, to preserve myself, to make myself, to achieve self-autonomy" ("Speaking" 169). In providing us with the tools to write our own stories, Mayorga and Grise continue Anzaldúa's legacy of inspiring us to write, to share our stories of family and community, for ourselves or for the stage. Our stories are not reduced to the five-by-eight cards V holds during her performance of *The Vagina Monologues*. For V, "it was as if the women I had interviewed were made present by those cards, and I needed them there with me" (Ensler, *Vagina* xxvi). Like the women whose stories are featured in *The Panza Monologues*, we are more than anonymous sources of stories to be mined, appropriated, and curated for someone else's creative work.

Mayorga and Grise's text doesn't stop with merely offering a model of an intersectional performance practice: It moves beyond the script to position the reader as a potential creator and performer. Sandwiched between the third and fifth chapters of the text is "A DIY Production Manual." The chapter is a rich repository of how-to sections that are aimed at helping readers understand the work and steps that go into putting on a performance. While previous chapters document aspects of the creation and progression of the play, Grise and Mayorga write that "this chapter thinks on the future, moves your thoughts forward, and urges possibilities" (159). Having labored in the world of theater, they are aware of the difficulties in the field for those who lack access to resources or whose stories are not valued by mainstream theater. With this in mind, Grise and Mayorga present the chapter as a blueprint for creating a performance: "Believe us when we say, through our own journey of creating and producing *The Panza Monologues*, we know the many types of obstacles you will face in the throes of trying to produce a piece of theater. Don't get discouraged; making theater is always hard work" (159–160). Many young people who are interested in theater and performance, especially those from marginalized communities, might not have the knowledge or the mentoring necessary to help them navigate the performance world. By sharing their own experience with this lack of support, Mayorga and Grise offer a useful critique of the field that reveals some of the gatekeeping mechanisms at play. They demystify the theater world through the creation of a comprehensive guide—a form of textual mentoring—to the complicated procedures involved in theater making.

The sections in chapter 4 all include practical advice and offer suggestions for putting on a performance or a screening of *The Panza Monologues*. The section "Guidelines, Advice, and Good Wishes for Staging a Production of *The Panza Monologues*" explains the purpose and importance of asking for permission to stage a production and the significance of royalties. It offers suggestions for creating promotional materials and guidance on staging. Mayorga and Grise even include a production checklist and sample form letters for permissions and royalty requests. The abundance of detail reflects the pedagogical intent behind their text, demonstrating a method of mentoring that transcends the page.

For those who might not be able to create their own production but who want to engage with the play in community, the text offers the section "Tupperware Meets Telenovela: How to Organize a *Panza* Party," a guide to viewing the DVD performance at home. Grise and Mayorga define panza parties as "viewing parties, sponsored by a 'fan,' ardent supporter, or ally who gathers together a group of people in their homes to view our DVD collectively and, thus, in community—much like the event of theatergoing" (190). They offer examples of various panza parties and provide resources for hosting them, including a checklist of activities to prepare for, put on, and clean up after the party. In their overview of the concept of the panza party, Grise and Mayorga mention marketing the DVD to libraries and universities for classroom use, but they write that "we also desired to put our portable *teatro* in the hands of people who don't normally have access to these places" (189). They understand that access to live theater productions is beyond the reach of many, and they use that knowledge to create not just a recording of the performance for future audiences but a practical guide for screening the performance in one's own home. While the energy of a live performance cannot be captured on camera, the play can inspire a different type of energy when screened for an audience invested in the message of the production.

The supplementary materials included in the last three chapters of *The Panza Monologues* build on the larger project of the script. They help the audience see their own stories as worth telling and provide the tools to explore their own histories and relationships with space and power. Grise and Mayorga understand what is at stake in publishing the script as part of a larger text. They explain, "As the contextual materials that you'll find in this book hope to suggest, publication of our script offers an occasion for redress, provocation, and an invitation to create further actions that ameliorate generations of silence" (xxix). The text provides an important framework for understanding the script, but more importantly, through its archiving of the process, it acts as a model of writing from the margins that offers a form of textual mentoring for those reading it. It gives us the tools necessary to embark on the process of claiming our own panzas in an effort to liberate ourselves and our communities.

Like other forms of creative expression, performance offers a powerful tool in educating an audience and challenging dangerous misconceptions about marginalized communities. It can inspire self-reflection and shifts in perception. While the centering of marginalized narratives can make important interventions in the hegemonic structure of mainstream theater, such work can also replicate problematic appropriations of those narratives. Even when well-intentioned, creative work that does not decenter whiteness can cause harm. There is no question that *The Vagina Monologues* has had a huge impact in the performance world and in the onstage representation of women's bodies. It offers a point from which to grow in more complex and intentional directions while also posing as a cautionary tale of the dangers of totalizing narratives that center single-identity-focused activism. The creators of *The Panza Monologues* took the structure that worked in *The Vagina Monologues*, but they avoided the limitations of V's production by rooting their project in an ethics of care and responsibility to the community whose narratives are featured in the performance. Their work goes beyond a simple critique of *The Vagina Monologues*. Mayorga and Grise create a pedagogical performance and build an instructive archive that can be activated by others looking to use performance as a tool for change. As an audience, we are left with inspiring stories of empowerment and radical representation, along with a guide to imagine and generate our own stories. The text of *The Panza Monologues* goes beyond the moment of performance by providing a rich repository of production history and resources for future artivists. *The Panza Monologues* reminds us of the potential of imagining a better world into being through the creation of performance in the service of community and offers an example of textual mentoring to employ in the conception of future expressions of resistance. The next chapter shifts focus to a community's use of performance as a project of activism and continues the project of building archives in the service of creating visions of change.

THREE

A Seat on the Bus

Radical Organizing and Performance in Envisioning Change

On September 1, 2012, a colorful bus christened Priscilla rolled into Charlotte, North Carolina, for an action at the Democratic National Convention. With its sides brightly painted with a blue-green sky filled with monarch butterflies, the bus proudly proclaimed, in bold, black letters, SIN PAPELES SIN MIEDO on one side and NO PAPERS NO FEAR on the other. Previously an old and nondescript 1972 MCI Challenger bus, Priscilla had metamorphosed into a striking work of art on wheels—the Undocubus. This Priscilla might not be a Queen of the Desert, but she too carried an important group of marginalized people and, recalling the civil rights activism of the Freedom Riders fifty years earlier, traveled through the Deep South.[1]

The bus began its journey in Phoenix, Arizona, and carried forty undocumented immigrants across eleven states over six weeks as part of a national immigrant rights action, the No Papers, No Fear Ride for Justice. The Undocubus concluded its multicity tour with a protest outside of the Democratic National Convention. As part of the national election cycle, members of the Democratic National Committee had gathered in Charlotte to nominate President Barack Obama for reelection in the 2012 presidential election. These immigrant activists made the trek across hostile territory and multiple checkpoints, continuously risking detention, in order to confront President Obama and the Democrats on their failure to pass comprehensive immigration reform and to challenge the administration's continued removal of undocumented immigrants. Their action culminated in an act of civil disobedience, the blocking of an uptown intersection. Ten Undocubus riders wearing white shirts echoing Priscilla's slogan and holding up individual signs printed with the word UNDOCUMENTED sat on a large banner that proudly proclaimed their lack of documentation and lack of fear. These ten activists were forcibly removed and arrested by police.

The message of the Undocubus riders and their supporters was communicated by both their actions and the images those actions inspired. The fusion of words and visuals illustrates the importance that collaborations between performance, art, and activism play in our current social justice movements. The image of ten individuals taking over public space—human beings who many believe should exist in the shadows because of their status—is made that much more compelling by the imagery used to create an empowering narrative of self-definition: a performance of agency and autonomy. Because the images of the bus and the Riders invoke a long history of struggle, it would be easy to see the Ride as simply employing a schema of the past. Looking closely at the different strategies that converged in the Ride, however, reveals a much broader narrative of community and belonging—one that embraces multiple historical moments of resistance to create a vision of change that is more intersectional in its mobilization.

The framing of the Ride through previous histories of resistance and the use of the performative strategies and artistic creations of the past highlight a strategy of necessity, or of making do with what is already available when resources are scarce. In analyzing this type of strategy, I rely heavily on the concept of *rasquachismo*—as coined and theorized by Tómas Ybarra-Frausto—a tradition of invention rooted in a working-class ethos that relies heavily on reimagining and repurposing that which might not be seen as valuable by those who are invested in mainstream notions of worth or beauty.[2] In particular, I draw on Amalia Mesa-Bains's feminist reading of rasquachismo and her insistence that "the source of rasquachismo rests in the everyday, the domestic sites of home and community" (300).[3] Centering an intersectional analysis of rasquachismo that acknowledges gender and the role of women in innovation helps identify the inclusive politics at play in the construction of the Ride.

In this chapter, I argue for a reading of the No Papers, No Fear Ride as embodying a form of rasquachismo, now imagined as a project of bringing together multiple movements of resistance in a new model for activism and coalition building. The two previous chapters focused on how performance has been used as an intellectual and a community project of artivism in the service of resistance. Both chapters engaged with specific feminist texts of the past in an effort to move beyond single-identity-focused activism. I now shift my focus to explore how social movements of the past shape and inspire current fights for justice and the role performance plays in strategies of resistance. I excavate the multiple sites of historical struggle and resistance invoked by the No Papers, No Fear movement and map out the hybrid vision of justice envisioned and performed by its Riders. I read the use of performance around the Ride as part of an activist project in the service of community and resistance. Unlike the previous chapters, the story that this chapter tells does not emerge from the structure of a published text. The journey of the Riders has been documented on multiple platforms and in diverse sources. Thus, the story I tell about the Ride is cobbled together from all of these many sources—my own form of literary rasquachismo. I begin by setting the stage with a history of the art and social movements that led to the No Papers, No Fear Ride, and how the Ride not only drew on but also departed from these histories. My analysis of different moments along the Ride involves an exploration of both visual and performative aspects. Given that the organizing of the Ride was deeply dependent on cultural activism, or a combination of creative expression and activism, I center the visual as an integral part in the creation of meaning and as part of a longer legacy of using art in the service of community resistance.

While the various aspects of the Ride could be analyzed separately, I read the Ride as a cohesive performance in order to identify the powerful organizing tool that art and performance provide for social movements. My understanding of the Ride as a performance is not based on a published script or on a single performance. It is instead based on my analysis of the organizers' documenting of the Ride, the action of the Riders, and the various strategies invoked throughout the journey. By reading the Ride as a form of performance, my analysis demonstrates the possibilities of using performance in the service of community. The Riders' faith in their message and their belief in the strength of their collective community overrode the fear of possible detention and deportation. In reading their journey through the lens of performance, I am not dismissing the reality of the risks the Riders took or minimizing the incredible toll such activism must have taken on the mind, body, and spirit of the Riders, their families, and their supporters. I analyze the No Papers, No Fear Ride action as a form of performance because it illustrates the amount of planning and creative organizing involved in producing such an action. For those who are unfamiliar with organizing, it is easy to overlook the amount of work or to dismiss the organizing logics of performance in orchestrating movements of resistance. By emphasizing the collaboration that exists between organizing and art making, my reading positions the Ride as a model of artivism and community building.

Like other art forms, performance has the capacity to move us. In her discussion of the July 2019 protests in Puerto Rico, Yarimar Bonilla argues that in a political movement "you need spectacle. You need performance. You need something that moves you and sways you" ("Puerto Ricans Stand Up"). Art allows individuals to understand a worldview outside of their own experience. For many creatives, theater and performance offer a radical space for imagining a different world and a more just vision of the future. As Cherríe Moraga powerfully argues, "Experience first generated through the body returns to the body in the flesh of the staged performance. In this sense, for me, it is as close to direct political activism as I can get as an artist, for theater requires the body to make testimony and requires other bodies to bear witness to it" (45). While many of the Riders on the Undocubus did not have a performance background, they were able to use their bodies in ways that enacted resistance and self-empowerment for multiple audiences. They might not have been trained actors, but they used their everyday practice of resistance—existing within a system of oppression—to organize a powerful action rooted in community strength and the power of rasquachismo.

The Riders used their experiences to produce a script that rejected the media narratives that ignored their humanity, reduced them to binary stereotypes of criminal or victim, or simply used them for political sound bites. They relied on their own stories of struggle, resistance, and joy to insert themselves into the larger conversation on immigration. The Riders and the organizers of the No Papers, No Fear Ride diligently documented various aspects of the journey. The footage of press releases, personal reflections, and video recordings of protests and rallies are all preserved on the movement's website. The site becomes a repository of their activism, documenting their process, their actions, and their stories. While the Ride might not have produced a published script or book, the website becomes an archive of resistance that lives on beyond the events that took place at the end of the summer in 2012.[4] In thinking about the legacy of the action and its Riders, I am deeply inspired by José Esteban Muñoz's vision of a future rooted in radical queer resistance. In *Cruising Utopia*, Muñoz argues that "the present is not enough. It is impoverished and toxic for queers and other people who do not feel the privilege of majoritarian belonging, normative tastes, and 'rational' expectation. . . . The present must be now in relation to the alternative temporal and spatial maps provided by a perception of past and future affective worlds" (27). I see Priscilla helping her Riders cruise in from the margins, take center stage with a vision of a more just future, and advocate for their community based on lessons learned from the past. I argue that the Ride and its archive is a form of navigational storytelling that can help mentor future artists and activists fighting for social justice.

Part 1: Setting the Stage

The Players

In order to fully understand the No Papers, No Fear Ride for Justice, we need to understand the historical moment that prompted the need for the action. The humanitarian crisis at the US-Mexico border is not a new one. While it would be easy to focus on the Trump administration's openly xenophobic and draconian anti-immigrant policies, especially given the vitriolic discourse employed, Republican administrations are not unique in their anti-immigration stance. We cannot forget that under President Obama, over three million noncitizens were removed—more than under previous administrations.[5] Immigrants and immigrant rights activists had hoped that the election of Obama would lead to a reform of policies that criminalized unauthorized immigrants. During his first presidential campaign, Obama declared "that he would position immigration as 'a top priority in [his] first year as president'" and stated, "'I am going to be fighting for comprehensive immigration reform, and we shouldn't pose the question that somehow we can't achieve that. I believe that the American people desperately want it. That's what I'm going to be fighting for as president'" (qtd. in Hernández 25).[6] Like many promises made during election campaigns, Obama's commitment to immigration reform foundered. Instead, enforcement efforts grew through programs like the Department of Homeland Security's Operation Streamline and Secure Communities, which have led to an increase in the criminalization of undocumented immigrants and a rise in deportation numbers. By the time the Democrats were preparing to hold their convention in advance of the national election, the Obama administration had deported over one million undocumented immigrants.

The No Papers, No Fear Ride also took place just months after President Obama used his executive power to defer the deportation of undocumented immigrants under the age of thirty who had arrived in the United States before the age of sixteen. The program, Deferred Action for Childhood Arrivals (DACA), marked a pronounced shift from the administration's previous enforcement and deportation policies. While the passage of DACA was welcome news, immigration rights advocates were disappointed overall by what was seen as President Obama's failure to live up to his larger campaign promises of fighting for comprehensive immigration reform. Even though DACA offered a segment of the undocumented population relief from deportation, such relief was limited and temporary. As legal scholar Anil Kalhan points out, "Deferred action constitutes nonbinding, revocable notification that authorities have chosen not to seek the removal of a particular individual—and nothing more"—and it can be curtailed at any time (67).[7] The Undocubus action drew attention to the limitations of DACA and made visible the diversity of immigrants having to live under the precarious status of being undocumented.

President Obama's earlier deportation policies contributed to the already problematic representation of immigrants from the Global South. The depiction of undocumented immigrants in popular media has been particularly vitriolic. The longtime practice of sensationalizing undocumented immigration and criminalizing immigrant bodies is a popular one that sells publications and generates online revenue. The narratives created by such a practice have naturalized and made familiar a narrative of xenophobia disguised in the discourse of national security and patriotism.[8] Mainstream audiences have become comfortable with the image of undocumented immigrants as criminals and aliens, even though immigrants commit fewer crimes than native-born populations.[9] The popularity that the myth of the immigrant as criminal continues to enjoy is evident in the political and media discourse around the immigration debate.

The media's power to provide information in turn shapes how the public thinks about that information, and we must pay close attention to how the media chooses to portray immigrant communities.[10] The public discourse on immigration affects the construction of immigrant subjectivities, which in turn influences the mainstream acceptance of those constructions (for examples, see Santa Ana; Lakoff and Ferguson). In his well-known study of the language used to report on Latinos in print media (specifically, the *Los Angeles Times* from 1992 to 1998), Otto Santa Ana found that while the nation is often represented as a physical structure (e.g., body, house, castle, ship), immigrants are framed as attackers of that structure (e.g., diseases, invaders) and, most egregiously, as animals (257–273). Unfortunately, the use of problematic metaphors is just one of many strategies that deny Latina/o/x immigrants the right to be seen as anything other than a threat to the nation. Another effective discursive tactic of dehumanizing undocumented immigrants is through the construction of illegality.[11] The rhetorical connection between the framing of undocumented immigrants as illegal and the practice of othering them positions these bodies as criminal and therefore corrupt (Lakoff and Ferguson). The prevalence of these discourses, racist nativism, and anti-immigrant sentiment in the United States is part of a larger ideology of white supremacy (Pérez Huber et al. 46). It is against this xenophobic backdrop that the performance of the Riders takes place.

Invoking Scripts from the Past

The group of activists involved in the No Papers, No Fear Ride reflected the diversity of the undocumented immigrant community and comprised an intergenerational coalition of workers, students, mothers, fathers, artists, and activists, queer and straight. In challenging the mainstream construction of undocumented immigrants as outsiders and criminals, organizers of the Ride sought to create a public image that instead humanized the Riders and emphasized their diversity, but also placed them within a longer history of civil rights movements. One of the challenges faced by immigrant rights activists is the assumption that certain immigrants, specifically those from the Global South, are not capable of assimilating and are therefore not "American." By inserting immigrants, especially undocumented immigrants, into the larger narrative of US civil rights, the organizers rejected the construction of national belonging that excludes nonwhite immigrants. Through its planning and execution, the Ride deliberately invoked images and discourse from the past in order to position the movement within a continuing legacy of activism. The activists employed successful strategies of previous social justice movements while also expanding constructions of national belonging and citizenship. The Ride exemplifies the practice of movement-to-movement influence that David Meyer and Nancy Whittier term "social movement spillover," which is "a product of both contemporaneous and successor effects, as movements influence each other directly, alter successive challenges, and affect the larger terrain on which they struggle" (280). The Ride engaged familiar scripts of the past as a strategy of social movement spillover to invoke older messages of equality and social justice and expand them to include undocumented immigrants.

The organizers of the Ride drew on some of the most enduring and powerful images of the fights for justice and equality of the twentieth century, including the mobilization of Chicano/Latino workers by the United Farm Workers on the West Coast and the African American civil rights movement in the South. I approach these earlier movements and actions as performance to show how they offer artistic strategies of resistance that can be replicated in current performances of resistance. Within this history of activism, one of the most iconic actions remains the Freedom Rides, in part because of the power of the movement and the impactful images it left behind. Even if one does not know the history of the Freedom Rides, the photographs of the movement—which captured the courage of the Freedom Riders and the violence they were subjected to by white mobs and local and state police—remain a visible history of courage and resistance.

The 1961 Freedom Rides were themselves inspired by a previous action, the 1947 Journey of Reconciliation, which was organized by members of the Fellowship of Reconciliation and the Congress of Racial Equality (CORE) who, like the Freedom Riders, sought to challenge segregation in interstate travel.[12] Among the leaders of the 1947 action were Bayard Rustin—who would continue his challenge to segregated busing in the Freedom Rides—and George Houser, a cofounder of CORE. The Journey was meant to gather information on the level of compliance around desegregation decisions and to learn more about the conditions of travel, while also developing strategies for managing conflict around desegregation actions. These strategies employed aspects of nonviolence modeled after the Gandhi-led nonviolent resistance movement in

India. As part of that nonviolent approach, the organizers created a clear set of guidelines that would help the riders respond to white hostility:

1. If you are a Negro, sit in a front seat. If you are white, sit in a rear seat.
2. If the driver asks you to move, tell him *calmly and courteously*: "As an interstate passenger I have a right to sit anywhere in this bus. This is the law as laid down by the United States Supreme Court."
3. If the driver summons the police and repeats his order in their presence, tell them exactly what you said when he first asked you to move.
4. If the police tell you to "come along," without putting you under arrest, tell them you will not go until you are put under arrest. Police have often used the tactic of frightening a person into getting off the bus without making an arrest, keeping him until the bus has left and then just leaving him standing by the empty roadside. In such a case this person has no redress.
5. If the police put you under arrest, go with them peacefully. At the police station, phone the nearest center of the NAACP, or one of their lawyers. They will assist you.
6. If you have money with you, you can get out on bail immediately. It will probably be either $25 or $50. If you don't have bail, anti-discrimination organizations will help raise it for you.
7. If you happen to be arrested the delay in your journey will only be a few hours. The value of your action in breaking down Jim Crow will be too great to be measured. (qtd. in Catsam 22)

I see the guidelines as part of a script in a larger performance of peaceful defiance. The list signals the intricate planning involved in creating the spoken dialogue and in orchestrating the physical actions that, once combined, produce a replicable act. The script offered the riders a discourse of resistance rooted in both legal and moral standings, and although they could not fully anticipate the actions of the audience they were confronting, Rustin and Houser prepared the riders for their important part in the performance.

Just as a stage performance involves planning and rehearsal, a performance of resistance also involves extreme attention to detail; and the stakes are much higher when one's physical safety is at risk. The list of instructions was just one part of planning the Journey of Reconciliation. In fact, Rustin and Houser traveled the route beforehand, "adhering to Jim Crow restrictions, in order to canvas the itinerary, line up lawyers, raise funds, contact local leaders, and organize meetings" (Catsam 21). As directors of the performance, they understood that the bus was only one part of the stage. An important aspect of the Journey would involve the individual testimony of the riders—a monologue of sorts—to educate and raise support for desegregation projects. In setting up the supporting cast and assigning specific roles to the participants, Rustin and Houser orchestrated a communal performance that was heavily dependent on the execution of multiple roles in the process of the Journey.[13] While the Journey of Reconciliation did not obtain the kind of media attention that future activism would attract, it helped document the multiple types of civil rights actions that existed before the tumultuous 1960s, and it influenced future actions. The Journey offered a powerful script for a performative nonviolent action that would live beyond the bus rides.

The years between the 1947 Journey of Reconciliation and the 1961 Freedom Rides saw important shifts in the fight for civil rights and racial equality.[14] Although the 1954 *Brown v. Board of Education* ruling is often seen as one of the most important juridical decisions of the period, it was a less well-known Supreme Court case that precipitated the Freedom Rides: the 1960 ruling in favor of Bruce Boynton in *Boynton v. Virginia*, which overturned his trespassing conviction for dining in a whites-only restaurant in a bus terminal. The ruling stated that segregation within facilities used by interstate passengers—including lunch counters, restrooms, ticket counters, and waiting rooms—was unconstitutional (Arsenault 106). The decision offered CORE, under the direction of James L. Farmer Jr., the opportunity to revisit the desegregation project of the Journey of Reconciliation, but this time with the objective of desegregating the spaces serving interstate travelers, not just the buses.

The initial plan for the Freedom Rides, including the name, was sketched by CORE staffers Gordon Carey and Tom Gaither and followed the outline of the original 1947 draft for a Washington, DC, to New Orleans journey created by Rustin and Houser (Arsenault 109). Unlike the previous journey, this ride would not be limited to the upper Southern states. The planned route would take Freedom Riders through Virginia, the Carolinas, Georgia, Alabama, Mississippi, and Louisiana, beginning in Washington, DC, and ending in New Orleans. As with the Journey of Reconciliation, a great deal of planning went into orchestrating the action. Like Rustin and Houser, Gaither performed a practice run of the route, and at every scheduled stop "he surveyed the layout of terminal facilities, met with Black leaders to arrange housing and speaking engagements for the Riders, and assessed the tenor of local race relations" (Arsenault 109). In this practice run, Gaither identified the stage on which this new performance would take place, the different audiences who would witness the enactment of resistance, and the receptiveness of various communities to the message of the performance.

The organizers understood the risk the Freedom Riders would be taking, and CORE was committed to preparing them with strategies of nonviolence. The plan, according to James Farmer, was to "recruit from twelve to fourteen persons, call them to Washington, DC, for a week of intensive training and preparation, and then embark on the ride" (qtd. in Arsenault 109). A large part of the training involved role-playing sessions that would help the Riders understand the possible reactions of those they would confront and aid them in planning their own actions. These sessions, which the organizers referred to as "sociodramas," involved some participants "playing the part of the Freedom Riders sitting at simulated lunch counters or sitting on the front-seats of a make-believe bus. Others acted out the roles of functionaries, adversaries, or observers. Several played the role of white hoodlums coming to beat up the Freedom Riders on the buses or at lunch counters at the terminals" (Arsenault 107). In training the Freedom Riders on nonviolent resistance and teaching them about the dangers involved in such direct action, the "sociodramas" also employed performance as a form of pedagogy. The Freedom Rides might not have the written list, or script, of the Journey of Reconciliation, but the riders had rehearsed and performed a script to follow when confronted by those determined to fight desegregation.

The thirteen original Freedom Riders left Washington, DC, on May 4, 1961, on two buses—a Greyhound and a Trailways—accompanied by three journalists who were documenting the ride.[15] Although they had trained for the action and had individual experience with organizing and activism, nothing could have prepared the Freedom Riders for the violence and vitriol with which they were confronted on their journey. In fact, the riders never made it to New Orleans. On May 14, the Greyhound bus was attacked and firebombed outside of Anniston, Alabama, while the riders on the Trailways bus were brutally assaulted by Klansmen in Anniston and then confronted and viciously battered by a violent white mob at the Birmingham bus station.[16] The level of violence was so frightening that CORE decided to cancel the Freedom Rides. Members of the Student Nonviolent Coordinating Committee (SNCC), led by Diane Nash, volunteered to continue the action. Nash "insisted that valuable civil rights momentum would be lost if the rides did not continue. Allowing white mobs to stop movement activities, she predicted, would encourage even more mob action, resulting in even more bloodshed" (Holsaert et al. 35).

Under the leadership of SNCC and CORE, and with sometimes limited support from organizations like the NAACP and the Southern Christian Leadership Conference, the Freedom Rides would continue through the summer of 1961. In the end, over sixty Freedom Rides took place, and 436 individuals from all over the country became Freedom Riders.[17] While the 1960s continued to witness violence against civil rights activists and the refusal of many white supremacists to desegregate their communities, the Freedom Rides stand as a testament to the power of individuals to fight for rights and justice. The organizers and the Freedom Riders changed how the nation understood activism, nonviolence, and direct action. Raymond Arsenault argues, "By demonstrating the moral power of nonviolence as well as the resolute determination of ordinary citizens to achieve simple justice, the Riders hoped to transform the civil rights movement into a broad-based and insistent freedom struggle. . . . Even those activists who set their sights on a less revolutionary goal saw the Freedom Rides as a progenitor of radical and accelerated change" (517). Regardless of each Freedom Rider's personal goal, the opportunity to effect change was a powerful motivator. The Freedom Riders knew that change would come slowly, but they imagined a world in which racial justice could be achieved and Jim Crow segregation would finally die. There was no guarantee that their actions would lead to quantifiable change, but they refused to give up on the vision of a better future. The activist script created by the Freedom Riders is a powerful one that has inspired resistance beyond the historical moment of the Freedom Rides. It inspired the 2012 No Papers, No Fear Ride for Justice and multiple iterations of opposition to structures of oppression.[18]

Expanding the Script: Riding for Immigrant Rights

The No Papers, No Fear Ride is not the first immigrant rights action to invoke the strategies of the Freedom Rides of 1961.[19] Among several groups in the United States that have employed the strategy of bus activism is the coalition that organized the 2003 Immigrant Workers Freedom Ride.[20] Considered by many as the beginning of a new immigrant civil rights movement, the Immigrant Workers Freedom Ride was made possible by a coalition that included various labor unions, immigrant rights organizations, and interfaith groups (see Atkin 216n1). In September 2003, the coalition organized nine hundred riders to board eighteen buses in ten cities to embark on a journey to Washington, DC (Wong and Bank Muñoz). The action sought to mobilize support for basic principles that would help guide future immigration legislation, including the principles of rewarding work, renewing democracy, restoring labor protections, reuniting families, and respecting the civil rights and liberties of all (Atkin 202). The ride serves as an important precursor to the No Papers, No Fear Ride for Justice and helps bridge the activism of the original Freedom Riders with the specific needs of the No Papers, No Fear Riders.

From the beginning, the Immigrant Workers Freedom Ride relied heavily on the historical memory of the 1961 Freedom Rides. The organizers clearly articulated a plan "to resurrect a familiar tactic of the Civil Rights Movement in a fight against the newest form of an old injustice, the exploitation of thousands of immigrant workers" (Allen). The action also relied on the backing of the famous Freedom Rider John Lewis, who wrote in support of the rides and spoke at the gathering in Washington, DC. While the action was made possible by the hard work of the movement's organizers and riders, Lewis's support was vital to legitimizing the connection that was being invoked between the Immigrant Workers Freedom Ride and the civil-rights-era Freedom Rides. Lewis's public praise for the action went beyond simple admiration. In an editorial published in *The Washington Post*, Lewis wrote, "Like the Freedom Rides of 1961, Freedom Ride 2003 calls on ordinary people to do extraordinary things: to put their bodies on the line at a moment in American history when immigration is a volatile issue everywhere; to stand up for their rights and the rights of many others; to call attention to bad laws that harm good people; and to challenge the federal government to act where it seems determined not to." The explicit connection between the two movements illustrates the commonalities that exist in the struggle of marginalized peoples to achieve social justice and equality. The organizers of the Immigrant Workers Freedom Rides strategically called forth a legacy of resistance to help position the rights of immigrant workers within a longer fight for civil rights. They relied on the visuals and the activist performances of the past to advocate for immigrant workers in the present.

Just as the Journey of Reconciliation helped set the stage for the Freedom Rides, the Immigrant Workers Freedom Ride helped set the stage for the No Papers, No Fear Ride for Justice. The 2012 No Papers, No Fear Ride helped expand the scope of the immigrant rights conversation by moving beyond the 2003 movement's focus on labor as its organizing principle.[21] Given the large role that the AFL-CIO and other unions had in organizing the Immigrant Workers Freedom Ride, it isn't surprising that labor and civic pride were such an important part of the mission of the ride. The assimilationist politics undergirding the 2003 ride were clearly present in the organizers' practice of discussing immigrants as good workers—that is, as worthy of being part of the nation because of the labor they offer rather than because of what they contribute to the nation as human beings. In fact, in his reflections on the 2003 ride, community leader and activist Alejandro Luis Molina writes, "In DC, we were scorned by some on the other buses because as usual, the compañeros/as of Centro Sin Fronteras and the Juan Antonio Corretjer Puerto Rican Cultural Center refused to stand for the US pledge of allegiance. In what many of the white union organizers took as an affront to the politics of the event, all of the people on our bus refused to take a novelty size American Flag, that was handed out as people crowded into the auditorium" (Molina and Reyes 136–137). This resistance to the discourse of civic pride did not sit well with those who wanted these immigrant activists to simply show their gratitude. It demonstrates the limitations of the Immigrant Workers Freedom Ride's single-identity-focused activism and the white organizers' lack of understanding of the intersectional identity of immigrants. They saw them as only workers. Almost ten years later, the No Papers, No Fear Riders began their own journey for immigrant rights. This ride, however, would brilliantly and joyously embrace the intersecting identities of the undocumented riders, refusing to ignore or erase the complex subjectivities of the immigrant community being represented.

Riding in Style: *Bajito y Suavecito*

Unlike the public buses that had carried previous riders, these new Riders traveled on a bus of their own, which they used to carry both activists and their message.[22] In decorating the fabulous Priscilla, the activists and Riders relied on the artistic strategy of lowriders that had redefined how working-class communities of color used vehicles to resist and transgress boundaries of belonging. At first glance, the connection between lowrider culture and Priscilla might not be clearly evident. After all, lowrider culture features custom cars that are dropped low to the ground in order to ride *bajito y suavecito*—low and slow—and is often dismissed as simply an aesthetic expression of Chicano culture. But a brief history of lowrider culture reveals strong connections between the issues of mobility, space, structural oppression, performance, and art. By situating the art that adorns Priscilla as part of a legacy of using automobiles as canvas, I read the art on Priscilla as more than a visual political strategy of disseminating a message. I position the art on the bus as an ongoing practice of using aesthetic expression to challenge exclusionary constructions of belonging, community, and justice. Like highly adorned lowrider cars, Priscilla's body becomes a canvas for artistic and political expression. Her bright colors, flying butterflies, and bold letters create a highly visible image of resistance that demands to be seen and acts as a set for the Riders' performance of dissent.

If one's only understanding of lowriding is informed by mainstream media, it is easy to dismiss it as a subculture stereotypically associated with gang members and violence.[23] Such a misunderstanding ignores the history of resistance and community formation that makes up lowriding culture. Lowriders are part of a broader car culture that expands the utilitarian function of motor vehicles beyond modes of transportation.[24] While lowrider culture has several possible origin stories, what remains consistent is the importance of the aesthetic and philosophy of *bajito y suavecito*, which stands in sharp contrast to the majoritarian hot rod culture of white men and the practices of raising a car's body higher above the ground and racing at high speed (Sandoval, "Politics" 183; Ortiz Torres 26–27; Chappell, "Lowrider Publics" 270–271).

Lowriding is also about a certain type of performance: a public enactment of masculinity connected to car culture and mobility. Unlike drag racing, another type of masculinity on display, lowriding rejects the fast pace of racing and embraces cruising, a type of movement meant to be seen and leisurely enjoyed.[25] The hydraulics that help lower and bounce the cars, initially invented to circumvent their policing, now function as part of the performance of lowriding.[26] The choreography between the hydraulics, the music that accompanies the ride, and the driving formation of the cars create a public performance that is augmented by the art that adorns the vehicles.[27] The cruising of the lowrider vehicle draws attention to its driver, making the driver hypervisible. The importance of this visibility lies in the claiming of public space by communities of color—in this case, Chicano and Mexican American youths—and the cultural affirmation communicated through the performance.[28]

Because lowrider culture is based on a performance of masculinity, which in turn is based on the visual performance of gender, the appearance of lowrider vehicles must go beyond a nice paint job. The aesthetic vision of lowriding transforms the body of a vehicle into a canvas upon which to make art and create meaning. Michael Cutler Stone's remark that "Chicano muralists are in fact engaged to paint murals on low rider cars" is especially useful when considering the cultural origins of Priscilla (11). The fact that muralists are transferring their art from the walls of neighborhoods to the hoods and doors of lowriders illustrates the level of importance that art plays in this car culture. The art of the lowrider becomes a hybrid political signifier that engages the aesthetics of the car owner, the talent of the muralist, and the resistant history of a community that refuses to be unseen. But the importance of lowrider art extends beyond its ability to make visible a community's cultural identity. The art of lowriding culture also documents alternative histories of community.

The story of lowriding is also one of community activism. In his work on the countercultural and activist aspects of lowrider groups, Rubén G. Mendoza finds that lowrider clubs were often modeled after the mutual aid societies that sought to provide for Chicano/Latino communities. There are countless stories of lowrider car clubs holding toy drives and fundraisers to benefit community groups.[29] In fact, in a 1980 interview with *Lowrider* magazine, Cesar Chavez recounts how lowriding car clubs helped the organizing efforts of the United Farm Workers: "We wanted to do a little car caravanning in the community . . . and we wanted them to be with us cause they had a lot of cars—they came and joined. And they've done it in a number of places where we've asked them to help. They come in and help" (J. Gutierrez 44).[30] Chavez's recollection not only connects lowriding culture to community activism but also links the use of lowrider art to previous moments of resistance—in this case, the fight for the rights of farmworkers. Beyond advocating for change in their own urban communities, lowrider clubs also fought for the rights of rural communities.

Understanding the complex history of lowrider culture helps further contextualize the history of collaboration found among different marginalized groups. In thinking through the possibilities of intersectional coalition building, I rely on Denise Sandoval's work on the historical connection between Chicano and African American lowriding communities. Sandoval argues that media representations of lowrider cultures in East and South Central Los Angeles overlook "that each of these communities, Black and Chicano, has shared a similar history of struggle in Los Angeles and that at moments cultural expressions, such as lowriding, have led to interconnections and the creation of multicultural spaces. It is the passionate love affair for lowrider cars that has often bridged the gaps between East Los Angeles and South Central or South Los Angeles" ("Politics" 177).[31] Although tensions existed between the two groups, lowrider culture offered a common interest around which to collaborate. Lowrider car clubs were instrumental in fostering alliances to challenge the spatial segregation of urban spaces.

Like previous historical moments of cultural exchange and resistance, Black and brown lowriding communities found commonalities in their status as second-class citizens of the nation. By embracing a lowrider identity, they insisted on being seen and commanding respect. Like the participants in lowrider culture, undocumented immigrants have had to confront rhetoric used to criminalize and ostracize them. For Chicano and Black participants in lowrider culture, the term "lowrider" began as an insult but "took on new meaning as youth and young adults redefined it as a source of cultural pride" (Sandoval, "Politics" 185). In the case of the No Papers, No Fear Riders, they embraced the term "undocumented" in a linguistic performance that manifests acceptance of the term not only as an immigration status but as an embodiment of their humanity.

Members of brown and Black lowrider culture were also united in their shared experience with discriminatory law enforcement. Unlike their white hot rod counterparts, brown and Black lowriders were subject to police surveillance and harassment.[32] While it might be tempting to frame such harassment as merely affecting a small group within a much larger community, Ben Chappell argues that "lowriders provide a focal point not only for police control over public space, but also for the symbolic exercise of state power over an entire community" (*Lowrider Space* 34). Through a public display of defiant masculinity, the practice of lowriding allowed men of these communities to resist imposed segregation and to transgress against racial codes that situated them as inferior to white men.[33] Given the role that spatial segregation plays in the structuring of inequality, it comes as no surprise that social justice organizing has focused on challenging the limitations placed on the physical movement and mobility of communities of color.

From the 1947 Journey of Reconciliation, to the 1961 Freedom Rides, to lowrider voter registration drives, motorized vehicles have played an important role in challenging segregation laws and advocating for the freedom of people of color to navigate space without the constant threat of violence. Priscilla has similarly helped her Riders confront the danger and possible detection that travel poses for undocumented individuals—in a very public way. The No Papers, No Fear Ride rejects the strategy of remaining under the radar and challenges the policing of the Riders' mobility in a way that is reminiscent of how lowriders resisted discriminatory local ordinances through their cruising or how Freedom Riders defiantly crossed the segregation lines of interstate travel. Echoing these histories of resistance, Priscilla's Riders refused to be reduced simply to their immigration status and boldly announced to the world that they were undocumented and unafraid. Situating Priscilla within this longer legacy of activism connects the Riders to those who helped set the stage for their public performance of affirmation and resistance.

Part 2: The Performance

In traditional theater and performance, staging and set design play an important role in telling a story, and the No Papers, No Fear Ride for Justice is no different. In thinking about the role of Priscilla in the enactment of performance activism, I position the Undocubus as the mobile stage on which part of the performance takes place. Like the earlier lowriders who performed resistance through their art and their defiant navigation of space, Priscilla announces the arrival of her Riders in style. Part of the affective work of the bus's aesthetics is based on the visual metaphors the art creates for its audience. The monarch butterflies on the side of the bus emanate from the back end, as if they've just been released, set free against the brilliant blue-green backdrop of the sky. The white rays depicted in the sky also radiate from the back, giving the overall mural a sensation of release and forward movement. The image invokes a feeling of liberation originating from a place of togetherness. Captured mid-flight on both sides of Priscilla's body, the butterflies exude a sense of freedom and hope for what is ahead.

The butterflies soar toward the message on the front portion of Priscilla's body: NO PAPERS NO FEAR / JOURNEY FOR JUSTICE on one side and SIN PAPELES SIN MIEDO / JORNADA POR LA JUSTICIA on the other. The phrases are stenciled in bold, black letters and outlined in white to contrast sharply with the brightness of the sky behind them. The optimism of the colors and images underscores the message of strength in the rejection of fear. The placement of the stenciled words at the closing end of the hopefulness of the mural reinforces the idea that in coming together and empowering themselves through their coming-out, Priscilla's Riders are heading toward a new way of navigating the world. Leaving their fear behind and working in community allows for a more hopeful future. The design on Priscilla makes clear the optimism of the Ride and the aspirations of its Riders.

Priscilla's art, particularly her monarch butterfly iconography, provides a beautiful visual aid that emphasizes the message that migration is an integral part of the natural world, regardless of constructed national borders. The monarch's journey between the United States and Mexico offers a perfect representation of the connection that exists between population movement and the land in the natural world. The monarch, like other migrating beings, does not recognize the man-made borders arbitrarily established between nations. The use of the butterfly as a metaphor for migration is also important because of the meaning of butterflies within a larger historical context of *jotería*. In his brilliant study of butterfly iconography and what he terms "mariposa consciousness," Daniel Enrique Pérez traces the different concepts that butterflies represent, including "nature, beauty, balance, the human soul, deities, love, rebirth, and transformation" (98). The members of the Ride invoke several of these meanings in their decision to use butterfly iconography. They write, "The butterfly is a symbol of freedom. . . . Like our community, the monarch is strong, beautiful and determined. . . . As we set out to change the world, each one of us changed ourselves. . . . As individuals and as a community, we took steps to fly free like the monarch; free from fear, free from intimidation" ("Meaning"). The power of their transformation and their rejection of living in fear is visually captured through the iconography of Priscilla's butterflies and the multiple monarch images surrounding the Riders' public coming-out.

The use of the butterfly imagery is especially poignant considering the linguistic practice of referring to men who have sex with men as *mariposas*, a practice Pérez traces back to sixteenth-century Spain (97). The term has historically been used pejoratively to describe the "non-normative gender and sexual behavior" of Latinx men (Pérez 99). The

Ride's embracing of the butterfly as a metaphor for the participants' struggle to be free is symbolic not just for its visual power but also for its acceptance of the queerness that butterflies also represent. As previously mentioned, the forty Riders were a diverse group of individuals that included several vocal queer Riders, including the well-known artist Julio Salgado. Unlike the original Freedom Rides, whose organizers had tried to hide Bayard Rustin's sexuality, this new Ride embraced the queerness of its members, including their art and their narratives, in the larger story of the action. The No Papers, No Fear Ride did not replicate the exclusionary, single-identity-based issue organizing that had plagued the earlier social justice movements and that had relegated the queerness of individuals like Rustin to the margins of the movements' history.[34]

The adoption of the monarch butterfly in the strategy of self-definition embodies an intersectional ethos of inclusion that incorporates the various identities of Priscilla's Riders. They are undocumented, but they are more than just their immigration status or their labor. Priscilla becomes the mobile stage on which to visually convey the message of the Ride, while also physically carrying the Riders on their journey. She is the embodiment of the Ride's rasquachismo, bringing together the resources at hand, making something beautiful, and providing a powerful backdrop against which the performance can take flight. Having set the stage and identified the context for the performance, I now turn to the actual enactment of resistance carried out by the Ride. In the analysis that follows, I weave together the multiple organizing parts of the Ride to tell a coherent story of community, performance, and empowerment. Given my reading of the Ride as a performance, my analysis follows the structure of a more traditional show.

Act 1: Phoenix, Arizona

"Get on the Bus"

Our performance begins with a story—one produced for a digital audience and aimed at spreading the news of the No Papers, No Fear Ride for Justice before the Undocubus began its journey.[35] On July 19, 2012, the movement's website posted the Ride's first video and captioned it with their overall goals: "This summer undocumented immigrants fed up with mistreatment are publicly coming out as unafraid to challenge their own fears in order for the world to recognize their humanity" ("No

Papers No Fear Ride" [blog post]). The video's description establishes that the Riders are undertaking the action in response to their unjust treatment, but it also makes the important claim that the Ride is about the Riders' own empowerment. By fighting against their own fears of detection and possible deportation, the Riders are taking control of their narratives. Unlike the participants in the 2003 Immigrant Workers Freedom Ride, these Riders are journeying in hostile environments to have their humanity recognized—not just their labor.

It is no coincidence that the No Papers, No Fear Ride originates in Arizona, the site of some of the nation's most draconian efforts to police undocumented individuals. From the passing of Senate Bill 1070, to Sheriff Joe Arpaio's "tent city" jail, Arizona is a model for state-level xenophobic and anti-immigrant legislation, regulation, and surveillance. Immigrant rights activists have had to become adept at crafting strategies of resistance in the face of such hostility. The text that accompanies the first No Papers, No Fear video states that the Ride "will challenge Sheriffs and proponents of anti-immigrant policies and set an example of courage to inspire a new day for migrant rights" ("No Papers No Fear Ride" [blog post]). In an effort to build coalitions and networks of solidarity, the Ride connects the anti-immigrant legislation and policies of Arizona to those in other states. For the Riders, what is happening in Phoenix to undocumented immigrants in their state is not an isolated incident but is part of a larger project of xenophobic anti-immigrant policies rippling throughout the nation.

Given the importance of making the Ride visible on a national scale, the beginning of the Ride had to make a statement. The 2012 civil trial against Sheriff Arpaio, *Melendres v. Arpaio*, offered the activists of Arizona the perfect opportunity to announce the Ride. The trial was a heavily covered media spectacle and was being closely monitored by many who viewed the trial as a test case on the legality of Arpaio's surveillance and aggressive policing of the immigrant community in Phoenix. The organizers of the Ride kicked off the action in conjunction with Arpaio's civil trial. Four members of the immigrant rights group Puente—Miguel Guerra, Leticia Ramirez, Natally Cruz, and Isela Meraz—chose to protest outside of the courthouse and volunteered to be arrested. The activists were aware of the risk of being handed over to immigration authorities after their arrest, but the threat did not dissuade them from their protest. In a later interview, Guerra made it clear that the threat of deportation had been worth it: "At least I know I played a part in history here, and can leave with my head held high" (qtd. in Pilkington). Upon their release, the organizers of the No Papers, No Fear Ride held a press conference announcing the participation of the four Puente members in the movement. By kicking off the action at such a heavily followed event, the organizers of the Ride used a strategy of rasquachismo, capturing media attention and harnessing the energy and momentum of the courthouse protests to create visibility for the Ride.

The introductory video itself offers a powerful message of resistance and hope, even as it describes the struggle faced by immigrants in Arizona. In the video, multiple activists discuss the motivations and frustrations behind the Ride. They begin by making sure the audience understands that SB 1070 is just the latest attack on their civil rights: "Arizona's human rights crisis didn't start when SB 1070 was introduced. A new phase of our human rights struggle did." By framing the rights of immigrants within a larger narrative of human rights, the Riders are expanding the conversation around undocumented immigration. It isn't merely an issue of legality but one of the rights of immigrants as human beings to be treated justly. The Riders go on to describe the failure of the federal government to protect their rights: "We witnessed Arizona's example spread through many states through copycat laws and federal programs. We hoped for immigration reform and instead found ourselves used as a political football by both Republicans and Democrats" ("No Papers No Fear Ride" [video]). They hold both political parties responsible for treating immigrants not as human beings but as tools in their own partisan fights. By historically contextualizing the Ride, the video offers an audience that might not be fully aware of the struggles of undocumented immigrants a brief but powerful glimpse into the motivations of the Riders.

Besides helping educate and prepare the audience for the performance, the video offers its participants an empowering message of self-determination. Instead of waiting for laws to change, these activists have taken it upon themselves to work toward change: "We announced to pledge that no matter what the courts decide, we will not comply. We began the process to defend ourselves in our homes, in our communities, in our schools." The discourse of self-defense is an important strategy that situates their immigrant community as being under attack by the unjust laws and policies put into place by Arpaio and like-minded law enforcement entities and politicians. Instead of the usual framing of undocumented immigrants as living in the shadows, afraid to be seen, the activists in the video make clear they are speaking and acting for themselves: "Two years later, what are we going to do? In Arizona and everywhere, we have no one but ourselves. . . . If the most humble among us are willing to stand up against Arpaio and [Immigration and Customs Enforcement], we set an example that we hope the president, the [Justice Department], and our advocates in DC would be brave enough to follow." They establish themselves as the model to follow, the ones who will lead the way toward change. But they do so while also holding their audience accountable: "SB 1070 and Arpaio create a moral dilemma that we must all answer. . . . Will you work to turn the tide or will you silently join the oppressors?" The rhetorical strategy of their last question makes it clear that no one is neutral in this fight. The video ends with the on-screen words "Get on the bus" ("No Papers No Fear Ride" [video]).

The visuals of the video help support the compelling message delivered by the featured activists. They speak directly and unflinchingly to the camera, offering their words while powerful images of resistance flash on the screen. We see young people engaged in protest and acts of civil disobedience. The photos capture standoffs with heavily armed police, as activists are led away in handcuffs. One image shows a defiant young woman standing firm in the face of a towering police officer in full riot gear. Many of the photos are black and white, reminiscent of older images of opposition. Interspersed within the narrative of the activists are clips of various actions and protests. The phrase "We will not comply" is made more powerful when the viewer witnesses a young girl, sitting on a homemade sign in the middle of an intersection, defiantly speaking the words into a bullhorn. The footage and photographs included in the video illustrate the diversity of the individuals advocating for their community. The musical track heard through the video, a version of Karl Jenkins's *Palladio*, swells to a crescendo as the urgency of the speakers' words are felt by the viewer. A more modern drumbeat is mixed into the song to inspire the viewer and to emphasize the strength of the activists' actions. The layering of the rousing music with the striking images of protest creates an effective performance of resistance.

It is important to note that although the video features images of a diverse group of activists, all of the speakers in the video are women. By acting as spokespersons for the Ride, these women are positioned as public-facing leaders of the action. In this way, the No Papers, No Fear Ride departs from the earlier Freedom Rides on which it is based. The success of the Freedom Rides was due in no small part to SNCC and its female leadership, including Ella Baker and Diane Nash, and to Freedom

Rider Lucretia Collins. Baker had organized the youth leadership conference that led to the creation of SNCC.[36] She would go on to mentor Nash, who would become a force to be reckoned with: a fierce fighter for civil rights and a giant problem for the men who underestimated her.[37] The fearless women of SNCC played a much more important part in the movement than the supporting role history has assigned them. The gender bias of the movement's male leaders influenced the roles women played in the movement and the lack of acknowledgment they would receive, while the gender bias of historians and scholars would affect how the narrative around the civil rights movement would be written for decades.[38] Unlike the earlier Freedom Rides, the No Papers, No Fear Ride centered the role of women in its media strategy and amplified their voices from the very start. The use of video, and its posting on the No Papers, No Fear website, contributes to the archiving of the organizing process and documents the inclusionary politics of the Ride.

Priscilla—the Spirit of Rasquachismo

Although I previously discussed Priscilla's visual impact, I now turn to a discussion of the process of overhauling the bus—a process that itself was an important part of the performance. Like the secondhand cars purchased and transformed into lowrider showpieces, Priscilla was a vintage bus that had undergone a complete overhaul. Previously utilized in organizing tours on climate justice issues, the 1972 bus was repurposed to carry the Riders on their journey and in the process came to embody a *rasquache* style of resistance to economic and political oppression. In her description of the bus, Chicana activist and Rider Marisa Franco discusses the decision—made with an understanding of the challenge—to use Priscilla for the trip. She writes that the decision was also about the spirit of resilience the Riders wanted to portray: "It was important to reflect a virtue of our community, that we roll with the punches. The fact that most of the time we don't have all the things we need, but we get it done somehow" (Franco, "Pricila"). In Franco's description of Priscilla's transformation, the effort to make her ready for the road emerges as part of the organizing and community-making process of the group: "When you work for something, when you sweat for it, the value transcends dollars and cents" ("Pricila"). Like the lowriders before her, Priscilla's worth exceeds the sum of her parts.[39] Just as "lowriders became narratives or visual texts of working-class life," Priscilla becomes a visual narrative of undocumented realities (Sandoval, "Politics" 181). In the words of the Riders, "We all rolled up our sleeves to transform [Priscilla] just like a catepillar [*sic*] becoming a monarch" ("Meaning").

Priscilla's transformation was documented through various images and personal reflections posted on the No Papers, No Fear website. The video "Timelapse: The Making of the (Undocu)Bus" captures the participants' process of bringing DJ Farias Portugal's sketch of Priscilla to life. Unlike the traditional practice of creating lowrider art in auto body shops—spaces predominantly populated by men—the art of the Undocubus is a communal project in which the community manifests the vision of the artist. We see multiple individuals, including children, laying down tape, cutting out stencils, painting the butterflies and the sky behind them, and finishing up with the large, black letters that communicate the movement's message. The video highlights the labor that goes into creating the Ride's artistic vision, and while we might not have their names, we are made aware that women and children are an integral part of this community art project. The video documents a strategy of engaging community in the creation of a vision of resistance.

Further making do with the tools at their disposal, the creators of "Timelapse: The Making of the (Undocu)Bus" use music to connect with the history of activism represented by the Freedom Rides. The song in the video, "Ain't Gonna Let Nobody Turn Me Round," is the Roots' version of a spiritual that became popular during the 1960s civil rights movement.[40] The song was first used in the summer of 1962 in Albany, Georgia, during actions against the segregation of travel on buses and trains.[41] The No Papers, No Fear organizers invoke the song's message of hope and resistance in a combination of visuals and sound that constructs a narrative of Priscilla's metamorphosis as one that goes beyond a simple makeover. By employing the song to tell the narrative of Priscilla's transformation, the video creates an effective digital performance of resistance that is rooted in both past movements and present-day communal visions of justice. The layering of such a dynamic historical song of protest over the visuals of the community transforming the bus adds an aspect of hope and resistance to the digital production, while also highlighting the diversity of the movement's participants.

The inclusive image of community members actively transforming Priscilla stands in stark contrast to the stereotypical masculinist image of lowriding. As with previous movements, lowrider culture and its activism have replicated various heteropatriarchal structures of oppression. While a community and family ethos might be at the center of lowrider culture, the organization of the participants has historically excluded women and queer-identified community members.[42] Denise Sandoval highlights the presence of women in lowrider culture and in the readership of *Low Rider* magazine—the culture's premier periodical—even as their involvement and contributions remain peripheral (Sandoval, "Cruising").[43] While the editors of *Low Rider* persisted in relegating Chicana lowriders to the fringe of the culture, women continued to fight for inclusion and created spaces for themselves within the main lowriding scene.[44] Queer members of the Chicanx community have found similar limitations placed upon their participation within mainstream lowrider culture.[45] The rigid performance of masculinity in car cultures leaves no room for sexual ambiguity. While the magazine, and the mainstream lowrider culture it represents, might ignore the presence of queerness within the community, it doesn't mean that queerness does not exist there.[46] The No Papers, No Fear Ride's emphasis on the diversity of the undocumented immigrant community is an important departure from the lowrider culture of the past. Instead, the Ride combines the historical lessons of art activism with an intersectional ethos of community to ensure that no Riders are left behind because of their gender or sexual orientation. Priscilla's rasquache aesthetics represent not only a bringing together of the resources available to the Riders but also an understanding of the importance of inclusivity learned from past movements' exclusionary politics.

Ultimately, Priscilla becomes more than the art on her body: She transforms into a communal space of belonging that transports her Riders. Like lowriders whose interiors are upgraded to match the grandeur of their exterior bodies, Priscilla's insides are transformed into a beautiful space for traveling, eating, and sleeping. Her interior becomes the heart of the bus that carries the Riders on their journey. In her reflections on the organization's blog, Franco makes the connection between lowriders and "Priscilla, my beloved low rider bus" ("Farewells"). She proudly writes of the Undocubus's makeover: "So we roll out of Phoenix, baby girl lookin' PIMP, [an] outside masterpiece painting project led by DeeJay Farias Portugal and Sandra Castro. . . . The inside became a colorful collage designed by Julio Sanchez, Leticia Ramirez and Nataly Cruz" (Franco, "Pricila"). Franco's description and her naming of the artists and Riders involved also underscores the role of women in the process.

In chronicling their Undocubus's transformation, the No Papers, No Fear organizers offer a digital mentoring text for future use. The painting of Priscilla becomes an evolution of the politics of lowrider culture and represents the empowering practice of rasquachismo on a grand scale.

Through the efforts of the community, the Undocubus transforms from a vehicle of transportation to a mobile stage for the performance of resistance and self-representation. Using the bus to communicate the larger message of the Ride is a visual strategy that prepares its audience to receive the stories the Riders carry with them. While Priscilla might not be cruising low and slow down the boulevard, she is disrupting a social system that rejects undocumented immigrants and is challenging their marginality and invisibility. After all, it is hard to miss a brightly decorated bus driving down interstate highways or cruising down the streets of cities. In making the Riders visible, Priscilla brings together the images of the Freedom Rides, the sensibilities of rasquachismo, and the political artistry of lowriding to assemble a new hybrid vision of resistance and activism. The beautiful image of the butterflies flying down the interstate highway sets the stage for each stop's actions.

Act 2: The Southern States

Testimonio Takes Center Stage

On the evening of July 29, 2012, the first group of No Papers, No Fear Riders loaded up the bus and said farewell to their community. Priscilla was leaving Phoenix for her first stop on the tour: Denver, Colorado. Along with enthusiasm for the Ride, the Riders and their supporters felt the weight of the risk the activists would undertake by making their status so publicly visible. So much of the journey was unknown: Not only would the voyage take the Riders away from their friends and family; there was also the fear that those riding the bus might not be able to return. In her reflections on their farewell, Marisa Franco writes that after the bus departed, driving away from the supporters "cheering the bus and its riders on, there was an element of sadness. Once we turned off into the main street, turned onto the I-10 everyone [became] silent, turning into themselves perhaps already feeling the distance of their families and daily lives" ("Farewells").

Press releases that coincided with each stop helped announce the arrival and actions planned by the Riders and local organizations.[47] Like preperformance advertisements announcing theatrical runs and premieres, the press releases informed communities of the Ride's arrival and garnered support and anticipation for the Riders' actions. As sources of information beyond mere dates and locations, the releases became useful tools for documenting the coalition of groups and individuals that helped make the Ride successful at every stop, and they drew connections between the realities of various undocumented immigrant communities along the route. Through their posting on the No Papers, No Fear website, the releases also compose part of the archive that documents the Ride and the strategies used in setting up the multiple stops, offering a source of textual mentorship for future activists.

Queering the Testimonio

During the tour, Priscilla helped perform the affective visual work of the Ride at every stop, but the Ride's performance of resistance relied heavily on the bodies and words of the Riders themselves. Throughout the journey, the undocumented Riders used their coming-out narratives to put a human face on the immigration debate. Employing a linguistic strategy made popular by the LGBTQ+ movement, Riders framed their public proclamations of being undocumented as a process of coming out. No longer willing to hide or to remain silent because of their status, the Riders came out at various points on their journey, always aware of the danger of being arrested but refusing to be afraid. My framing of the discourse of coming out is based on an understanding that "for sexual minorities, the term *coming out* rhetorically linked various forms of disclosure to different audiences—including parents, family, coworkers, and the media. When used by the immigrant youth movement, it implicitly draws a parallel between undocumented immigrants and sexual minorities, suggesting that both are unjustly oppressed" (Enriquez and Saguy 110).[48] The embracing of coming-out narratives as a rhetorical strategy illustrates the No Papers, No Fear movement's understanding of the power of this linguistic schema, and it in turn validates and acknowledges the influence of queer undocumented youth.[49]

The Riders' coming-out narratives did not just disclose their immigration status: Their personal stories also made evident the types of discrimination and unjust treatment facing undocumented immigrants. The practice of using oral stories to inform an audience of the conditions that undocumented immigrants face in their everyday lives is rooted in the historical tradition of the *testimonio*. In his work on testimonio, John

Beverley loosely defines the genre as a "novel or novella-length narrative in book or pamphlet (that is, printed as opposed to acoustic) form, told in the first-person by a narrator who is also the real protagonist or witness of the events he or she recounts, and whose unit of narration is usually a 'life' or a significant life experience" (12–13). Beverley acknowledges that testimonio-like texts have existed in the past—for example, oral histories and memoirs—but argues that testimonio "coalesces as a new narrative genre in the 1960s and further develops in close relation to the movements for national liberation and the generalized cultural radicalism of that decade" (13). While the conventional practice of testimonio articulates history through the perspective of marginalized individuals in the form of nonfiction literature, most often framed and transcribed by an interlocutor, testimonio has grown beyond the written format and the reliance on an intermediary.

While the traditional coming-out narrative is a form of resistance to queer invisibility and centers the desires and needs of the body, the methodology of the testimonio is reliant on a process of speaking back to power that involves an analysis of intersectional oppressive structures and the impact of those structures on marginalized individuals. In their discussion of the roots and evolution of testimonio, Kathryn Blackmer Reyes and Julia Curry Rodríguez argue that "the objective of the *testimonio* is to bring to light a wrong, a point of view, or an urgent call for action. Thus, in this manner, the *testimonio* is different from the qualitative method of in-depth interviewing, oral history narration, prose, or spoken word. The *testimonio* is intentional and political" (525).[50] The customary coming-out narrative is based on an individual's story of disclosure, and while it can become part of a larger LGBTQ+ history, it is not based on recounting a collective experience. In contrast, testimonio uses the story of the individual as part of a collective action. In this way, "the cornerstone of *testimonio*, like oral history, is not the speaking of truth, but rather, the telling of an account from an individual point of view whose conscience has led to an analysis of the experience as a shared component of oppression" (Blackmer Reyes and Curry Rodríguez 528). Through testimonio, marginalized individuals use their personal narratives to discuss the experiences of subjugation faced by their community, and thus testimonio offers a collective strategy of bearing witness and using one's voice to talk back to power.

Testimonio is also an important tool for education and inspiration. In framing my argument about the type of mentoring that testimonio offers,

I rely on Dolores Delgado Bernal and her coauthors' findings that testimonio "lends itself to a form of teaching and learning that brings the mind, body, spirit, and political urgency to the fore. Whether in a formal classroom or in myriad informal learning environments, such as the home, *testimonio* has the potential to provide a way to theorize and learn from body experiences of oppression and resistance" (367).[51] As a pedagogical tool, testimonio offers a means of using personal stories to educate an audience in an effort to gather support in the struggle to resist oppression. The No Papers, No Fear Riders used the methodology of testimonio to theorize their marginalization and to produce their own testimonios, often captured on video and archived on their website, to educate their audience. Reading the Riders' coming-out narratives as a form of testimonio also allows for an understanding of the collective risk involved in disclosing their immigration status. For many undocumented immigrants, disclosing their status also means disclosing the status of family members. It is not simply an individual decision, and the Riders' testimonio gestures toward the impact that exposure has on their community.

Disclosing their individual immigration status through a narrative that centers the collective gave the Riders the opportunity to embody their resistance through the process of crafting and performing testimonio. Given the importance of education, resistance, and inspiration in the activism of the Riders, testimonio enabled them to go beyond merely describing their individual experiences. The narrative structure of testimonio generates a more performative type of speech, because it "simultaneously engages the personal and collective aspects of identity formation while translating choices, silences, and ultimate identities" (Delgado Bernal et al. 364). The exercise of repeatedly disclosing their status, reciting the phrases "undocumented and unafraid" and "sin papeles sin miedo," and narrating the impact of their status on their communities illustrates the Riders' deliberate and intentional use of their testimonio as a guiding script that articulates a comprehensive structure for the larger communal narrative. Sixty-five years earlier, the organizers of the Journey of Reconciliation had composed a set of guidelines to script their resistance. Now the Undocubus Riders used their coming-out testimonios to create their own playbook of defiance. By combining their coming-out with the practice of testimonio, the Riders created a linguistic performance of resistance rooted in various historical movements that voiced opposition through communal storytelling. By privileging their stories and experiences as sites of knowledge, they offer a model for others to follow.

"We Exist"

In recognizing the Riders' use of the coming-out testimonio as a linguistic strategy rooted in queer activism of the past, it is important to underscore the No Papers, No Fear Ride's acceptance of queerness as an integral identity formation in the undocumented community, and not as an appropriation of the language of the LGBTQ+ community. Unlike earlier movements, the Ride does not attempt to underplay the queerness of its participants, and, in fact, the movement features queer testimonios on its blog. One example is a video defiantly titled "I'm a Queer Undocumented Mexican. We Exist. We're Involved" ("Gerardo"). The video's narrator, Gerardo Torres, describes his work as a community activist and holds a picture of himself with his parents as he declares, "I am a queer undocumented Mexican. . . . I want to make [people] aware that the queer community is alive. We are part of the whole movement" ("Gerardo"). The family photo strategically situates his queerness as existing within a traditional family structure, normalizing his identity. In his biography posted on the No Papers, No Fear website, Torres writes, "I want people to know that the queer undocumented community is also affected by these laws" ("Bio: Gerardo Torres"). He uses his voice on the blog to help the movement's audience understand that queer immigrants do not exist on the margins: They are a central part of the immigrant rights struggle. In the movement's press releases, the organizers also included Torres's queerness in their descriptions of him as a Rider.

Torres himself draws the connection between his activism as a Rider and his understanding of a queer history of resistance. In a blog entry that narrates his confronting of Kris Kobach, one of the architects of SB 1070, during a hearing before the US Commission on Civil Rights, Torres writes,

> I should also say that being part of the . . . LGBTQ community, and knowing our history, has been important. I have seen how as people who are queer, we have learned to speak from our experience, for ourselves. I think of people like Harvey Milk, who has taught us that we can be politicians, and come out, and demand to be accepted as who we are; Bayard Rustin, who shows us that we can be great organizers and part of amazing movements for change, to fight for our civil rights. . . . They have left us a great legacy, that we have an obligation to carry on and pass on to new generations.

Torres emphasizes the importance of the work of past queer activists on his own understanding of struggle and of what is possible. He situates himself and his fellow queer Riders within this larger history of queer activism and coalition building, and in the process he inserts this queerstory into the larger narrative of the Ride. The title of Torres's blog entry, "Fearless and Speaking for Ourselves," also highlights the agency that queer Riders experience in telling their own narratives of immigration, and it illustrates the power that discourse and language play in defining our movements. In fact, it was Torres's planned participation in the Ride that forced him to reveal his queerness to his cousins, aunts, and uncles, because he wanted "'to be the voice of the queer community,' and the only way to do that is to embrace his homosexuality publicly" (Santos).

The importance of the movement's embracing of queer individuals alongside its employment of queer liberatory discourse cannot be understated. Just because a movement employs the discourse of queer activism doesn't mean the movement accepts—or even tolerates—queerness. Two years earlier, for example, a group of undocumented students undertook their own form of public protest, called the Trail of DREAMs. The action featured four students—Gaby Pacheco, Isabel Sousa-Rodriguez, Felipe Matos, and Carlos Roa—who undertook a 1,500-mile walk from Miami to the White House (see Jobin-Leeds and AgitArte). Along the way, the activists learned the strategies of resistance employed by previous civil rights movements and built coalitions with various groups.[52] Although the students were supported by many, sometimes that support was conditional. Even as "the Trail of DREAMs walkers dared undocumented people to come out, they hid the fact that" Isabel and Felipe were a queer couple; in fact, the two were asked by several churches to sit separately at events (Jobin-Leeds and AgitArte 92).[53] Isabel has expressed regret that the couple weren't more assertive in standing up for themselves, but the choice to respect their intersectional identities was not left entirely up to them.[54] As young adults, and as undocumented immigrants, they were surrounded by older adults with more power who should have advocated for the young couple. Marginalized individuals should not be made to choose between their intersecting identities. It was one of the most painful mistakes made in previous movements and one that replicates the structures of inequality that activists are fighting to dismantle.[55]

The No Papers, No Fear Ride's celebration—not just tolerance—of the queerness of some Riders and organizers offers a model for the type of intersectional organizing that is vitally important for the growth and survival of our movements and the support of our communities. In his blog entry “Letter to My Mother,” Marco Flores recalls a conversation with fellow Rider Chela (Isela Meraz):

> We were at ease discussing our existence as *familia*, our life as *queer gente* within the movement. Because within the undocumented movement, our queerness is often pushed aside, and at times, even erased. The fear of adding more complexity to an already difficult fight leads to our own exclusion from the fight for immigration justice. We are asked to downplay our *jotería* for the public, because there is no room for sexual politics in the undocumented movement. We have to choose one self over the other. We can never be queer *and* undocumented, because to be both simultaneously would be a “sort of distraction” that would weaken the movement. But in the midst of the UndocuBus riders, I could for once exist as my undocumented *and* my queer self. It meant piecing myself together for the first time; I felt whole within my own fragments.

Flores’s powerful written testimonio of his experience with his fellow Undocubus Riders, and the feeling of belonging he experienced among them, offers a striking contrast to the ostracizing or closeting of queer people in previous movements. His ability to feel whole, to be seen and accepted for all of his different identities, exemplifies the inclusiveness of the Ride and illustrates the potential for self-empowerment that intersectional organizing offers. By embracing the diversity within the immigrant community, the Ride strengthened connections across difference and made it easier for others to join the movement.

Empowerment on the Road

At their various stops, the Riders encouraged local undocumented immigrants to share their own stories, invoking the communal aspect of testimonio to help make connections across multiple geographical sites. During the group’s first stop, undocumented immigrants from the local Denver community offered their own public coming-out testimonios, initiating the movement’s practice of including local voices in a larger community narrative of empowerment and defiance (F. Lopez). Everywhere along their route, undocumented immigrants joined the Riders in publicly performing their coming-out and testifying to the conditions they faced as a result of their immigration status. Their coming-out testimonios offered the Riders an opportunity to connect with undocumented immigrants throughout their journey and to address the role that local politics play in immigrants’ living conditions. In New Orleans, the Riders held a rally outside an immigration court with and in support of the Southern Thirty-Two, a group of day laborers unjustly arrested in an immigration raid in Kenner, Louisiana ("Justicia"). In Atlanta, the Riders joined a coalition that included the Georgia Latino Alliance for Human Rights and Southerners on the Ground for a rally and public offering of coming-out testimonios outside of the city detention center ("Aug.24.2012"). In Asheville, North Carolina, the Riders deliberately held their action outside of Shogun Buffet, the site of an immigration raid that had placed twelve of the restaurant's workers in deportation proceedings ("No Papers No Fear Delegation"). When the Riders arrived in Laurel, Mississippi, they held an education and organizing workshop with local poultry-processing workers and discussed tensions with the local chapter of the Laborers' International Union of North America around the union's support for E-Verify and its unwillingness to protect the rights of immigrant workers (Mangandi).

One of the most inspiring performances of undocumented immigrants coming out through their testimonio occurred in Sylva, North Carolina, where Riders and local supporters protested outside the offices of Jackson County Sheriff Jimmy Ashe. The protestors questioned the legality of law enforcement checkpoints set up in predominantly Latinx and immigrant communities. A video of the action outside the sheriff's office, published on YouTube, served to digitally archive the protest and make it accessible to a wider audience ("Sylva"). The demonstration featured the testimonio of various community members, including Claudia Arellano and Jose Gonzalez, members of Coalición de Organizaciones Latino-Americanas, who gave personal accounts of being racially profiled at the checkpoints. In the video, we witness several Riders asking to speak to Sheriff Ashe and being told he isn't in the office. The woman working the front desk informs the Riders that they can leave him a voicemail message to set up an appointment to meet with him. We witness Riders Kitzia Esteva and Martin Unzueta calling the sheriff and leaving messages regarding their concern for the treatment of immigrants in Jackson County. The video captures several individuals speaking on their phones outside of the office, indicating the activists' concerted effort to flood the sheriff's phone line. Rider Marisa Franco, having asked to speak to one of the sheriff's subordinates, is filmed talking with an unidentified deputy, sharing the community's concerns and questioning Ashe's refusal to meet with community members. Franco reminds the deputy that Ashe is an elected official who serves the community. The deputy's discomfort is clear as he asks that the camera be turned off and then condescendingly wishes her a good day and closes the door ("Sylva").

When the sheriff won't meet with them or take their calls, the Riders organize to make their presence known and to further document their grievances. In the video, Franco instructs those who feel comfortable doing so to enter the office and vocalize their testimonio through a concise script: to state their name, where they are coming from, their immigration status, the fact that they are not afraid, and their request to speak to the sheriff. The activists' plan—knowing that Sheriff Ashe will not meet with them and that they will be turned away—is for the next person in line to recite the same script. In the video, undocumented activists line up to leave their testimonio with the receptionist. They form a long line that snakes out the door, continuing past the entrance to the building and beyond the view of the camera. The repeated oration of the activists' testimonio clearly frustrates the receptionist, who seems uncertain how to handle all the BIPOC immigrants confidently stating their names and defiantly declaring their status. She looks bewildered and unsure of how to document what is happening and looks to others in the office for assistance ("Sylva"). The sight of these activists—individuals who have been marginalized and made to be afraid through the practice of checkpoints—standing up for their rights and speaking their truth is a powerful testimony to the strategies of resistance employed by the Riders and their supporters. The danger of undocumented immigrants declaring their immigration status in the middle of a police station cannot be overstated, especially when we consider that Sheriff Ashe had made his stance on anti-immigrant policing practices clear. The condescension of the deputies and the staff and the refusal of the sheriff to meet with the Riders and local activists did not dissuade them from speaking out and using their narratives to resist their unjust treatment. The Riders' use of their coming-out testimonios encouraged local immigrants to join in a public act of resistance that empowered the entire community.[56]

Inspiring their audience through the use of coming-out testimonios was not the Riders' only pedagogical tool. Along the way, the Riders held workshops aimed at helping local activists organize around specific challenges facing their immigrant communities. In Denver, the Riders held a workshop with local organizers to discuss the impact of Colorado Senate Bill 90—an anti-immigrant law similar to section 2B of Arizona's SB 1070—and to share strategies for organizing against such legislation. In keeping with their practice of understanding the specificity of identity within immigrant communities, the organizers held breakout sessions whose topics included "Women and Families," "LGBT Rights," "Labor," "Students and Youth," and "Barrio Defense Committees in Depth" (F. Lopez). The sessions offered those in attendance the opportunity to participate in various conversations that intersected with their identity as undocumented immigrants. The breakdown of the sessions also makes clear that the movement comprises a multiplicity of people, including women, youths, workers, students, and queer individuals. In her reflections on the Denver stop, Rider Daniela Cruz discusses the connections the activists made across geographical spaces. She observes that the struggle of immigrants in Colorado "reminded me of the struggle we have been fighting in Arizona, and affirmed that immigration laws affect people in a lot more states, and how this fight doesn't belong to just one community but to ALL of us" (Cruz).

In keeping with their focus on the local, the Riders tailored their outreach activities to the specific needs of local communities at each stop. In Austin, Texas, the Riders participated in a teach-in that included the testimonio of individuals who had experienced detention. During their stop in New Orleans, Riders from the Arizona organizations Puente and the Southside Worker Center went on an outreach trip to connect with the city's day laborer population (de la Fuente). Visiting a corner of Gretna Boulevard where many laborers get picked up for day work, the Riders connected with the local undocumented community in their own territory. Instead of simply informing the day laborers of the Ride, Eleazar Castellanos and other Riders shared their testimonio and discussed strategies for protection against unfair labor practices—strategies that had helped immigrant workers in Tucson. The health promoters from Puente provided the day laborers with basic health screenings, including checking their blood pressure and blood sugar levels, and offered information on chronic illnesses that affect the immigrant community ("Promotoras"). Through these outreach efforts, the Riders connected with a population that might have gone overlooked and shared information on their rights as immigrants and workers. All of these activities have been documented and archived by the No Papers, No Fear movement, living beyond the moment of their performance.

Building Coalitions

Beyond educating the Ride's audience, each of the stops along the route offered the Riders the opportunity to make alliances and create coalitions. Like the Freedom Riders before them, the Undocubus Riders relied on the support of community organizations committed to social justice, including religious groups and churches. The Riders were hosted by Church of the Savior in Knoxville, Iglesia El Siloe in Charlotte, and Unitarian Universalist churches in Denver, Knoxville, and Memphis. The Riders found support in other immigrant rights organizations, including the Tennessee Immigrant and Refugee Rights Coalition, Allies of Knoxville's Immigrant Neighbors, the Latin American Coalition, La Familia Unida, and United for the Dream, to name a few. Support also came from organizations committed to broader issues of social justice, including the Twomey Center for Peace Through Justice in New Orleans, Southerners on New Ground in Atlanta, Knoxville United Against Racism, the Memphis Gay and Lesbian Community Center, and the Mid-South Peace and Justice Center. Each of these organizations offered its own form of support and collaboration. The number and diversity of the groups that chose to champion the Riders and their message illustrates the possibilities that intersectional coalition building offers to justice movements.

Two of the Rides' most historically rich connections happened in New Orleans and Selma. In Louisiana, the New Orleans Worker Center for Racial Justice hosted a conversation between the Riders and several veterans of the civil rights movement. The Worker Center was founded as an intersectional organization in response to the devastation left behind by Hurricane Katrina. The organization's website notes, "Against the backdrop of a political economy that pitted communities of color against each other, a group of black and immigrant workers came together from public housing developments, FEMA trailer parks, day labor corners, and labor camps across Louisiana to build a new freedom movement: multi-racial; committed to racial, gender, and immigrant justice; and dedicated to building power at the intersection of race and the economy" ("Our History"). The Worker Center's history of coalition building between, and advocacy for, Black and immigrant workers offered the Ride's organizers a powerful model of activism and cross-organizational collaboration.

A video of the meeting filmed by Rider Barni Qaasim captures the inspiring conversation between the No Papers, No Fear activists and Doratha Smith-Simmons, a member of CORE who shared her experiences as a young civil rights activist during the 1960s. Speaking of young people's commitment to the civil rights movement, Smith-Simmons recalls, "When we as young people joined CORE, we were prepared to die for what we believed. . . . I think individually I may have been afraid but, as a group, we were not afraid. We were as one" ("No One"). The power of Smith-Simmons's narrative of activism lies not only in her history of bravery but also in her acknowledgment that despite the fear she might have felt as an individual, she found strength in working together with her fellow CORE members.

Smith-Simmons's narrative resonates strongly with the Riders' own message of fearlessness.[57] Her testimony also highlights the importance of song in the creation of a performance of resistance. She tells the Riders, "Another thing that kept us from being afraid was singing, music. And we were singing, and a-singing, and a-singing. And the police came up and said, 'Stop the singing.' So, what did we do? We sang louder, 'Ain't gonna let no police dog turn us 'round, turn us 'round, turn us 'round . . . we gonna keep on walking, keep on talking, marching up to freedom land'" ("No One"). As she sings the words that made those CORE members feel less afraid, we watch as the Riders sing along. The meeting's participants understand the power that music plays in creating a soundtrack to their movements. The performance of those songs of resistance give the activists courage in the face of violent oppression. As the Riders resumed their journey through the Southern states, they deepened their connections to veterans of the civil rights movement.

In a second example of the coalitions that developed between civil rights veterans and the Riders, the organization Saving OurSelves (SOS) invited the Riders to visit Selma, Alabama, to learn more about the civil rights activism of the area. Extending one of the major goals of the 1960s civil rights movement, the mission of SOS is "to wage a campaign and re-ignite a movement to restore and maintain unfettered voting rights, which must be secured in order to secure labor, women, immigration, health and other vital rights essential to a just, democratic nation" ("Our Mission"). The video of the Selma gathering documents the Riders' visit to Edmund Pettus Bridge and the National Voting Rights Museum. The opening caption, also written in Spanish, notes, "Riders visit the site of Bloody Sunday in Selma, Alabama[,] where African American activists were brutally beaten by state troopers. Black people were kept from voting by white supremacists" ("'When I See Injustice'"). We hear a version of "Ain't Gonna Let Nobody Turn Me Round" as Faya Ora Rose Touré, a civil rights activist and artist, appears on-screen to narrate the story of the 1965 attack on marchers as they attempted to cross the bridge. We watch as Riders cross the same bridge, holding signs and banners and invoking the name of Rosa Parks in their chants. Alabama State Senator Hank Sanders marches with the Riders as he recounts the incredible violence faced by the marchers on the bridge. The video offers powerful visual testimony of the Riders following in the footsteps of those brave marchers forty-seven years later. In tracing the marchers' footsteps and invoking Rosa Parks, the Riders honor the legacy of activism and civil rights struggles that preceded their movement, using the event as a visual reminder of the work that remains to be done to achieve equality and justice.

At the National Voting Rights Museum, Sam Walker—whom the video's caption identifies as a foot soldier of the civil rights movement—tells the Riders about his experience of being incarcerated, as an eleven-year-old boy, for his activism. The Riders then participate in a roundtable discussion with other activists, including Joanne Bland, the cofounder of the National Voting Rights Institute, and Annie Pearl Avery, a civil rights veteran who shares an inspiring message of fighting against injustice even at the cost of one's freedom. Avery's testimony is especially poignant, as she recounts the multiple places where she was jailed and gassed by police for her activism. By the end of the video, it is clear that both communities understand the difficulties faced by each movement and the commonalities between them. Bland observes, "Our histories are so intertwined. We must stand together," while Rider Mari Cruz echoes this message of solidarity, stating, "We as a Latino community are here with you" ("'When I See Injustice'"). The impact of the visit to Selma is clearly captured in a conversation between Riders Maria Huerta and Isela Meraz, posted the same day on the movement's blog. Huerta concludes, "The overall message we got from the people there was to connect—to form *un puente*, a bridge—between our community and the African American community. Because in the end, our struggles [are] one" (Huerta and Meraz). The opportunity to meet with individuals who were part of the movement that inspired so much of the Undocubus action allowed the Riders to contextualize their own history of struggle and to envision their fight for justice as a much broader one. The videos that capture these significant meetings not only connect two social movements but also illustrate the power that performance and the visual embodiment of resistance play in effecting change.

Coming Out in Birmingham

One of the Ride's most inspiring stops happened in Birmingham, Alabama, on August 17, 2012, when a group of Riders attended the US Commission on Civil Rights hearings on the impact of state-based immigration laws. Four brave Riders—Gerardo Torres, Mari Cruz Ramirez Jimenez, Maria Huerta, and Juan Jose Mangandi—interrupted the proceedings with their coming-out testimonios. Holding up white signs stenciled with the word UNDOCUMENTED, each of the Riders stood in turn during the testimony of Kris Kobach, the author of SB 1070 and one of the undocumented community's most vocal opponents. Each Rider interrupted Kobach's statement, pushing back against claims that such anti-immigrant legislation was not a form of racial profiling. In his description of the action, Gerardo Torres described the importance of their acts of intervention: "We had not been included as part of the group to testify, so we stood up, uninvited, and told our stories."[58]

While their fellow Riders engaged in peaceful protest inside the hearing room, a group of Riders outside committed their own acts of civil disobedience, this time centering the performance of resistance to detention. Invoking the spirit of rasquache productions of the past—most famously embodied by the actos of Teatro Campesino in the organizing work of the United Farm Workers—Riders put on a performance using a handful of props and their bodies to tell a story of defiance. Teatro Campesino used the short skit form of the acto as a tool to "Inspire the audience to social action. Illuminate specific points about social problems. Satirize the opposition. Show or hint at a solution. Express what people are feeling" (Valdez 12). The Riders' performance outside of the hearings employs the actos' enactment of resistance in a modern effort to organize and inspire the movement's audience.

Using a bus, La Luna, as a mock Department of Homeland Security vehicle, one Rider acted out the role of an Immigration and Customs Enforcement agent while other Riders played detainees.[59] In true rasquache fashion, the performers used garbage bags painted with white stripes to symbolize prison uniforms. As the ICE agent berated two detainees, another group began to fight back, tearing off their makeshift prison uniforms and unshackling themselves, physically and symbolically setting themselves free. In a blog post about the performance, the Riders describe wanting "to show how [I]mmigration abuses their power by hitting people, screaming at people and treating us like animals and the importance of organizing together in order to resist" (Ramirez et al.). As part of their performance, the Riders freed monarch butterflies from a box, again drawing the connection between the butterflies' freedom to fly unencumbered and the Riders' own quest to be free. While the peaceful demonstration inside the building by Torres, Ramirez Jimenez, Huerta, and Mangandi helped make an intervention in the official hearings, the performance of the Riders outside of the hearings gave the Birmingham action a powerful dimension of embodied resistance.

Theater of the Streets

The inspiration of Teatro Campesino and popular theater was present at other stops along the Riders' journey. For Rider Juan Jose Mangandi, a member of Teatro Jornalero Sin Fronteras, "Theater is a medium to send a message. Not only to those who oppose us. It is also a message of hope to people so that they are aware that they are not alone. We are 12 million people living the same drama" ("Juan Jose Mangandi"). Mangandi's likening of the reality of living as an undocumented immigrant to a drama conveys the constructed and performative nature of citizenship and national belonging. Such an acknowledgment allows for the creation of narratives to dismantle the drama and offers Mangandi and fellow activists the use of theater to create stories to "help people to find pride. Help them make sense of life." His words are visually emphasized in the video by clips of activists performing in a parking lot in Memphis, Tennessee ("Juan Jose Mangandi"). In a video filmed by fellow Rider Jorge Torres in Memphis, we see a more in-depth view of Mangandi's work through various skits involving Riders and members of the Tennessee Immigrant and Refugee Rights Coalition, who organized the event to support the Ride ("Memphis"). We witness a dramatized border crossing and the terrible reality of the death of a migrant traveler. We watch as Mangandi prays over the fallen woman, asking the spirit of the desert to take care of her soul, and prays that her children never have to migrate. The simple skit with deep significance captures the dangers of crossing the border, the potential loss of life, and the mourning of a community. The actors don't need complicated sets or elaborate costumes to convey their message to their audience. There is power in the simplicity of their performance and beauty in the communal mourning it inspires.

In Atlanta, Georgia, Torres's camera captured the collaboration between the Riders and the Georgia Latino Alliance for Human Rights (GLAHR).[60] As part of their activities around the Ride, GLAHR organized a series of short theater pieces performed by their Teatro de los GLAHRiadores—a play on the word *gladiador* (gladiator). Torres's video records the group's performances, beginning with an actor in a George W. Bush mask invoking the discourse of terrorism to explain draconian immigration policies ("Teatro de los GLAHRiadores"). The plastic mask is reminiscent of the masks used by actors in Teatro Campesino's actos, and it embodies the type of rasquache aesthetic that is such an important aspect of this type of activist theater. The skits offer three different examples of how the immigrant community is policed in Georgia, including the practice of racially motivated traffic stops, the detainment of workers, and the racial profiling of young immigrant men. The performances offer their audience an opportunity to learn more about their rights, the options they have under detention, and the impact on their lives of the collaboration between local police and ICE—or what the skit's Bush character calls the "PoliMigra." The performance ends with one of the GLAHR actors voicing solidarity with the Riders: "We're all undocumented! We're all on the Undocubus! No papers, no fear!" (my trans.; "Teatro de los GLAHRiadores"). Using the tools of art and theater creates solidarity between the Riders and the members of GLAHR that goes beyond workshops, protests, and civil disobedience.[61] The theater and art produced in collaboration helped the actors and those in the audience imagine a different world in which their humanity is recognized and their human rights are acknowledged and upheld.

The theater performances were also part of larger cultural celebrations in local communities. Beyond focusing on the dangers of being undocumented and the fear of detention and deportation, the community gatherings offered the Riders and their supporters the opportunity to celebrate the strengths of the immigrant community. Unlike the mainstream narrative that frames oppressed communities as always suffering and abject, the Riders' collaborations with local groups included events that featured the talent and joy of immigrant communities. These events offered immigrants and their supporters an opportunity to create community through a celebration of storytelling, art, music, and culture. In Austin, the Riders joined the Workers Defense Project for a fandango that included music, poetry, testimonio, dance, and breaking bread together ("Austin"). In Memphis, in addition to the teatro performances captured in Jorge Torres's videos, we also witness a group of children dancing *ballet folklórico*, joyfully celebrating traditional Mexican dance ("Memphis"). In North Carolina, the Riders began their journey through the state with "Undocunight: Una Noche de Sueños y Esperanza," a cultural and story-sharing event hosted by community supporters in Asheville ("No Papers No Fear Delegation"). During the final stop of their journey, in Charlotte, the Riders held the event "Sin Papeles y Sin Miedo: Festival de Canto, Poesía y Arte" at Fiesta Jalisco, a local Mexican restaurant. The festival culminated with a special concert by Los Jornaleros del Norte that honored the Riders and their journey. These celebrations not only reiterated the power that making music, dancing, and sharing stories can play in sustaining hope within social movements but also rejected the abject figure of the undocumented immigrant popular in mainstream narratives.

By the time Priscilla arrived at her destination, the Riders had created a strong network of support based on the relationships they had built along the way. In developing this support, they relied on all of the tools at their disposal: the linguistic use of testimonio and coming-out narratives, community-building skills to engage with local immigrant communities and to create new coalitions between movements, public performances of dissent, and the creative use of rasquache theatrical productions. It would be easy to overlook the importance of the stops along the way in order to focus attention on the action at the Riders' final destination. By reading each moment as part of the whole performance, however, we gain a clearer picture of the organizing logic of the Ride. The organizers, the Riders, and their allies employed strategies of the past and acts of community empowerment to create a coherent performance of resistance. Priscilla's journey to North Carolina tells a story of activism rooted in community, resilience, and courage. The Riders would need the communal strength they had developed on their journey to sustain them through the last act of their performance: the action at the Democratic National Convention.

Act 3: Charlotte, North Carolina

Confronting the Democrats

The performance of the No Papers, No Fear Ride for Justice culminated in the final scene with which this chapter began: the acts of protest and choreographed civil disobedience on the opening day of the 2012 Democratic National Convention. Like the Ride's stops in other cities, this event was highly planned and coordinated among the movement's activists, their supporters, and local groups. Priscilla rolled into Charlotte on September 1, 2012, heralded by a press release announcing the Riders' arrival and the events planned during their stay in the city ("Charlotte"). The release acknowledged the specific local legislation affecting the lives of immigrants in North Carolina and highlighted the collaboration between the Riders and community groups, including the Latin American Coalition, La Familia Unida, and United for the Dream. The press release worked to garner support for the Riders, increase the visibility of the upcoming action, and draw media attention to the Riders' planned civil disobedience.

In preparing for the final action, the Riders participated in the March on Wall Street South on September 2. The march's coalition of different activist groups offered the Riders the opportunity to build alliances with other organizations working toward social justice and equality. The motley group of activists who participated in the march were using the convention gathering as an opportunity to protest issues ranging from climate change, to housing affordability, to education ("DNC Time"). The Riders' participation was part of a larger strategy of coalition building that drew visibility and awareness to the connections among immigration, worker exploitation, and the private prison system that profits from the detainment of undocumented immigrants.

Given the number of other organizations and groups who had arrived in Charlotte to protest at the Democratic National Convention, it was also important for the Riders to make their presence known among the crowd. Giant cardboard butterflies, held aloft on poles by the Riders and their supporters, flew above the march's sea of activists and organizers. Some of the brightly colored butterflies carried the Ride's message on their wings: NO PAPERS NO FEAR and SIN PAPELES SIN MIEDO. Many activists wore their own sets of wings, while others carried colorful cloth banners with abstract wings and the words MIGRANT JUSTICE emblazoned on them. The artistic props helped make the Riders visible within a large contingency of dedicated social justice activists representing multiple organizations and causes. As in most performances, the visuals of the action played a vital role in telling the Riders' story and spreading their message.

Much like their use of imagery during the March on Wall Street South, the Ride's activists and artists spent the night before the Riders' big action spreading their visual message throughout the city. The film *Migration Is Beautiful*, part of the documentary series *Voice of Art*, captures these artivists spray-painting images on banners, stenciling letters on signs, cutting out wings, painting butterfly costumes, and screen-printing flags. On the night before the big action at the Democratic National Convention, Favianna Rodriguez and her fellow artists went out into the city. Rodriguez explains that "to spread awareness in Charlotte, a crew of us set out late at night to hit the streets with migrating butterflies" (*Migration*). We watch as Rodriguez and the group of artists begin to decorate the city with oversized posters. Under the cover of darkness, they use buckets of wheat paste and paint rollers to create the scenery—a rasquache communal set—for the action.[62] On the side of a building, the activists post a giant, yellow, diamond-shaped sign, announcing in bold, black letters, BUTTERFLY CROSSING and MIGRATION IS NATURAL. The sign features at its center Rodriguez's artistic rendering of a monarch butterfly with migrant faces in its wings. The deliberate use of the diamond-shaped road sign alludes to the movement of migrants up ahead. We see artist-activists pasting the same sign on the side of a transformer and at various sites throughout the city. As night fades in the video, the morning light comes up and illuminates the posters.

In another scene in *Migration Is Beautiful*, the camera captures the street artist Adapt and his crew wheat-pasting a poster of a group of immigrants being loaded into a detention van. In the poster, the unidentified individuals are handcuffed and shackled to each other, with a couple of them holding rolled-up paperwork. The group is being led into the vehicle by an unidentified man wearing a US Marshals Service jacket. The group of immigrants—ordinary-looking men and women dressed in nondescript clothing—stands in stark contrast to the racist stereotype of the dangerous undocumented immigrant from the South, a criminal who is here to prey on the innocent and law-abiding American public. The powerful image is rendered in black and white, with the exception of the phrase FIRST THEY CAME FOR THE IMMIGRANTS, written in bold, red-orange, graffiti-style letters on the front passenger's side of the van (*Migration*). The use of bold color in an otherwise black-and-white poster forces its audience to see the connection between the action of the image—the removal of human beings from their community—and the message of the words.

Adapt's message is a version of what is now known as the "Bystander's

Credo,"[63] Martin Niemöller's often-quoted poem based on various lectures he gave after the end of World War II:

> First they came for the Socialists, and I did not speak out—
> Because I was not a Socialist.
> Then they came for the Trade Unionists, and I did not speak out—
> Because I was not a Trade Unionist.
> Then they came for the Jews, and I did not speak out—
> Because I was not a Jew.
> Then they came for me—and there was no one left to speak for me. (Marcuse 173)

While different versions of the credo exist, in modern use and interpretation Niemöller's words function as a call to action. The quotation invokes the threat that the persecution of one group poses for all, and the danger of one's silence in the face of such oppression. It alludes to the moral responsibility of advocating for those who are being oppressed. Adapt's art piece connects the detention and removal of undocumented immigrants to a longer history of persecution in the name of the nation-state. For an audience perhaps unaware of the policing of immigrant communities, the image is intended to inform and to move them to action. This compelling black-and-white image with its vivid text, along with Priscilla's vibrant presence as she cruised through Charlotte and the colorful butterflies pasted all over the city, helped set the scene for the next day's performance of civil disobedience.

Performing Resistance

While the artivists were busy preparing the props and staging for the next day's action, the organizers of the No Papers, No Fear Ride were planning the group's final performance. In her story on the action, Elise Foley writes about the meeting at Iglesia El Siloe where organizers called for volunteers to participate in the civil disobedience. Ten Riders stepped forward: Rosi Carrasco, her daughter Sol Ireri Unzueta Carrasco, Eleazar Castellanos, Yovani Diaz, Gloria Esteva, Maria Cruz Ramirez, Julio Cesar Sanchez, Gerardo Torres, and Martin Unzueta, Rosi's husband and Ireri's father ("Undocumented Activists"). Given their undocumented status, the ten volunteers were aware that their arrests would come with the threat of immigrant detention and possible deportation. These ten Riders would become the primary actors in the movement's final performance of resistance, standing in place of the many undocumented immigrants who were fighting for their right to live without fear of detection or detention.

The group strategically choreographed and planned the action. Some of the organizers scouted the downtown area to plan their route and determine where the ten volunteers would perform the culminating action. The volunteers themselves "practiced the movements over and over in the hot sun. . . . Some protesters, both those planning to be arrested and others, wrote phone numbers on their bodies so they would know who to call if they were put in jail" (Foley). The rehearsals for the action, and all of the planning leading up to it, demonstrate the amount of thought and attention to detail that the Riders' civil disobedience demanded. The hard work and sacrifices made by the Riders and their supporters during the six weeks leading up to the Democratic National Convention culminated in a successful display of resistance and self-determination.

In various videos that document the action, we watch as the Riders disembark from Priscilla and make their way toward the intersection of East Fifth and North College, outside of the Time Warner Cable Arena (*Migration*; "Undocumented Activists"; "Undocubus Ride"; Hannely and Piotrowski). The banners and flags created by Favianna Rodriguez, César Maxit, and their fellow artists fly over the assembled group of activists. At times we see the Riders holding hands, offering each other support. At one point, Yovani Diaz walks with his hand on Rosi Carrasco's shoulder in a gesture of solidarity and encouragement. Along the route, the Riders speak to members of the media, offering their testimonio as they walk confidently, with their fists raised high, down the streets of Charlotte. A camera captures Rosi Carrasco reading from a statement that explains the purpose of the protest, while her daughter Ireri amplifies her voice with a megaphone. Rodriguez and others are costumed in colorful butterfly wings as they maneuver their way through the crowd. We watch a group of organizers rush to set the stage upon which the ten Riders will perform their act of civil disobedience.

Acting as the physical stage for the protest is César Maxit's beautiful banner. At first glance, the butterfly at the center of the banner looks like the other butterflies displayed on the Riders' journey, but a closer look at the image reveals layers of meaning. In *Migration Is Beautiful*, Maxit explains the significance of the various parts of his butterfly design. The monarch displays wings containing four power fists—one of the most recognizable symbols of resistance—that face the four directions, symbolizing the right of individuals to travel in any direction they choose. Surrounding the fists are small, white footsteps that echo a circular north-south migration pattern. At the tip of each wing, Maxit has painted a migrating family. The monarch on the banner is framed by two milkweed plants, the only type of plant monarch caterpillars eat and on which monarch butterflies lay their eggs (Brigida). Visually linking the banner to the design of Priscilla, the banner's radiating yellow rays against a blue sky make the butterfly look like it's about to fly away. Bold, black letters proudly state SIN PAPELES / SIN MIEDO above the butterfly, and NO PAPERS / NO FEAR below.

The ten Riders are wearing Maxit's butterfly on their T-shirts. Set against a brilliant white background, the butterfly is framed by the Ride's slogan in dynamic bright-orange lettering and the word MIGRANT in black letters. MIGRANT is again framed by two milkweed plants. In smaller font below, we see the phrase "All humans have a right to migrate. All migrants have human rights." Below the words are pre-Columbian butterfly pictograms. Maxit's creation generates a visual narrative that challenges the modern construction of national boundaries and the criminalization of migration. The use of pre-Columbian images on the banner and the T-shirts situates migration from the Global South as existing within a longer historical practice of human mobility and movement. By using a beautiful butterfly to connect migration to a larger discourse of human rights, the image challenges the practices of criminalizing immigrants and framing them as inferior or subhuman.

As the ten activists approach the laid-out banner, they chant, "No papers, no fear! Dignity is standing here!" They position themselves at the sides and the back of the banner, leaving the front clear. Led by Rosi Carrasco they stand around the banner and hold up, defiantly above their heads, individual cloth banners stenciled in vibrant orange paint with the word UNDOCUMENTED. The Riders' decision to stand, and eventually to kneel, at what amounts to stage right, upstage, and stage left positions those walking in front of the convention center as spectators to the performance. Once settled, the Riders begin to perform their coming-out testimonio, amplified by the megaphone held by Isela Meraz. In addition to offering their own narratives, the Riders call on President Obama to stop the deportation of undocumented people, to end the collaboration between police departments and ICE, and to advocate for their civil rights. Supporters, police officers, and members of the media surround the Riders as the group, led by musicians, sing,

"Sin papeles y sin miedo" and "Queremos trabajo, la migra al carajo." In between the testimonios, Meraz leads the crowd in chants like "Education not deportation," "No minutemen, no KKK, no racist USA," and "Undocumented and unafraid." The chanting encourages the supporters surrounding the Riders to become part of the performance. We see the ten Riders singing along and moving to the music that acts as a soundtrack to their action. Although we witness expressions of joy and pride on the protestors' faces, it is impossible to forget the danger they are in, as they are also encircled by a disproportionate number of law enforcement officers in various uniforms.

A large police presence, the individuals heavily armed and many wearing body armor, surrounds the ten Riders as they remain kneeling on the banner. These looming figures convey a threatening presence with their impassive faces and intimidating demeanor. Silence falls across the crowd when an officer of the Charlotte-Mecklenburg Police Department announces on a megaphone, "Can I have your attention please? You're impeding traffic here at Fifth and College. I'm instructing you that you need to leave this intersection. You need to remove yourself from this intersection. If you do not leave, you will be arrested. You have five minutes to leave this intersection" ("Undocumented Activists"). The activists respond by defiantly chanting, "Compañeros aguanta, el pueblo se levanta" and "Sí se puede," to give each other courage and remind themselves of what is at stake. When the officer reiterates, "I need you to leave this intersection, or you will be arrested for impeding traffic," he is answered with a chorus of "Whose street? Our street!" ("Undocumented Activists").

The police respond to the disobedience by arresting the ten Riders performing the resistance. As they are led one by one into the prisoner transport vans, the Riders continue to chant and speak to the media, ensuring that their resistance will be documented. When Mike Burke from *Democracy Now!* asks Ireri Unzueta Carrasco if there is anything else she would like to add, she smiles and responds, "I am proud to be doing this with my parents," before she is led into the van ("Undocumented Activists"). In explaining the importance of the performance's embodiment of resistance, Favianna Rodriguez vocalizes the precarious position that the ten Riders have been placed in by being arrested. She explains that "part of the tradition that we have as activists [is] to take over public space, to send a message, to get arrested so that we are making a statement with our bodies" (*Migration*). The weeks-long activism of the Ride becomes embodied through the performance of resistance carried out by the ten courageous Riders.

Given the policing structures in place in North Carolina, it would have been easy for local law enforcement to transfer the ten Riders to the custody of ICE.[64] The visibility of the action, however, made such a project much more complicated for the agencies involved. In a press release the following day, the organizers informed the public that "all arrestees were released instead of being placed in deportation proceedings, confirming the message riders have set out to express through the tour: the migrant community is stronger and safer when organized and out of the shadows" ("Undocumented People"). Placing the Riders in deportation proceedings would have generated a public relations nightmare that law enforcement agencies thought best to avoid. In this case, being unafraid and coming out publicly helped protect the undocumented members of the community.

The ten Riders who used their bodies to advocate for their community were certainly courageous, but their action was made even more powerful, and memorable, through the visual imagery of resistance—the staging, costumes, and props—that complemented their performance. Images of the ten Riders kneeling on Maxit's banner can be found all over the internet, offering a vibrant archived snapshot of the action and ensuring the life of the action beyond the moment. The No Papers, No Fear Ride for Justice challenged the script that defined the mainstream stereotype of the undocumented immigrant, and did so in a way that offers a model for future movements to follow. The documenting of images, processes, and strategies of refusal through the media and on the movement's own website offers an archive of resistance that present and future activists can use to imagine new strategies of opposition.

Beyond the Curtain Call

In their much-cited article "The Framing of Immigration," George Lakoff and Sam Ferguson advocate for the rights of undocumented immigrants and argue that "they must be given an opportunity to come out of the shadows and lead normal lives as Americans" (11). While this chapter has illustrated the various ways the No Papers, No Fear Ride for Justice, and other immigrant rights and artivist movements, has advocated for coming out of the shadows, these activists are not waiting for permission or an invitation to do so. What makes the current wave of immigrant activism especially powerful is the undocumented immigrants' refusal to rely on others to speak for them or to frame their arguments. It is also important to acknowledge that their construction of American identity is rooted in difference and inclusiveness. Like the Freedom Riders before them, these activists have claimed a public presence to assert for themselves their rights as students, workers, and community members.

While art, theater, and performance play an important role in many social justice campaigns, the art that set the stage for the No Papers, No Fear action uniquely captured the spirit of movement embodied in the journey of people who cross constructed national boundaries. Gloria Anzaldúa argues that "art and la frontera intersect in a liminal space where border people, especially artists, live in a state of 'nepantla' . . . that uncertain terrain one crosses when moving from one place to another, when changing from one class, race, or sexual position to another, when traveling from the present identity into a new identity" ("Border Arte" 180). The art created by the Riders and their supporters—from the mural adorning Priscilla's body to the butterflies worn proudly by the activists—comes from the space of liminality that places undocumented immigrants in the outermost margins of the nation. The artists' ability to create images that so beautifully captured the message of the Ride comes from their positioning within a larger Latinx, both immigrant and nonimmigrant, community that supports its undocumented members. The butterflies not only act as a metaphor for migration but also come to signify the embracing of a new identity, an empowered existence that rejects fear, silence, and invisibility.

One of the most important texts that recorded the role of art and performance in the action is the documentary film *Migration Is Beautiful*, published in three parts on YouTube. The film documents the efforts of artists and activists to bring visibility to the issue of immigration and to humanize the narrative around undocumented immigrants.[65] It also acts as an additional form of digital testimonio, as it captures the personal stories of artists, activists, and immigrants. The film primarily focuses on Favianna Rodriguez's work with the undocumented immigrant community and her strong belief that social change can be inspired by art and cultural organizing. Rodriguez insists, "Behind every migrant is a story of family love. I thought if there were ways we can highlight that instead of the negative stories you hear over and over, there might be a way to change people's lives about how they see migrants" (qtd. in K. Puga). Rodriguez's project of changing individual perceptions rewrites the script that negatively defines immigrants in mainstream narratives of migration.

The use of art and performance in the No Papers, No Fear movement gives the Riders agency to write their own script. In his blog entry "Letter to My Mother," Rider Marco Flores writes,

> For a while now, I've been thinking about the significance of the arts in the undocumented movement. Art has provided a vital energy to this trip. I firmly believe that we are all artists, and we have the right to create art. Our life depends on our ability to be able to tap into a creative world that can give us tools for change. Art is being able to re-create our humanity in the face of people who deem us only as "illegal." The power of art to nurture collective activism is immense, and such were my nights with the UndocuBus riders, who would stay up until sunrise to complete banners, posters, speeches, *cuentos*—the stroke of a brush on a canvas or the rolling of words off one's tongue inspire us. Together, we, as undocumented artists, create the tools necessary for each day's struggle. Art became more than a language; it too becomes our instrument of growth and empowerment.

Flores's words capture the importance of what imagination and ingenuity offer the movement. They bear witness to the power of artistic creation to help write a new script for the public, while at the same time offering activists a tool for survival, resistance, and self-definition.

Through Priscilla, the art and the performative acts of the Riders and their supporters created a vision of activism that relies on performance, discourse, and coalition building to shape a hybrid movement we can all learn from and follow. The Riders are indeed, to invoke Muñoz, cruising utopia in their own beautiful lowrider bus, offering us a glimpse of hope through their drafting of a roadmap to liberation based on a vision of a future that acknowledges everyone's humanity and right to self-determination. The deliberate documenting and archiving of the processes of organizing the Ride, creating its art, and performing its acts of resistance leave behind a plethora of sources that can help mentor future activists and inspire new movements rooted in freedom for all. While the fight for immigrant rights continues with no end in sight, the 2012 No Papers, No Fear Ride for Justice is a reminder of the power of performance as a tool for activism and change. The action of the Riders and their supporters inspires me to imagine that a better future is possible, even when inhabiting a present mired in oppression and injustice. In the herculean task of looking beyond the pessimism of our current moment, the Riders' performance of resistance remains a powerful enactment of optimism.

CONCLUSION

Mentoring and Imagining Visions of Change

IF WE ARE TO CREATE A WORLD IN WHICH THE STRONG AND THE WEAK SURVIVE, THEN WE MUST WRITE NEW STORIES THAT ENGENDER SOLIDARITY, MUTUALITY, AND SHARED PROSPERITY.

RUHA BENJAMIN, *IMAGINATION*

In January 2009, eight years before I experienced Luis Alfaro's *St. Jude*, I was introduced to the work of the queer Xicana/x artist Adelina Anthony. I was back in Texas, my home state, visiting a good friend, who excitedly drove us from San Antonio to Austin to attend the premiere of *La Sad Girl* at allgo.[1] The audience was a vibrant mix of queer people of color and allies who enthusiastically welcomed Anthony, performing as the titular character, onto the stage. As part of Anthony's triptych series *Las Hociconas, La Sad Girl* is positioned between *La Angry Xicana?!* and *La Chismosa!!!* Although I had previously seen Anthony onstage as Luna in a production of Cherríe Moraga's *The Hungry Woman: A Mexican Medea*, I wasn't prepared for her transformation into the character of La Sad Girl. A combination of dark humor, social commentary, and biting critique of the structures of oppression, the performance centers a character who is both vulnerable and slightly terrifying. Dressed as a Xicana goth in all black and wielding a whip, she commanded the stage and enthralled the audience. While I loved the embodiment of her character, the literary nerd in me delighted in Anthony's use of language.

Even before La Sad Girl's entrance, the importance of language in the performance was evident. On the stage was a giant dictionary, while the upstage wall featured the scrawled words JOTA and PUTA, interconnected by the letter *T*, mimicking a crossword puzzle. "Jota" is a pejorative word for lesbian, while "puta" remains a popular way of calling a woman a whore. For many audience members, the words would have been a painful reminder of the language that has been used to marginalize queer women within the Chicanx/Latinx community. Anthony, however, takes these words and appropriates their power, turning them into a tool that rejects the moralistic authority behind them. She embraces them in the performance, claiming to be "an artist and a political puta" (Anthony 32). As La Sad Girl, Anthony boldly discusses her queer desire—using words like "pussy," "choochie," and "panocha"—and often addresses the audience as "jotería," centering queerness not only on the stage but also in the space of spectatorship. She laments the condition of straight people who are "born that way, or . . . [choose] that kind of lifestyle." She usurps Darwin's evolutionary theory by claiming, "It's about survival . . . of the finest," and subverts Descartes's philosophy, turning "I think, therefore, I am" into "I fuck, therefore, I am" (Anthony 35). The huge dictionary on the stage becomes another site of linguistic cooptation. By referring to it as "Webbie's Dick" instead of its official name, *The Merriam-Webster Dictionary*, Anthony irreverently mocks the dictionary's patriarchal authority over language. All of these verbal maneuvers center Chicana/x subjectivity and queer desire. I walked out of the performance grateful to have been in the audience to witness Anthony's linguistic dexterity, humor, and embodiment of queer existence.

It was Anthony's linguistic play and her appropriation of philosophical discourse in the creative reclamation of knowledge production that first planted the seeds for *Beyond the Moment*. I was inspired to think through the practice of using hegemonic apparatuses of oppression to deconstruct, upend, and create tools of liberation. When I first saw *La Sad Girl*, I was in the process of writing my first book, which also included several theater productions. I understood the stage as an incredible space of possibilities—a place where visions of justice and social change could be embodied in meaningful and beautiful ways. *La Sad Girl*, however, offered me a glimpse of the possibilities of engaging with existing structures that oppress and using them in playful, queer, and evocative ways to undermine their power.

While Anthony's performance helped seed the ideas for this book, it was our interactions in the classroom that encouraged the interdisciplinary development of my argument. I invited Anthony to Wellesley College to perform the entire triptych, over a period of several years. Her first performance electrified the Wellesley audience in attendance. The students had no idea what to do with Anthony. She inspired them but also made them deeply uncomfortable with her critique of heteropatriarchy and her bold embodiment of queerness on the stage. I saw my queer students of color fall in love with Anthony's performance and witnessed their awe at seeing parts of themselves represented unapologetically. The performances were impactful and exciting, but it was the conversations that the performances generated that deeply influenced the evolution of this project.

During her visits to Wellesley, Anthony met with several classes to discuss her performance, her process, and the educational trajectory that had led her to the stage. I wasn't new to the power of theater. I had had the privilege of learning about Chicanx/Latinx theater and performance from the brilliant Jorge Huerta and was mentored by the incomparable Alberto Sandoval-Sánchez. What I hadn't had the privilege of witnessing was a classically trained dramatist discussing her process to groups of young people hungry for her stories. In our various classroom discussions, I watched Anthony discuss her rejection of a Western theater canon in favor of embracing works that spoke more deeply to her own identity. I was inspired by the conversation about her process and her centering of a queer Chicana identity in all of her performances. I loved how she explained to students the method of inviting nonqueer Chicana audience members into the performance through the metaphor of concentric circles: each circle creating a space for entrance based on an audience member's identity, but not at the cost of decentering the queer Chicana body. Given that Anthony had been mentored by Cherríe Moraga, it was easy to see how her work continued Moraga's legacy of creating radical theater in the service of community. Anthony's engagement with my college community expanded my knowledge and understanding of the pedagogical potential of theater and performance, and it encouraged me to think creatively about my own teaching and mentoring.

When writing about the creators discussed in this volume, I have placed a strong emphasis on the process and collaborative spirit behind their performances. In that spirit, it feels important to discuss my own process and methodology, especially as they are rooted in community and collaboration. As I began organizing this book project, I sat with the lessons I had learned from Anthony's and Alfaro's performances. I was inspired by their theater practice and knew I wanted to write a book that both centered an analysis of those performance practices and addressed the importance of what remained after the audience left the theater. The works of Coco Fusco, Virginia Grise and Irma Mayorga, and the No Papers, No Fear Ride for Justice movement provided the primary source material to develop my argument, which advocates for the importance of theater as a site of resistance but also as a site for learning and mentoring. These artivists constructed archives rich with creative materials and inspiration for future forms of resistance. I have sought to identify and document the interventions these archives are making in our understandings of the movements of the past, our work in the present, and our visions for the future.

My insistence on situating the performances in the book as forms of textual mentoring is rooted in my own experiences as a queer woman of color in academia. My entry into the professoriate would not have been possible without the faculty of color who mentored me through graduate school and beyond. In the process of conceptualizing this project, I became an active member of the women of color faculty on my campus. Since entering the classroom, mentoring my students has always been an important part of my pedagogy. After becoming tenured, however, I realized that I had knowledge that could help pretenure faculty navigate Wellesley. In collaboration with three colleagues who had also been recently tenured, we created a mentoring group for women of color on our campus. This work led me to serve on the board of the Faculty of Color Working Group and the advisory committee of the Women of Color in the Academy. My participation in both organizations deeply informed my understanding of mentoring and community building. As part of our involvement with the working group, M. Gabriela Torres, Melva Treviño Peña, and I created a mentoring program with the goal of helping BIPOC faculty navigate the challenges of academia.[2] These joint efforts transformed my research, teaching, and mentoring. It is the knowledge I gained through such experiences of collaboration and community building that frames this book's concept of textual mentoring.

For many creators and scholars of color, finding effective mentoring can be extraordinarily difficult. Looking to traditional mentoring programs for guidance is often a frustrating exercise. Many mentoring programs, both within academia and beyond—the nonprofit sector, cultural centers, and other entities—replicate systems of inequality, even as they attempt to support BIPOC artists, scholars, and community activists. It is thus important to create systems of support that more accurately reflect the challenges faced by BIPOC communities and the values they hold important. Not everyone, however, has the privilege of finding mentorship that centers marginalized identities and affirms their place within the institution, organization, and community. It is in this absence that textual mentoring has the potential to help inspire, inform, and resist. After all, mentoring is not an academic skill and should not be framed as such. It is a skill of survival that has been used by marginalized communities to help navigate violent systems of oppression. My concept of textual mentoring centers the experience of the creator and the process of creation as sites of learning and inspiration. Theater and performance are a powerful site of imaginative resistance, and positioning this art form as another tool in an arsenal of refusal allows it to live beyond the ephemera of the stage.

The performances I've discussed in this book offer a model of creative resistance that, read as examples of textual mentoring, provide an aspirational methodology of liberation. They leave behind an archive of embodied refusal, a model of using performance to resist and transform, and possibly heal. The book's interdisciplinary methodology is part of a strategy to combine the many aspects of theater that have inspired me and my teaching. My analysis of these performance texts is deeply inspired by Moraga's belief that "the revolutionary promise of theater of liberation lies in the embodied rendering of our prisons and, in the act, our release from them" (49). Performance has the power to transform how we see the world: to help us recognize more clearly the structures that keep us oppressed. In this way, performance can also inspire how we navigate those structures. By making the construction of the structures of oppression tangible, performance makes them vulnerable to deconstruction. Recognizing performance's potential to inspire resistance and reimagine a radical future, artivist theater and performance can reconfigure present struggles for social justice. By generating a new archive for those looking to the arts for cultural models of activism, *Beyond the Moment* contributes to a study of performance that recognizes an artistic legacy of resistance within the genre.

The past few years have seen a rise in fascism, the emboldening of right-wing groups, the eroding of civil rights, and attacks on reproductive justice. Wars continue to be waged and supported by the US government, comprehensive immigration reform remains a dream, and health care outcomes for our communities continue to decline. It is hard to see the promise of cultural activism in the face of so much oppression and inequality. As an educator, however, hope is an integral part of my pedagogy. I have to believe that teaching remains a site of resistance, and that artivism is vital to fostering visions of change. Ruha Benjamin reminds us that "we shouldn't shine a light only on the deadly imaginations and social orders that are killing us but experiment and play with new prescriptions, visions, and forms of social organization" (16). Imagination can act as an antidote to the pessimism that permeates our present moment. The visions of resistance and change created by the performances in *Beyond the Moment* reinvigorate previous moments of defiance, document present actions of opposition, and imagine future articulations of artivist liberation. Performance and theater that go beyond the moment of embodiment have the power to build a legacy of learning and inspiration that makes up a radical imagination, which "can inspire us to push beyond the constraints of what we think, and are told, is politically possible" (Benjamin 23). The works and creators featured in this book inspire me to think creatively about art, activism, and pedagogy. They help me hold on to the hope for a more just future and make it possible for me to enter the classroom, the auditorium, and the organizing space with a sense of optimism. They help me imagine a different world for my children, my students, and future generations.

Acknowledgments

Beyond the Moment is a project that has been with me for a decade. It was born in community, nourished, and sustained by so many extraordinary individuals. I could never have finished this manuscript without the support, love, and inspiration from members of my various communities. I hope everyone who has made an impact in my life knows that their influence is captured in these pages.

Writing is hard, as it can be an isolating and frustrating process. But I have found community rooted in care among various writing groups. I have had the great fortune of being surrounded by fellow academics who are trying to reconfigure our writing practices to be more collaborative and supportive. I am grateful for the encouragement and camaraderie of my writing companions, women who helped me work through my ideas, assisted with writing challenges, and held me accountable. Thank you to my Newhouse writing group—Mary Kate McGowan, Veronika Fuechtner, and Sara Kippur—for cocreating a virtual writing space that has continued far beyond our fellowship year. I am also grateful to the incomparable Mattis sisters, Nadine and Jacquie, who created Easton's Nook, a space of belonging for so many writers of color. The Nook played a vital role in helping me develop the ideas for this book; every time I walk through its doors, it feels like coming home. Thank you to Juliana Anderson, whom I love to call a unicorn therapist—a queer, immigrant, woman of color—for helping me reclaim my voice and find my way back to my writing. Words cannot fully express my gratitude for my dearest friend, Charlene Galarneau, whose friendship has seen me through some of my most challenging times. Our friendship and writing partnership have nourished one of the most important relationships I've cultivated in academia. Thank you for the beautiful care with which you've approached my work, and for the spaces you've created to cultivate my growth as a scholar. My gratitude to Cathy Hannabach, Rachel Fudge, and Micha Rahder at Ideas on Fire for helping me shape the unruly mess of words into a coherent manuscript.

Being a queer woman of color in academia can be incredibly alienating, and for many years I struggled to find a place where I felt genuinely supported and seen. I cannot overstate how important it was for me to find a home at my institution that embraced me in all of my complexities. The Suzy Newhouse Center for the Humanities became the place where I could be myself without fear. Under the direction of Eve Zimmerman and Lauren Cote, the Newhouse became the space where I felt I belonged. Eve and Lauren brought me into the center when I needed a safe space to land and created the conditions where I could find my footing and begin to thrive. Eve's mentorship and support encouraged me to pursue the directorship of the Newhouse. As part of Team Newhouse, working with Lauren and my fellow director, Julie Walsh, has been one of the most rewarding experiences at Wellesley. I will be forever grateful for the opportunity to be a part of a team whose values are aligned with my own and who have never asked me to compromise who I am and what I believe. Thank you, Julie and Lauren, for helping me grow as a leader and community member. Thank you also to the brilliant and generous Newhouse Fellows, who have made directing the Newhouse such a joy. Working with the Newhouse community has been a constant reminder of what is possible when we create spaces of possibilities, resistance, and joy.

In the past few years, I have enjoyed the privilege of developing and running multiple mentoring programs. I am grateful to the amazing Tracey Cameron for helping mentor me as I took on the role of faculty director of our Mellon Mays Undergraduate Fellowship program (MMUF). Her guidance and wealth of knowledge about MMUF was vital to my introduction to the program. My partner in crime, the kind and thoughtful Teó Barbalho, has made being the faculty director of MMUF a true pleasure. In partnership with the Newhouse, we have built a program for our students that makes me proud to be an educator. Thank you, Teó and Lauren, for helping care for our extraordinary fellows! Thank you also to Mellon Mays Fellow and research assistant extraordinaire Angelica Delgado Navarro for helping with the completion of the manuscript.

Another program I am proud to have helped build is a mentoring program for early-career women of color faculty. I am grateful to my wonderful colleagues Soo Hong, Smitha Radhakrishnan, and Mala

Radhakrishnan for agreeing to join me in the project of creating a support system for our community. Our work came out of our desire to create the kind of mentoring we wish we had encountered during our own path to tenure at Wellesley. My appreciation for the women who make up this group cannot be fully expressed. Our built community has dramatically changed my relationship to our institution. I now feel a sense of belonging at Wellesley that has made this academic space feel more welcoming. This group has been a continuous source of inspiration and joy. My sincere gratitude to all of you for helping make our institution a better place for our students, our colleagues, and ourselves—and thank you to President Paula Johnson for her continued support.

In 2019 I was invited to join the Faculty of Color Working Group to help support the advancement of faculty of color in the New England area. My participation in the program has led to one of the most important collaborations of my career. As part of the responsibilities of the mentoring subcommittee, I worked with M. Gabriela Torres and Melva Treviño Peña to create and implement an interinstitutional mentoring program. The process was extraordinarily rewarding and helped shape many of my ideas on mentoring. The collaboration led to the fostering of community and connections between wonderful colleagues across the area. Almost as important is the friendship and loving relationship that was born out of our work together. Amigas, I will be forever grateful for your beautiful spirit of generosity and care.

I have learned so much about pedagogy and mentoring from all of the extraordinary students I have had the privilege to work with inside and outside of the classroom. I am grateful to all of the students who have challenged my thinking, encouraged my growth, and made teaching a truly joyful experience. I am also indebted to the Mellon Mays Fellows I have been lucky to work with, and learn from, in my role as faculty director of our Wellesley program. All of these young people have inspired me to be a better educator, scholar, and human being. They have helped me remain hopeful in times when hope has been hard to sustain. They remind me of why I became an educator, and they motivate me to continue fighting for equity in education. They give me the strength to continue resisting injustice in our world at large.

I am thankful to my friend Mared Alicea-Westort for her many years of partnership and collaboration in advocating for our students and the Latinx community at Wellesley. I am grateful for the love and friendship extended so generously by Betty Tiro, whose support of me has never wavered. Thank you also to my colleagues and coconspirators in the American Studies Department, Petra Rivera-Rideau and Genevieve Clutario, for creating a department environment rooted in an ethics of community and mutual support and admiration. Working alongside you is a true pleasure, and I am so lucky to be able to call you my friends.

Thank you to the extraordinary mentors who have seen me through the many years I've lived far from home. Mari Castañeda, you model the possibilities of a type of leadership that is generous and kind but rooted in conviction and an ethics of care. Alberto Sandoval-Sánchez, mi corazón, your brilliance and generosity knows no bounds. This book could not have been written without your encouragement and inspiration. Mil gracias to the both of you for your unwavering support of the many Latine/Chicanx faculty you have mentored through the years. You have taught us all the real meaning of mentorship. Thank you also to my queerxs, L Heidenreich and Rita Urquijo-Ruiz, for all your years of friendship and support. Adelina Anthony, thank you for the work you create to help heal our communities, and for inspiring me and my students to see the beauty in our queerness. My deepest gratitude to Catrióna Rueda Esquibel, who was not only my first Chicana mentor but also my first queer mentor. After so many years, I continue to carry with me the lessons I learned from her about how to mentor queer students of color.

It has been almost two decades since I left my home in the Southwest. Living in the Northeast has not been easy. Being away from family, from the warmth of the desert sun, and from the land that calls me home has been difficult. I have survived and thrived only because of the community that has sustained me, my own familia from scratch. Mil gracias to my hermanas Lorgia García Peña and Nikki Greene for all the years of support and care, and for helping me find a home in Boston. I love you both so much and am forever grateful for your willingness to share your families with me. To my crew, Soo Hong and Laura Grattan, thank you for always having my back and reminding me of why we do the work we do. Your moral compass, deep love, and unwavering commitment to our students and our communities encourage me to be better. Your friendship is a gift.

Thank you to my extraordinary family. I am grateful to my father, Ernesto Mata, for fostering my love of the written word and for always believing in me—mil gracias, Papi. To my sister, Tina Mata, thank you for the many years you supported my work by caring for my little family.

I am so proud of the adults my children have become. Alyssa and Jaime, you continue to inspire me with your fearless activism and vision of a just future. Your steadfast love and support mean the world to me, and I am so grateful for every moment I have the privilege of sharing with you. Thank you to Chris Guzaitis, who has been my ride or die for over two decades. Bestie, words can never capture the gratitude I feel for all that we have shared. You have helped raise my children, encouraged my growth, made space for me to write and create, and generously read countless drafts. You push me out of my comfort zone and support my love of all that is queer and campy. Our friendship is the stuff of dreams—a partnership that continues to sustain and inspire. Thank you.

My most heartfelt gratitude to the amazing artists, writers, and creators who continue to imagine a world beyond our current moment.

Notes

Introduction. Ritual, Resistance, and Remembrance Onstage

1. The performance is named after the hospital, but the title also invokes the religious image of Saint Jude of Thaddeaus, the patron saint of lost causes and one of the Twelve Apostles.
2. While these songs have enjoyed popularity outside of specific religious traditions, they are often sung in Pentecostal services to inspire congregations. I recognized them from my own brief stint with Pentecostalism.
3. I was assigned the eighth audience reading, and my friend was assigned the first, which she generously allowed me to keep.
4. For the use of performance in organizing and advocating for marginalized communities, see D. Soyini Madison's *Acts of Activism*, which traces the use of performance in the defense of human rights and the embodiment of social justice by Ghanaian activists in Ghana and the United States. For additional discussions of performance as a tool for resistance, see Shannon Jackson's *Social Works*, an exploration of socially engaged experimental art making through a perspective of performance; and Baz Kershaw's *Politics of Performance*, a study of British alternative theater and its oppositional practices.
5. Román demonstrates the importance of performance in the creation of our national imaginary and explains how contemporary performance engages with current issues that affect identity and ideas of national belonging (3–4).
6. Sánchez and Pita's argument speaks directly to the 2005 nationwide pro-immigration marches and the organizing necessary to create community networks of resistance.
7. These contradictions include the critical divide along class lines, divisions based on intersecting subject formations, generational differences, and tensions based on national origins.
8. The use of "Latinx" becomes a linguistic intervention, and while some critics have positioned the term as an academic one imposed by intellectual elites, I push back against this assertion. Like many educators, I learned to use the previous @, the current *x*, and the recent *e* from my students—young people who have educated each other in the classroom, in their neighborhoods, and in their digital communities.
9. For more on the complicated constructions of Latinx community, see *Embodied Economies*, Israel Reyes's insightful analysis of transcultural capital, collective

action, and constructions of upward mobility in Latinx Caribbean cultural productions.

10. While the performances I write about are not actual reenactments of previous performances, I am inspired by Rebecca Schneider's approach to history and temporality in her study of reenactment and repetition and the attempt to "literally touch time through the residue of the gesture or the cross-temporality of the pose" (2). In *Performing Remains*, Schneider explores "the warp and draw of one time in another time—the *theatricality* of time"—and the process of keeping alive an event or set of acts "in order to pass on the past *as past*, not, indeed, as (only) present. Never (only) present" (6–7). Both of our projects seek to theorize what remains after an embodied performance and to explore the citationality of previous acts of theatricality.
11. In *Gender Trouble*, Butler argues that "gender proves to be performance—that is, constituting the identity it is purported to be. In this sense, gender is always a doing . . . there is no gender identity behind the expressions of gender; that identity is performatively constituted by the very 'expressions' that are said to be its results" (25).
12. Here I am invoking Michael Omi and Howard Winant's foundational concept of identity formations laid out in *Racial Formation in the United States*, which illustrates the fluidity of race and traces the various processes that influence the constructions of racial identity.
13. HBO's official description for the fourth season of *We're Here* invites the audience to follow "renowned drag queens Sasha Velour, Priyanka, Jaida Essence Hall, and Latrice Royal" as they spread "love and connection through the art of drag across small-town America" ("We're Here"). The show's formula centers on the stars teaching queer and heterosexual residents of small towns to perform drag in service of local LGBTQ+ community members. Each episode culminates with these new drag performers taking to the stage to perform for their friends, families, and communities. The use of drag as a tool for teaching residents of these small towns about their LGBTQ+ neighbors, and the issues facing them, denaturalizes the performance of gender. Drag becomes a pedagogical tool as it entertains those in the audience and those watching the drag process unfold on their screens.
14. *Matachines* are dancers who participate in ritual dance troupes, most often associated with Catholic celebrations. Their performances are a syncretic blend of religious colonization and Indigeneity. On December 12, 2022, TikTok user Yadi1207 posted a video of members of Danza San Lorenzo performing in their Wichita, Kansas, neighborhood after a white neighbor called the police and the fire department on the troupe ("Proud").
15. The second volume of Hector Galán's 1995 documentary *Chicano! The History of the Mexican American Civil Rights Movement* features powerful archived footage of the collaboration between the United Farm Workers and Teatro Campesino.
16. Jorge Huerta's *Chicano Theater* was the first published book-length study of the works of Luis Valdez and Teatro Campesino, but the legacy of scholarship on

Teatro's work is as rich as the primary texts. Dozens of essays, book chapters, and creative texts have been written on various aspects of Teatro's scripts and performances. Many of these scholarly treatments have been written by scholars outside of the United States and in languages other than English, highlighting the scope of influence of the work.

17. In *El Teatro Campesino*, Broyles-González used archival materials and interviews with the women of the teatro to prove that they were as integral and creative a part of the collective as Luis Valdez and the men of the group.
18. As Diana Taylor suggests, debates about "the 'ephemerality' of performance are, of course, profoundly political. Whose memories, traditions, and claims to history disappear if performance practices lack the staying power to transmit vital knowledge?" (*Archive* 5).
19. Contemporary artists like Favianna Rodriguez have popularized the terms "artivist" and "artivism" through their self-identification with and insistence on using such descriptors. The term "artivism" has a longer history and has been used to describe the political-creative practice of earlier artists. In their essay on Judy Baca's work, particularly her teaching and mentoring of BIPOC youth, Chela Sandoval and Guisela Latorre write that the term "is a hybrid neologism that signifies work created by individuals who see an organic relationship between art and activism," and that it has been central to Baca's long history as an artist, activist, and educator (82).
20. For more on critical readings of the archive as a site of power within the field of archival science, see Schwartz and Cook; Manoff; Carter; Pell; and Edquist.
21. In reflecting on the relationship between performance and the archive, I am inspired by Taylor's concept of the repertoire, or the notion that performance can be transmitted through a "nonarchival system of transfer," and her argument for "a repertoire performed through dance, theater, song, ritual, witnessing, healing practices, memory paths, and the many other forms of repeatable behaviors as something that cannot be housed or contained in the archive" (*Archive* xvii, 36–37).
22. As "a collection of materials that serve to inspire, inform, and shape a theater project's conception or execution by providing contextual information about a play," the casebook "can also function as an archive of participants' activities" (Grise and Mayorga xxxv). The casebook, however, is traditionally focused on a specific theater piece, while the texts at the center of my analysis offer strategies for radical performance and visions for resistance and change that go beyond the boundaries of the script.
23. I find Audrey Murrell's definition of mentoring—"a collaborative relationship between two or more individuals that supports the career and/or personal development throughout one's career"—to be more useful when thinking about the potential of mentoring as a collaborative process, not simply as a one-directional sharing of information (2). While a plethora of scholarship on mentoring exists, I rely on Beronda Montgomery's mentoring roadmap; Murrell and coauthors' research on identity-based peer mentoring; and Murrell's discussion of mentoring relationships as forms of networks. My understanding of mentoring is also

deeply informed by my experience with the collaborative project of designing a new mentoring program, with M. Gabriela Torres and Melva Treviño Peña, for the New England Humanities Consortium's Faculty of Color Working Group.

Chapter 1. Performing Violence: Coco Fusco's Guide to Resistance

1. Produced by Dana Roberson and Mary Mapes and reported on air by Dan Rather, the news story was the first to make public the horrors being experienced by detainees in a military campaign the American public had been assured was one of liberation—toppling Saddam Hussein's dictatorship. While initially lauded for breaking the story, CBS faced criticism when it came to light that the network had sat on the story for several weeks at the request of the Defense Department. See Folkenflik for more on the debate around the decision.
2. As Charles Hanley reports, "Detailed allegations of psychological abuse, deprivation, beatings and deaths at U.S.-run prisons in Iraq were met by public silence from the U.S. Army last October—six months before shocking photographs stirred world outrage and demands for action."
3. Allegations of abuse in US-run detention centers were nothing new. In fact, the International Committee of the Red Cross's "Report on the Treatment by the Coalition Forces of Prisoners of War and Other Protected Persons in Iraq" documents a multitude of cases of abuse and torture taking place at various detention sites, including Abu Ghraib, Camp Bucca, and Camp Cropper. Delivered to the coalition forces in February 2004, the report details various instances of abuse from 2003 and notes that the committee had previously voiced their concerns, both orally and in writing, to the coalition forces. For the full report, see Danner (249–275).
4. While some observers were stunned by the depravity captured in the images, those familiar with the underhanded nature of intelligence gathering and military operations, especially members of targeted communities, were not surprised.
5. For example, George Mariscal's edited volume *Aztlán and Viet Nam* features creative and scholarly works that engage with the grassroots opposition of the Chicana/o community to the Vietnam War. Several Teatro Campesino actos, including *Soldado Razo* and *Vietnam Campesino*, performed resistance to the war and drew connections between the oppression of the Vietnamese people and of the Chicana/o community in the United States.
6. Venues included Performance Space 122 in New York, as well as sites in Miami, Connecticut, Philadelphia, and New Zealand, and at the 2008 Whitney Biennial (Fusco and Muñoz 140).
7. Fusco's documentary film *Operation Atropos* (2006) is based on her experiences with Team Delta and the interrogation course.
8. The guide includes an illustration of the smaller units that make up the zones in the theater of operations and discusses the roles of the players within those zones. Looking closely at the guide's illustrations of the theater of operations, it is easy to see how the diagram looks like a typical proscenium stage, with the

combat zone located downstage and the communications zone located upstage (War Department 11).

9. Although a script for *Our Feminist Future* is published in *A Field Guide*, no published version of Fusco's *A Room of One's Own: Women and Power in the New America* was available for analysis at the time of this writing.
10. In his write-up of the symposium for *The New York Times*, art critic Holland Cotter writes that "the MoMA audience was almost entirely white" and notes that on another panel, "only one panelist, the young Kenyan-born artist Wangechi Mutu, was black. And the renowned critic Geeta Kapur from Delhi had to represent, by default, all of Asia. 'I feel like I'm gate-crashing a reunion,' Ms. Mutu joked as she began to speak, and she wasn't wrong."
11. The audience's attendance at the symposium gestures to their investment in the art world, especially given that the symposium had sold out weeks in advance, and suggests some hesitancy or resistance to connecting the military's authoritarian structure and the art world's heteropatriarchal structure (Cotter).
12. Fusco draws attention to the shared approaches of both arenas when her character applauds the art world "for its strategic integration of women" and focuses attention on "the fact that some of the tactics we developed for gender management have also been useful to you" (*Field Guide* 99).
13. The original version of the performance, *A Room of One's Own: Women and Power in the New America*, which specifically references Virginia Woolf's work, was also set up as a military briefing.
14. In her discussion of gender and the disciplinary subjugation of detainees, Fusco points out that "the level of gendered provocation rises when women soldiers are used in interrogation to coerce and delude prisoners by representing sexually charged cultural stereotypes of femininity." She goes on to write about several strategies, including using women as "bait" or having them play the role of the "befuddled interrogator" or "the compassionate solace-provider"—whom she terms "the bimbo who can't do her job, or the sympathetic mom who wipes your tears" (*Field Guide* 43).
15. Fusco discussed the use of this "bimbos and babes" strategy in her interviews with female service members. She writes, "When I asked a few young women who had served how they felt about being asked to use their sexuality as part of their patriotic duty, they seemed to have difficulty understanding the question, or perhaps they thought it was too sensitive to answer. Only one said it made her think of Playboy bunnies dancing for soldiers in the USO—a famous scene from *Apocalypse Now*" (*Field Guide* 49).
16. The discourse of assimilation also tries to obfuscate the fact that women in the military are still subject to a high incidence of rape and sexual assault. Their "womanness" is not simply overcome because they wear the uniform.
17. Eisenstein further argues that "women in the military may make the military look more democratic as though women now have the same choices as men" (30).
18. The notion of female soldiers helping carry out armed forces operations helps soften the image of the military campaigns. These women become representatives of the democracy the United States claims to be upholding in its foreign

policy. Integrating female soldiers into the "liberating" process of military occupation allows the military to invoke gender equality as it attempts to represent foreign governments as less modern and more violent.

19. For more, see Enloe's introduction to a series of articles on Abu Ghraib published in the *International Feminist Journal of Politics*.
20. Chew's argument aligns with the observations Fusco made while researching women in the military. Fusco writes that in her interviews with servicewomen, "they all describe the military as an exceptional educational and work opportunity and as an economic solution. . . . Though many complain about sexual harassment, they believe in the system that is in place to address the bad behavior of the perpetrators, rather than viewing the culture of the military as a prevailing factor that remains untouched by this mechanism of redress. If fault is found, it always lies within individuals who do not live up to the promises of the institution, not with the institution itself" (*Field Guide* 61).
21. As Isis Nusair points out, "Militarized and masculine presumptions about the oriental other were at the heart of the acts of sexual domination at Abu Ghraib. These were not singular or pathological events, but systematic oppressive acts integral to power relations and complex productions and significations of gender, race and sexuality" (182).
22. The Western misunderstanding of non-Western cultures is often a contradictory one. In her essay on Abu Ghraib, Jasbir Puar writes, "At the heart of Orientalist notions of sexuality is the paradoxical view that the Orient is both the space of 'illicit and dangerous sex' and the site of carefully suppressed animalistic sexual instincts" (526).
23. The audience of the performance at MoMA would have been familiar with the Abu Ghraib story. The symposium took place only four years after the violence at Abu Ghraib was made public, and the continued think pieces, exposés, and declassified documents would have allowed the torture scandal to remain in the public eye. Those who watch the performance online might lack the context to make the connection—some are perhaps too young to remember Abu Ghraib—thus demonstrating the pedagogical importance of *A Field Guide* and its context.
24. As a Cuban American, Fusco's racial identity is formed at the intersection of various colonial legacies. In her performance of *Norte: Sur*, a collaboration with Guillermo Gómez-Peña, she writes, "My name is Coco Fusco, and actually, I was born in the U.S. and am genetically composed of Yoruba, Taino, Catalan, Sephardic, and Neopolitan blood. In 1990, that makes me Hispanic. If this were the '50s, I might be considered black" (Fusco and Gómez-Peña 170).
25. The performance was filmed as part of the documentary *The Couple in the Cage: Guatinaui Odyssey* (1993), directed by Paula Heredia.
26. For an insightful discussion of the assimilation of women of color into the military, see Shigematsu.
27. The military's empty promise of the rights of full citizenship, both economic and political, through service is now being parroted by minority subjects, but unfortunately not ironically. In his discussion of Fusco's *A Field Guide*, Olguín

recounts a presentation at the 2012 conference of the National Association for Chicana and Chicano Studies, during which military veteran Dolores Mondragon argued that military service "offered new opportunities for Latina 'empowerment'" (199).

28. The Church Report's focus included military sites in Afghanistan, Iraq, and Guantanamo Bay. The Green and Schmidt-Furlow Reports focused on the involvement of the CIA and the FBI, respectively.
29. The report argues that "most, though not all, of the violent or sexual abuses occurred separately from scheduled interrogations and did not focus on persons held for intelligence purposes. No policy, directive or doctrine directly or indirectly caused violent or sexual abuse. Soldiers knew they were violating the approved techniques and procedures" (Fay and Jones 5).
30. The report goes on to argue that "the aberrant behavior on the night shift in Cell Block 1 at Abu Ghraib would have been avoided with proper training, leadership and oversight" (Schlesinger 13).
31. Taguba's conclusion makes two points: "Several US Army Soldiers have committed egregious acts and grave breaches of international law at Abu Ghraib / BCCF and Camp Bucca, Iraq. Furthermore, key senior leaders in both the 800th MP Brigade and the 205th MI Brigade failed to comply with established regulations, policies, and command directives in preventing detainee abuses at Abu Ghraib (BCCF) and at Camp Bucca during the period August 2003 to February 2004" (326).
32. It is important to point out that the Taguba Report was the most scathing of the reports, even as it straddled the parameters of what would be considered acceptable for the investigation. Taguba's investigation and report would lead to his retirement at the behest of General Richard Cody in January 2006 (Hersh, "General's Report").
33. The Schlesinger Report claims, "We should emphasize that tens of thousands of men and women in uniform strive every day under austere and dangerous conditions to secure our freedom and the freedom of others. By historical standards, they rate as some of the best trained, disciplined and professional service men and women in our nation's history" (Schlesinger 18). Similarly, the Fay-Jones Report argues that "although a clear breakdown in discipline and leadership, the events at Abu Ghraib should not blind us from the noble conduct of the vast majority of our Soldiers. We are a values based profession in which the clear majority of our Soldiers and leaders take great pride" (Fay and Jones 6). Even the Taguba Report, which is the most critical of the lack of leadership and oversight, stresses that "throughout the investigation, we observed many individual Soldiers and some subordinate units under the 800th MP Brigade that overcame significant obstacles, persevered in extremely poor conditions, and upheld the Army Values" (Taguba 49).
34. Danner's observations are substantiated by Taguba himself. In a discussion with the journalist Seymour Hersh, Taguba claimed, "'From what I knew, troops just don't take it upon themselves to initiate what they did without any form of knowledge of the higher-ups.'" Hersh notes that Taguba's "orders were clear,

however: he was to investigate only the military police at Abu Ghraib, and not those above them in the chain of command. 'These M.P. troops were not that creative,' [Taguba] said. 'Somebody was giving them guidance, but I was legally prevented from further investigation into higher authority. I was limited to a box'" (Hersh, "General's Report").

35. The Taguba Report documents many instances of abuse that were not captured in the public photographs. The report offers a much more violent account of the treatment of detainees at Abu Ghraib, including references to "ghost detainees" and the military's attempts to hide them from the oversight of the International Committee of the Red Cross (26–27).
36. These techniques violated the United Nations Convention against Torture and Other Cruel, Inhuman or Degrading Treatment or Punishment, but were justified by various legal documents produced by Alberto Gonzales, counsel to the president, and multiple members of the Justice Department's Office of Legal Counsel. The January 25, 2002, memo authored by Gonzales for President George W. Bush argued that detainees identified as members of al-Qaeda and the Taliban were not protected under Geneva Convention principles and could therefore be denied POW status—an important designation meant to guarantee humane treatment for prisoners of nations engaged in armed conflict. Gonzales's memo provided the legal rationale for the White House memo signed by President Bush thirteen days later, which declared al-Qaeda and Taliban detainees "unlawful combatants," stripping these individuals of Geneva Convention protections and creating a different class of prisoners. The legal and discursive construction of individuals as unlawful combatants was the first step in justifying the abusive treatment prohibited under previous legal protections. It set up a linguistic signification that framed Muslim detainees, even those with no clear links to al-Qaeda or the Taliban, as enemies capable of "horrific acts against innocent civilians" in official documents that dictated policies of engagement in the so-called war on terror (Bush).
37. The Schlesinger Report makes specific mention of the Office of Legal Counsel in its findings, while the Taguba Report references the investigation into Camp Bucca, another site of detainee abuse.
38. The Justice Department's 2009 Office of Professional Responsibility report offers an important behind-the-scenes analysis of the torture memos and documents. The 261-page report specifically addresses the process under which several important memoranda—including the 2002 Bybee memos, the 2003 Yoo memo, and the 2005 and 2007 Bradbury memos—were written (Office of Professional Responsibility).
39. This collaboration led to expanded powers for military and CIA interrogators under the legal protection of President George W. Bush and his administration.
40. The fifty-page report, signed by Assistant Attorney General Jay S. Bybee but primarily authored by Deputy Assistant Attorney General John C. Yoo, is part of a series of Office of Legal Counsel memoranda written to advise the White House on the legality of employing so-called enhanced interrogation techniques against detainees in the process of intelligence gathering. The memo was leaked

to the press in June 2004 and was widely criticized by members of the legal community, including "a group of more than 100 lawyers, law school professors, and retired judges, who called for a thorough investigation of how the [Unclassified] Bybee Memo and other, related [Office of Legal Counsel] memoranda came to be written" (Office of Professional Responsibility 3).

41. The memo concluded that "torture as defined in and proscribed by Sections 2340–2340A, covers only extreme acts . . . where the pain is physical, it must be of an intensity akin to that which accompanies serious physical injury such as death or organ failure. Severe mental pain requires suffering not just at the moment of infliction but it also requires lasting psychological harm." The memo goes even further, arguing, "There is significant range of acts that though they might constitute cruel, inhuman, or degrading treatment or punishment fail to rise to the level of torture" (Bybee, Unclassified Memo 46).
42. The memo goes even further in excusing this level of violence by stating, "Even if the defendant knows that severe pain will result from his actions, if causing such harm is not his objective, he lacks the requisite specific intent even though the defendant did not act in good faith" (Bybee, Unclassified Memo 4).
43. This argument was emphasized in a July 13, 2002, letter John C. Yoo sent to John A. Rizzo: "Specific intent can be negated by a showing of good faith. Thus, if an individual undertook any of the predicate acts for severe mental pain or suffering, but did so in the good faith belief that those acts would not cause the prisoner prolonged mental harm, he would not have acted with the specific intent necessary to establish torture" (qtd. in Office of Professional Responsibility 48). For a more in-depth discussion of the discourse of intent in defining acts of torture, see Hathaway et al.
44. These enhanced interrogation techniques, as outlined in the memo, were to include attention grasps, walling, facial holds, facial/insult slaps, cramped confinement, wall standing, stress positions, sleep deprivation, insects placed in a confinement box, and waterboarding (Bybee, Classified Memo 2). The techniques were based on the US military's Survival, Evasion, Resistance, and Escape (SERE) training program. SERE training was developed to "prepare trainees for the demands they may face as prisoners of war and to improve their ability to resist harsh treatment," including techniques used "by the German, Japanese, Korean, Chinese, and North Vietnamese military in past conflicts" (Office of Professional Responsibility 34). The problem with using SERE techniques as a basis for interrogation lies in the fact that those techniques are used differently when training US military personnel. The use of SERE techniques for training is meant to help prepare trainees for possible capture and interrogation. The methods are not used punitively, and the trainee understands that it is only an exercise.
45. A Physicians for Human Rights report on the use of psychological torture by the US military found that sleep deprivation causes a "host of negative psychological effects," including cognitive impairment and delayed response to stimuli, and that it affects thinking, attention, short-term memory, and speech (Borchelt et al. 69). As Darius Rejali notes, "Experts now agree that sleep deprivation 'is

a basic, and potentially dangerous, physiological-need state, similar to hunger or thirst and as basic to survival.' Additionally, sleep deprivation reduces a body's tolerance for musculoskeletal pain, causing deep aches first in the lower part of the body, followed by similar pains in the upper body" (290). For more on how sleep deprivation has historically been used as torture, see Rejali (291–292).

46. The Office of Professional Responsibility investigation found that "CIA personnel were concerned that they might face criminal liability for employing some of" the enhanced interrogation techniques (37).
47. While John Yoo was a primary architect of both the Unclassified and Classified Bybee Memos, his role in crafting the torture memos is more visible in the Yoo Memo, an eighty-one-page memorandum that shifts the focus from interrogations at the hands of the CIA to those performed by military personnel. The Yoo Memo, declassified on March 31, 2008, was delivered to William J. Haynes II, general counsel for the Department of Defense, on March 14, 2003. It upholds the basic tenets of the first Bybee memo and extends the legal protection against criminal charges to military personnel in the interrogation of detainees considered enemy combatants. While the memo was withdrawn nine months after it was submitted, it offered the military the same type of legal permission to use torture that the previous Bybee memos had offered to the CIA. The Justice Department's investigation documents the collaboration between the Defense Department and the CIA, including memos prepared by Defense and shared with the CIA, and vice versa (see Office of Professional Responsibility 75n68). Even more telling are the investigation's findings that prove the behind-the-scenes conversations and collaborations between the White House, the CIA, and the military in legally justifying interrogation tactics that would normally be considered abusive, if not outright torture.
48. Even after the Yoo Memo and the Unclassified Bybee Memo were withdrawn, in late 2003 and early 2004, respectively, the Office of Legal Counsel drafted other memos that continued to support the use of enhanced interrogation. In the process of drafting the replacement for the Bybee memos, the office's acting Assistant Attorney General Dan Levin vocalized his critique of the memos, "having the same reaction I think everybody who reads it has—'this is insane, who wrote this?'" (Office of Professional Responsibility 124). The memos' overall message was that enhanced interrogation was permissible, even though ample proof existed that such techniques violated standards of interrogation aimed at protecting the human rights of detained individuals. They point to a corrupt system of intelligence gathering that ignores international law on the treatment of prisoners of war and justifies unmitigated violence on human beings in the name of national security.
49. It wasn't until I had spent countless hours reading investigative journalism accounts of the torture of detainees, along with declassified military reports, Justice Department reports, and administrative memos, that I got a glimpse of how complicated and entrenched the use of torture is in the military and intelligence communities. It would be impossible for the average US citizen who gets

their news from mainstream sources to understand the extensive use of torture in interrogations.

50. At the time of her talks, Woolf was already a successful writer and had published several well-known novels, including *Mrs Dalloway* (1925) and *To the Lighthouse* (1927). *Orlando* (1928) was published the same year as her talks.
51. In her groundbreaking creative collection, *In Search of Our Mothers' Gardens*, Alice Walker invokes the poet Phillis Wheatley to question Woolf's assertion that one needs space and money to write poetry. Walker asks, "What then are we to make of Phillis Wheatley, a slave, who owned not even herself? This sickly, frail black girl who required a servant of her own at times—her health so precarious—and who, had she been white, would have been easily considered the intellectual superior of all the women and most of the men in the society of her day" (235). Walker's query is a necessary reminder that Woolf's status as a middle-class, white English woman restricts her ability to recognize oppression beyond her own positionality.
52. *Three Guineas* is particularly insightful in making the connection between the performance of masculinity, patriotism, and violence—topics Fusco would take up almost seven decades later. Published in 1938, on the eve of Britain's participation in World War II, *Three Guineas* reflects Woolf's preoccupation with the coming war and the role of patriarchy in armed conflict. In her first letter, Woolf attempts to answer the unnamed correspondent's question of how to prevent war. She begins by identifying what she sees as the reasons men fight: "War is a profession; a source of happiness and excitement; and it is also an outlet for manly qualities, without which more would deteriorate" (*Three Guineas* 8). While Woolf notes that not all men believe in war, she argues that the majority support it and that what helps bring about this consensus is patriotism, the love of country—in this case, England—and the pride of citizenship.
53. Jane Marcus argues, "We can look at the way Woolf authorizes her portrait of the Englishwoman as a white slave . . . in the field of gender trouble in the scopic regime of the master/slave dialectic, by appropriating the history of bondage of the black body to tell the story of the white woman's oppression" (24). While Marcus is referencing Woolf's specific use of "slave" when discussing white women's condition in *A Room of One's Own*, her argument also applies to *Three Guineas*.
54. In his brilliant critique of queer militarism, Dean Spade argues, "We have nothing to gain for being the new poster children for a US military branded as inclusive because it lets women serve in combat and has openly LGBT service members. This is shoddy window dressing for the realities of US militarism, which is bad for the world and certainly bad for populations, like women and LGBT people, who are targets of sexual and gender violence" (Spade and Belkin).
55. Women in the US military have long been excluded from participating in direct combat and have been relegated to roles seen as less dangerous. In 1988, the Department of Defense adopted the "risk rule," which "excluded women from noncombat units or missions if the risks of exposure to direct combat, hostile fire, or capture were equal to or greater than the risks in the combat units they

supported" (Kamarck 4). The rule was rescinded in 1994, just six years later, when Defense approved a new "direct ground combat definition and assignment rule" (Kamarck 6). Even after the department rescinded the "risk rule," women were still banned from serving in units that engaged directly in combat. In 2012, four women sued the Department of Defense to change the combat exclusion, leading to the ban's formal lifting in 2015 (Moore).

56. In *A Field Guide*, for example, Fusco spends time explaining Woolf's experience with war, her writing against it, and the simplicity of her ideas around gender. In her discussion of *Three Guineas*, Fusco writes that Woolf's text is "shrill and quaint" but that she envies the ease with which Woolf could simply draw a line between the sexes. Fusco writes, "You contemplated war at a time when the lines were drawn quite clearly between men who had all the power and made decisions and fought wars, and women whose professional, economic, and intellectual aspirations were thwarted by their exclusion from public life and restriction to the private sphere" (*Field Guide* 15).
57. In discussing the naïveté of her feminism, Ehrenreich writes, "We had a lot of debates over whether it was biology or conditioning that gave women the moral edge—or simply the experience of being a woman in a sexist culture. But the assumption of superiority, or at least a lesser inclination toward cruelty and violence, was more or less beyond debate. After all, women do most of the caring work in our culture, and in polls are consistently less inclined toward war than men" (3).
58. For an interdisciplinary discussion of the current role of US women, feminism, and imperialism, see Riley et al.
59. For more information on the leaked and incredibly disturbing record of al-Qahtani's treatment ("Interrogation Log"), see Zagorin and Duffy.
60. Al-Qahtani's lawyer writes, "There are at least ten separate instances when the interrogation log reports that interrogators used a technique labeled 'invasion of space by a female' or that Mr. al Qahtani is repulsed, angered or otherwise bothered by a female interrogator invading his personal space. The details of what this involved are generally lacking. 'Invasion of Space by a Female' is used to describe a number of tactics, from a female interrogator straddling Mr. al-Qahtani and molesting him while other military guards pin his body to the floor against his will to a female interrogator rubbing his neck and hair, often until Mr. al-Qahtani resists with force and is subdued by military guards" (G. Gutierrez 17–18).
61. In the absence of consent, her touch becomes a form of assault—abuse further evidenced by the fact that al-Qahtani was forcibly held down to facilitate the violence. If a female detainee was being forcibly straddled by a male interrogator and sexually touched, it would be much easier for an audience to recognize it as sexual abuse.
62. In her study of Jane Welsh Carlyle's letters, Jean Wasko writes, "For the letter, equated by Henry Tilney with the diary, is, in fact, a unique social medium, quite unlike that other peculiarly female genre, which allowed a woman to construct herself in private" (5). James Daybell argues that "reading letters with attention

to epistolary conventions and cultural practices, erodes (but does not entirely erase) simplistic notions of early modern subjectivity, and provides fruitful avenues for investigating the complex nature of women's 'private' and 'public' conscience" (518). For a short primer on the use of letters by women, including links to multiple essays on the topic, see Luu.

63. Throughout the essay, Fusco documents specific ideas Woolf wrote about and provides footnotes as a reference for her audience.
64. Basically, Fusco is mitigating the fact that theater can be "an unstable vehicle for expression, as capable of obscuring problems as it is of clarifying them" (Taylor, "Theater" 168).
65. For more on the memo and FBI responses to abuse at Guantanamo, see Reuters.
66. Going even further in documenting the level of discussion taking place around the treatment of detainees, Harrington writes that Marion Bowman of the FBI's Office of General Counsel had discussed the contents of that communication with the general counsels of both the Department of Defense and the National Security Agency. According to Harrington, Bowman "was assured that the general concerns expressed and the debate between the FBI and [the Defense Department] regarding the treatment of detainees was known to officials in the Pentagon," but there was no record that those "specific concerns regarding these three situations were communicated to [Defense] for appropriate action" (qtd. in Fusco, *Field Guide* 90).
67. The memo also demonstrates that the torture experienced by this detainee was not unique. The special agent was informed that the female interrogator's "treatment of that detainee was less harsh than her treatment of others" and that the witness "had seen her treatment of other detainees result in detainees curling into fetal position on the floor and crying in pain" (qtd. in Fusco, *Field Guide* 90). While she might have hidden her behavior in the interrogation room in this specific case, the witness's account makes it clear that her abuse of the detainee was not an isolated incident. The fact that her colleagues were aware of her abusive behavior and that nothing had been done to curb it implicates those in command who allowed it to continue.
68. The illustrations also capture some of the coercive tactics used against Mohammed al-Qahtani, documented in "Interrogation Log."
69. The exhibition opened at the International Center of Photography in December 2003 and was "the first comprehensive look at how ideas about race have shaped our understanding of what Americans look like and the role that photography has played in conveying those messages" ("Only Skin Deep"). The exhibition catalog, which features Fusco's introductory essay, was published in 2003 (Fusco, "Racial Time").
70. The photos also became a way for individuals to center the emotions evoked by them. In her critique of two 2004 exhibitions of the Abu Ghraib photos—at the International Center of Photography in Manhattan and the Andy Warhol Museum in Pittsburgh—Liz Philipose argues that "to view the photos is to compound the humiliation and this was, in part, the purpose of their original circulation" (73). In discussing the Manhattan exhibition, she writes, "Blurring

genitals in photographs is meant to protect the dignity of the viewers; blurring the faces of the detainees might have gestured toward the dignity of the viewed" (73). Discussing the symposium that accompanied the exhibition, Philipose further argues that although its organizers were well intentioned and sincere, "we have to note that the sentiments are all about us. It is we who are centralized in the display of those photos. It is our emotions, our responses, our sadness and our pain that is at stake in displaying those photos as museum exhibits" (73).

71. In his critical reading of comic strips, including Fisher's *Mutt and Jeff*, Ian Rakoff argues, "In 1895 the comic strip arrived and before long the selling of newspapers became reliant on these strip cartoons because they taught the immigrant masses English, the language essential for citizenship" (76).
72. The illustration of the establish your identity technique features a nude detainee, facing toward the female interrogator, who is sitting on a chair. We see the back of the detainee, and his posture conveys shame: His head is facing slightly down, his shoulders are hunched forward, and it looks like his hands are covering his genitalia (Fusco, *Field Guide* 114–115).
73. The reports were quick to censure then Brigadier General Janis L. Karpinski for her failure as a commander, and she became the convenient scapegoat, becoming the only commander to be demoted. Ryan Ashley Caldwell notes that although the prison was under the direct command of General Karpinski, her command was ignored by her male superiors when "it came to all decisions regarding Abu Ghraib. As [Karpinski] points out, she was kept 'out of the loop,' and she makes it clear that she believes that this is because she is a woman" (38).
74. In her reading of the photographs of Abu Ghraib, Laura Frost illustrates how their framing as a form of pornography worked to minimize the abuse captured in the photos. Frost points out that the men in the photographs have received far less attention than the women, especially England: "Of the abusive U.S. soldiers in the photographs, only the women have been subject to eroticized, sexualized readings" (141).
75. Frank Spinner argued that the "joke" of pretending to electrocute a detainee was part of an underlying relationship between detainee and captor: "They still had duties to do as soldiers and guards, yeah, they had to engage in sleep deprivation and this guy was still somebody who needed to be interrogated, but even in that strange context of what—the events that occurred at Abu Ghraib there were actually relationships that developed with these inmates. . . . There were relationships beyond what is shown in the pictures that the government has put before you" (qtd. in Caldwell 24). Spinner's opening remarks for Harman's defense trial are printed in full in Caldwell.
76. There are countless examples of white American women participating in various forms of colonial and imperial violence. I find LaNitra Walker's example of the connection between Abu Ghraib and the US history of lynching especially helpful. Walker argues that "the complicated relationship between race and gender in the images of torture from Abu Ghraib prison was already part of America's visual vocabulary through the legacy of lynching photographs" (190). She goes on to write that "in lynching photographs, women and girls are frequently

pictured as part of the crowds pointing at the hanged body, smiling with excitement, or posing for the camera. After a woman made her accusation of rape (or the accusation was made for her), her work as conspirator in the lynching was finished, and she could join the crowd to witness the event" (192).

77. The ability of white women to rely on their whiteness when attempting to impose their privilege is evident today in countless videos, including footage of so-called Karens and Beckys invoking a discourse of public safety and threatening to summon the police. In the "Turn It Off" acting challenge, a disturbing trend on social media, women filmed themselves crying for a few moments and then suddenly stopping: "The most alarming clips feature white women dramatically letting their tears roll down their faces while maintaining perfect eye contact with the camera, only to flash an ice-cold smile in the last few seconds" (Kozma). Social media users were quick to point out the danger that white women's tears pose for communities of color: A Twitter user noted, "The way white women weaponize their tears is the scariest, most dangerous thing ever. I don't think a lot of white women understand* that a lot of Black people are most scared of them than anyone else . . . **then again maybe there is an understanding, and that is also weaponized." A TikTok user similarly stated, "We know under a system of white supremacy, who is the most dangerous. This is not a trend. . . . This is just our lives" (qtd. in Kozma).
78. In a 2019 US House subcommittee hearing on efforts to increase diversity in the military, Representative Jackie Speier reported, "There are approximately 1.3 million Active Duty members in the military; 83 percent are men and 16 percent are women; 17 percent are Black or African American; 16 percent are Hispanic or Latino; 4.5 percent are Asian; and around 30,000 are noncitizen; 70 percent are White" (Subcommittee on Military Personnel 2).

Chapter 2. Topographies of Resistance: On Monologues and Embracing the Panza

1. In addition to reporting on the success of the event, the website of the Feminist Majority Foundation offered those unable to attend the gala an opportunity to buy their own burqa swatch as a form of "remembrance" ("Eve Ensler's Tribute").
2. Along with centering the name of the play, the book's main title page repeats the phrasing of Grise and Mayorga's creative position: "written, compiled, and collected by." The starkness of the white page and its black lettering stands in direct contrast with the opposing page, which acknowledges the contributions of Renaud González, Mata, and Salazar, printed in white text against a bold black page outlined in a white border.
3. In my analysis, I rely on the 2001 "V-Day Edition" of *The Vagina Monologues*, which is a much shorter text than the 2014 second edition of *The Panza Monologues*. The V-Day version includes a foreword by Gloria Steinem; a brief introduction by V; an essay on V-Day by Karen Obel, director of the V-Day foundation's college initiative; and a short summary of the mission and work of the V-Day foundation, by its executive director, Willa Shalit.

4. In the introduction to the monologue "The Vagina Workshop," V does acknowledge Betty Dodson's work and dedicates the monologue to her, but there is no clear explanation of what role, if any, Dodson played in the development of the monologue (Ensler, *Vagina* 41).
5. According to the V-Day foundation, in the decades since its premiere, the play has been published in more than forty-eight languages and performed in over 140 countries ("V [formerly Eve Ensler]").
6. Ariel is Ariel Orr Jordan, the partner whom V credits with helping her conceive *The Vagina Monologues* (Ensler, *Vagina* xxv). She thanks him in her acknowledgments as the person who "co-conceiv[ed] this piece with me, whose kindness and tenderness were a salve, were the beginning" (182).
7. In contrast, V is writing from the center, and through her practice of locating the margins as simply sites of oppression, she further marginalizes the voices of the nameless women represented in her monologues.
8. While Grise is the sole performer onstage, the script is the creation of both Grise and Mayorga, and I reference both as creators in my reading of the script. While Grise might vocalize the lines, both Grise and Mayorga are responsible for the words.
9. Mayorga and Grise's glossary, in addition to offering definitions and translations of the script's Spanish-language words and phrases, also provides important context for their usage in the community and includes brief histories of culturally significant foods and geographic locations.
10. A common critique levied against *The Vagina Monologues* is the rigidity around the production and the inability of organizers to incorporate the stories of community members involved in the performance. In her analysis of *The Vagina Monologues*, based on her experience as an organizer, a producer, and an actor for a 2006 performance of the play, Alyssa Reiser criticizes V's possessiveness around the monologues and includes a description from the 2006 V-Day organizers' kit to illustrate her point: "'Do not use the book of the play or versions of the script from previous campaigns. The new script must be followed. You may not edit any introductions or monologues. And you may not exclude or change the order of any of the monologues.'" Reiser condemns the production's "ridiculous amount of strict rules and guidelines . . . and harsh legal and financial penalties for violators" (4). In discussing her decision to create her own production based on the stories of local women in Hong Kong, Sealing Cheng argues that the "prohibition of any alteration to the prescribed text forecloses the possibility of any discussion or dialogue" (23).
11. For a critique of V's use of women's stories of suffering, and an insightful reading of *The Vagina Monologues* as a form of docudrama that inspires an emotional response but not a deep understanding of the issues being discussed, see Striff.
12. In her discussion of gathering Mata's panza story, Mayorga notes that Mata led the protest movement "against Levi Strauss after the company closed its factory on the south side of San Antonio in 1990, leaving 1,150 mostly female workers without jobs and with unjust severance pay" (Grise and Mayorga 17). The

plant operations were subsequently moved to Costa Rica. In January 2004, Levi's closed the last of its US factories, both also in San Antonio (Associated Press).

13. In a 2001 interview that documents the accomplishments of Mata and her fellow Fuerza Unida organizers, Mata says, "I feel so proud that I'm still here, 31 years later. We continue to make changes, and we're here for our community, we're here for all people" (Sauers).
14. In her podcast *Rebel Eaters Club*, Virgie Tovar discusses the impact of diet culture on BIPOC communities and offers ways of resisting the damaging messages around traditional foods. Her first episode, with Mia Feuer, specifically details the societal shift that takes us from loving our culturally specific foods to hating them as we learn to hate our bodies (Tovar).
15. The messaging around diabetes is especially fraught and laden with assumptions. What makes the rhetoric around diabetes different from the discourse of other complex diseases—like heart disease, hypertension, and asthma—is the extent to which genetics have been used to explain causality. In *Making the Mexican Diabetic*, Michael Montoya illustrates how "geneticists, epidemiologists, government analysts, and journalists frame diabetes as an ethnoracial disease. In fact, it is hard to find a discussion, popular or scientific, about diabetes without a discussion of its impact on people of color" (5). The fact that Latinos and other people of color are diagnosed with the disease at much higher rates has led to the idea that diabetes is in our blood. The danger in framing diabetes as genetic lies in the erasure of the structural inequalities that contribute to illness and disease. As Montoya argues, the "enclosure of the biological constitutes a sociocultural black-box effect and ensures that social worlds of those who disproportionately experience chronic disease remain irrelevant and extraneous" (185).
16. George Sánchez points out how an emphasis on assimilation through diet was one way of involving Mexican women in the process of becoming "American," which entailed teaching them to move away from Mexican staples like tortillas, rice, and beans. He writes that "malnourishment in Mexican families was not blamed on lack of food or resources" but on eating the "wrong" types of foods (102).
17. A type of problematic discourse surrounding weight loss after a breakup equates losing weight and controlling the body with healing from heartbreak. It has also become a popular way of situating weight loss as a form of revenge against a former partner or against others who have done harm. The practice is so popular that cultural productions have been created to profit off the idea. For example, the reality television show *Revenge Body with Khloé Kardashian* (2017–2019) appropriated the discourse of bodily empowerment and wellness to create a show aimed at helping participants get "healthy"—that is, lose weight—in order to prove their worthiness to those who have wronged them.
18. As S. Strings and coauthors point out, "A growing body of research shows that the overreliance on BMI contributes to weight stigma, which can lead to worse health outcomes. . . . To the extent that people of color have higher BMIs on average than White persons, they are often targets of fatphobia" (30).

19. Grise and Mayorga's use of statistics and their focus on Texas and, specifically, San Antonio helps their project avoid the problematic ambiguity found in V's narratives. As Erin Striff argues, the intentional minimalism of *The Vagina Monologues* means that it lacks "public documents or images to back up or locate in a larger social or historical context the events taking place on stage. In this respect the view imparted is a relatively limited one, created to appeal to a broad audience by virtue of its sharply defined focus" (73).
20. In V's recollection of her play's development, she makes ambiguous reference to the process and its contributors, writing, "I definitely do not remember writing the piece. Simply put, I was taken—used by the Vagina Queens. I never outlined the play or consciously shaped it" (Ensler, *Vagina* xxv). The individual creator, through which the imagined "Vagina Queens" worked, is at the center of her description. As previously mentioned, the only actual person V credits is her partner, Ari Orr Jordan, "who got me to take it seriously and helped me conceive the piece and make a plan" (xxv).
21. In contrast, V creates a narrative that ignores her role in shaping and curating the script, and renders invisible the individuals who helped bring the script into being. She claims that "to some degree, *The Vagina Monologues* has never really been any of my business. . . . Vagina stories found me, as did the people who wanted to produce the play or bring it to their town" (Ensler, *Vagina* xxv–xxvi). While her words might come across as humble and self-effacing, they obscure the power V has as the creator of *The Vagina Monologues* and her ownership over the production.

Chapter 3. A Seat on the Bus: Radical Organizing and Performance in Envisioning Change

1. For a queer audience, and those familiar with the film, the name of the bus invokes Stephan Elliott's 1994 Australian comedy *The Adventures of Priscilla, Queen of the Desert*.
2. In a pivotal essay, Ybarra-Frausto theorizes rasquachismo as a social aesthetic and strategy of survival and resistance: "In an environment always on the edge of coming apart (the car, the job, the toilet), things are held together with spit, grit, and movidas. . . . Resilience and resourcefulness spring from making do with what is at hand (hacer rendir las cosas). This use of available resources engenders hybridization, juxtaposition, and integration" (86).
3. Mesa-Bains argues that "in its broadest sense [rasquachismo] is a combination of resistant and resilient attitudes devised to allow the Chicano to survive and persevere with a sense of dignity. The capacity to hold life together with bits of string, old coffee cans, and broken mirrors in a dazzling gesture of aesthetic bravado is at the heart of rasquachismo" (300).
4. I read this archive as a version of the type of digital activism theorized by Marcela Fuentes. For Fuentes, "Digital networks work as vehicles of communication toward a future street mobilization, and they also function as sites of activation in the present tense . . . digital networks and interactive new media have

contributed new tools to activists and supporters. These tools help organizers and social movements expand their base and spheres of action" (2).

5. According to data compiled from Department of Homeland Security reports, the Obama administration removed 3,094,208 individuals, while the George W. Bush administration removed 2,012,539 and the Clinton administration removed 869,646 (Chishti et al.).
6. Latino voters overwhelmingly supported President Obama in the 2008 election by "a margin of over two to one," or 67 percent of the Latino vote (M. H. Lopez). The percentage increased to 71 percent in the 2012 election, the highest "vote share among [Latino] voters" since 1996, when Bill Clinton earned 72 percent of the Latino vote (Lopez and Taylor).
7. In fact, on September 5, 2017, the Trump administration announced it would end DACA (Romo et al.). One year later, on November 8, 2018, the US Court of Appeals for the Ninth Circuit found the cancellation "legally deficient" and rejected the administration's bid to end DACA (Kendall).
8. In her work on concentration camps and the role that dehumanization plays in the detention of certain groups, journalist Andrea Pitzer argues that the targeting of immigrants is not new. In fact, "every single administration at least back to Reagan . . . has a hand in the way that immigration has been used as a political football in which everybody wants to look tougher than the next person" (qtd. in "America's Concentration Camps?").
9. Andrea Pitzer has found studies going back to "World War I that revealed that immigrants commit less crime than U.S.-born populations. And so this idea of the immigrant as a criminal threat, which is a very old idea, has been debunked for a century. And yet, it is still picked up. It is still used" (qtd. in "America's Concentration Camps?").
10. In his study of linguistic metaphors around immigration in the news media, Otto Santa Ana argues that the media has "an institutionalized right of narration to the public," enjoying a type of access to the US public that other entities do not possess, and that even the US president must negotiate with the media for broadcasting time (50).
11. Eric Haas argues that at a basic level, the use of the term "illegal" when discussing immigrants "makes us think that a minor part of someone is all that they are"; in fact, the word "hides our shared humanity" (1). The rhetorical practice further creates a discourse of fear and mistrust that diminishes "our ability to empathize" (2).
12. Sixteen men—eight Black and eight white—began their Journey of Reconciliation in Washington, DC, and rode buses through Virginia, North Carolina, Tennessee, Kentucky, and back through Virginia. The Journey was in part intended to explore the compliance of individual states to the 1946 Supreme Court decision in *Morgan v. Virginia,* which struck down Jim Crow segregation in interstate transport. The decision was based on the case of Irene Morgan, an African American woman arrested in 1944 in Saluda, Virginia, for refusing to give up her seat on a trip to Baltimore. The NAACP and Morgan appealed her conviction on the grounds that segregated seating on interstate buses placed undue burden

on interstate conveyors and therefore violated the Commerce Clause of the US Constitution. For a more in-depth and complex history of the events that led to the Journey, the reception of the riders in various states, and the action's aftermath, see Catsam (13–45); and Arsenault (24–68).

13. The cost of the performance, however, was not the same for all the activists. Of those arrested and harassed, only three ended up serving prison terms. Bayard Rustin, Igal Roodenko, and Joe Felmet served twenty-two days on a chain gang in North Carolina. Although Andrew Johnson had also been convicted and sentenced to the same punishment, he chose not to return to North Carolina to serve his time (Catsam 40–42).
14. During those fourteen years, *Brown v. Board of Education* ended de jure segregation in education, the Montgomery bus boycott mobilized thousands in mass protest, civil rights activist Rosa Parks was arrested for refusing to give up her bus seat, and the nation witnessed the birth of the Southern Christian Leadership Conference, the rise of Martin Luther King Jr. as a leader in the movement, and the creation of the Student Nonviolent Coordinating Committee (SNCC). While these are only a few of the events that define this era of civil rights activism, they help illustrate the escalation of direct action and public resistance to segregation leading up to the Freedom Rides.
15. The journalists were Charlotte Devree, Simeon Booker, and Ted Gaffney. The Riders were CORE director James Farmer, Jim Peck (an original rider of the Journey of Reconciliation), Genevieve Hughes, Joe Perkins, John Lewis, Walter Bergman, Frances Bergman, Albert Bigelow, Jimmy McDonald, Ed Blankenheim, Hank Thomas, Charles Person, and Reverend Benjamin Elton Cox. Journalist Moses Newson would join the Riders in Greensboro. For information on the Riders and journalists, see Arsenault (112–119, 123).
16. Raymond Arsenault documents the violence that greeted the Riders, the white supremacists who helped organize the mobs, and the racist law enforcement officials who openly colluded to support the violence and protect those performing the violence (153–189).
17. Arsenault provides an appendix with detailed and comprehensive information on the activists who participated in the Freedom Rides, as well as a brief section on the Journey of Reconciliation (546–600).
18. The legacy and inspiration of the Freedom Rides extend beyond US national borders. Just four years after the 1961 action, in February 1965, a group of University of Sydney students led a bus tour of New South Wales, Australia. Dubbing their action a Freedom Ride, the activists hoped to highlight the segregation policies affecting Aboriginal Australians (Edmonds). Fifty years later, in 2011, a group of activists organized the Palestinian Freedom Rides. On November 15, 2015, six Palestinian activists boarded "segregated 'Jewish-only' buses that connect Israeli settlements in the West Bank to occupied East Jerusalem" (Griffin 79). For these activists, the ability to ride the buses is "part of their struggle for freedom, justice and dignity," and thus it represents the Palestinian people's demand "to travel freely on their own roads, on their own land, including the right to travel to Jerusalem" (Griffin 76–77). It is important to note that unlike

the original Freedom Rides, these two actions were not based on the type of segregation being experienced by African Americans in the US South. These rides are based on a resistance to settler colonialism and the effects of this colonial history on Indigenous communities. Both Palestinian and Aboriginal Australian communities are fighting to have access to land and resources that once belonged to them.

19. I want to briefly reference the tradition of caravans used in social protests outside of the United States. While many caravans travel by foot, the use of buses has now become part of the practice. In her reading of the performance of the devotional and the saintly in the Caravana de Madres Centroamericanas (Caravan of Central American Mothers), Ana Elena Puga points to the organized use of the caravan as a form of protest in Latin America—in this case, to protest the violent disappearance of Central American migrants in Mexico. She reads the *caravana* as a type of stage in motion, functioning "as a transnational pilgrimage to the memory of the disappeared relative, whether it is undertaken only once or many years in a row. It temporarily spotlights and claims the spaces traversed by undocumented Central American migrants in Mexico" (A. E. Puga 268). In addition to identifying the performative strategies of the caravanas, Puga offers a powerful reading of the images on the 2013 bus of the caravana mothers and their disappeared adult children.
20. One of the most consistent campaigns modeled on the Freedom Rides is Nuns on the Bus, a project of NETWORK, an organization of progressive Catholic nuns that lobbies for social change. Beginning in 2012 with their first ride for economic justice, Nuns on the Bus has carried out eight nationwide bus tours as part of its efforts to "promot[e] a just society where all people can flourish" (Olson).
21. The organizers of the Immigrant Workers Freedom Ride explained that their goal was "to demonstrate a broad national constituency for meaningful reform of immigration laws, while also encouraging civic pride by new and future citizens. In particular, the [ride] will educate the public and elected officials about three key requirements of new immigration policy: legalization and a 'road to citizenship' for all immigrant workers in this country; the right of immigrant workers to reunite their families; and protecting the rights of immigrants in the workplace" (Allen).
22. Rider Marisa Franco writes that the group "could have eaten the cost of a chartered bus, complete with a driver and avoided lots of sleepless nights and headaches" ("Pricila").
23. Writing about the cultural symbolism of lowriding in the early 1980s, Luis Plascencia notes that some in the community viewed lowriding as "a new, antisocial, gang-related, drug-promoting, crime-inducing, degenerative, self-indulgent, gaudy, and wasteful activity" (141). Michael Cutler Stone highlights the 1979 film *Boulevard Nights* as a "sensationalized cinematic conflation of low riding and gang warfare set on Whittier Boulevard in East Los Angeles. The film aroused conflictive sentiments among Chicanos, and its opening generated a community picket line" (13).

24. Plascencia traces the origins of lowriding to a 1938 auto repair shop in Sacramento, California, owned by Harry Westergard, who customized a 1935 Ford convertible with the types of alterations that would become popular in lowriding culture. Plascencia then traces the evolution of car customization to George Barris, who would become known as the King of the Kustomizers, who relocated to the Los Angeles area in the 1940s (143). For the artist Rubén Ortiz Torres, lowriders are connected to the Southwest, where in the 1940s "big cars whose trunks were loaded with materials rode very low and close to the ground" (28). Stone points to the surge in car ownership after World War II and the importance of the so-called 52–20 Club, the twenty-dollar-per-week benefit for returning veterans, in the rise of lowriding (8).
25. Ortiz Torres writes that cruising is the updated version of "the old Mexican practice of walking around the plaza on Sundays in order to socialize and flirt with the girls" (28).
26. Like the cars themselves, the hydraulic systems that raised and lowered the cars were put together with repurposed parts—in this case, from World War II airplanes. The first system was installed by Ron Aguirre in 1958 and changed the mobility of lowriders, as it allowed drivers to circumvent vehicle codes aimed at criminalizing them. Drivers could raise their cars if law enforcement was present. For more info on lowrider hydraulic systems, see Sandoval, "Politics"; and Chappell, "Lowrider Publics" (270–271).
27. For the role of music in lowriding culture, see Thayer.
28. In the words of Ortiz Torres, lowriders "drive slow, pumping their music and blocking traffic, messing with a social system that is not eager to accept them" (28). For information on Ortiz Torres's lowrider art, see Chavoya.
29. Denise Sandoval writes, for example, that the Dukes Car Club "organized car shows to benefit the broader Chicano community, from César Chávez and the United Farmworkers, to Mecha and other Chicano organizations, to even local prisons. They owned the 'Dukes' Bus,' which they filled with club members and took to prisons to put on lowrider shows for the inmates . . . activities [that] reveal the importance of la familia and the community to the lowriders, who do more than just cruise the streets. The Dukes believe in 'giving back to the community'" ("Politics" 193).
30. Chavez makes it clear that he chose to do the interview with *Low Rider* magazine because they "have a tremendous influence and impact," a recognition of the audience that reads the magazine and their support for the United Farm Workers' organizing efforts (J. Gutierrez 54).
31. For more on the cross-racial collaborations facilitated by lowrider culture, see Sandoval, "Politics."
32. While I am not equating the policing of Chicano lowriders by local law enforcement with the surveillance and detainment of undocumented immigrants, I am drawing a parallel between police departments and federal agencies like Immigration and Customs Enforcement (ICE), which are all agents of the nation and responsible for carrying out repressive and discriminatory state policies against minoritarian subjects. These law enforcement agencies illustrate the

local and federal use of ordinances and legislation to criminalize and control the movements of individuals. Police departments used anti-lowriding ordinances to penalize Chicano and Black community members who challenged the lines of spatial segregation, while Customs and Border Protection and ICE use anti-immigrant legislation to interrogate and apprehend anyone who lacks proper documentation and who calls into question the validity of constructed national borders. These discriminatory practices are based on a white supremacist law enforcement model that criminalizes communities of color.

33. Such transgression in some spaces was not allowed for either group. According to Denise Sandoval, "Lynwood was called 'Lynchwood' by Chicanos and African Americans, because if they drove into that neighborhood, they were quickly escorted out by the police. They learned early on that Lynwood was only for white people" ("Politics" 190). The fact that the neighborhood had such a vile nickname underlines the type of violence that people of color might expect if caught in the area.
34. Rustin helped organize the 1947 Journey of Reconciliation, and his planning for the action would provide the blueprint for the Freedom Rides fourteen years later. An avowed pacifist, it was Rustin who helped mentor Martin Luther King Jr. on the Gandhian principles of nonviolence. Rustin was also the chief organizer of the 1963 March on Washington, where King delivered his famous "I Have a Dream" speech. In his biography of Rustin, John D'Emilio writes, "If Rustin has been lost in the shadows of history, it is at least in part because he was a gay man in an era when the stigma attached to this was unrelieved. . . . Friends, mentors, and close allies repeatedly abandoned him because of how he chose to love" (3).
35. I read the organizers' use of digital media as an example of what Fuentes theorizes as the assemblage between the physical and the digital. For Fuentes, reading such an assemblage through the lens of performance allows us to "discern the ways in which spatiality, temporality, embodiment, and participation, all central aspects of the doings of performance, are tactically redefined in contemporary entangled activisms that expand previous notions of social mobilization and political efficacy" (3).
36. In her biography of Ella Baker, Barbara Ransby makes clear that "it was Baker, not King, who nurtured the student movement and helped to launch a new organization. It was Baker, not King, who offered the sit-in leaders a model of organizing and an approach to politics that they found consistent with their own experience and would find invaluable in the months and years to come" (197).
37. Arsenault writes that when Diane Nash was identified as the leader of the new Freedom Rides, US Attorney General Robert Kennedy ordered John Seigenthaler to figure out a way to stop them. Seigenthaler called Nash and pleaded with her to end the action, but Nash refused. After Seigenthaler told Nash she was going to get the activists killed, Nash informed him that "if the first wave of Nashville Freedom Riders" died, then other Riders would "follow them" (Arsenault 177). Nash's role in coordinating the Freedom Rides was so important that she was denied a spot in the action. In fact, the SNCC organizers believed

Nash was "too crucial to the entire operation to be placed in jeopardy" (Arsenault 178).

38. Evelyn Simien and Danielle McGuire argue, "While many studies acknowledge the key role of women's involvement, they often assign them a kind of secondary or supportive role. By identifying women as either behind-the-scenes activists or helpmates, much of the master narrative obscures the various leadership experiences of women who participated in the movement on a local and national level—and highlights their collective versus individual efforts to strategically plan, mobilize, and execute tactical strategies on the ground" (414).
39. In discussing the necessity of learning to maintain and rebuild one's vehicle, Stone argues that "low riding reflects the historical weight of pervasive socioeconomic realities which . . . have necessitated the utilization of second-hand resources in survival and the expression of cultural ideals" (10).
40. The Roots' recording of the song was featured in *Soundtrack for a Revolution*, a 2009 documentary film by Bill Guttentag and Dan Sturman that examines the importance of music in civil rights activism.
41. Reverend Ralph Abernathy introduced the song during a community meeting at a church, and it became a standard at protests. In one instance, "a nationally televised CBS documentary showed spirited students rhythmically clapping and singing 'ain't gonna let Chief Pritchett turn me 'round' while the policemen picked them up, two to a student, and carried them into the [holding] wagons" (Carwan and Carwan 57). The images of resistance captured in that CBS documentary offer a visual legacy of the power of song to inspire collective action and resistance. For more information on how "Ain't Gonna Let Nobody Turn Me Round" and other songs inspired and mobilized communities, see Carwan and Carwan.
42. Paige Penland, a former writer and editor for *Low Rider*, uses the magazine's archives to provide a visual history of lowriding in her book on the culture. The book's section on "the women of lowriding" offers a brief history of Chicanas' involvement in the car culture. Penland writes that "since the 1940s, women have rolled right with their Lowrider Movement, but have had to work harder for the driver's seat" (44).
43. In her study of *Low Rider* magazine, Sandoval analyzes reader letters to understand the construction of Chicana identity within lowriding and in the magazine's marketing. Sandoval argues that although the magazine's audience has grown in terms of numbers and geography, those changes are not reflected in *Low Rider*'s visual discourse. Sandoval finds that "what has not changed over time is [*Low Rider*'s] consistent use of women's bodies to 'speak' to its readers. Indeed, the eroticization of the female form in relation to the low rider cars, car shows, and magazine representations is an endemic part of the vocabulary of low rider culture in general" ("Cruising" 181). Sandoval's finding that the magazine's focus will always be on "satisfying the male readers" highlights the assumption that all of *Low Rider*'s readers are male and heterosexual ("Cruising" 191).
44. The filmmaker Gloria Morán documented the struggles of female lowriders in her 2013 short film *The Unique Ladies*, highlighting their struggle to fully

participate in lowrider clubs and subsequent decision to create their own club where they could be active participants in the culture. In his discussion of the documentary, Ben Chappell argues that despite the barriers to women's participation in lowrider clubs, "the nature of lowriding as a material aesthetic opens up a way for people to contest their own exclusion—by doing it better, making it harder for others to deny their status as lowriders" ("Lowrider Publics" 275).

45. In his discussion of the lowrider magazine *Firme*, Richard T. Rodríguez includes a fascinating reading of a 1981 interview, "A Gay Life Style (Only if La Familia Approves)." Rodríguez argues that the interview points to the existence of debates regarding gay identity within the lowrider community and the larger Chicanx community. For Rodríguez, the interview is evidence of the interventions queer Chicanx individuals have made in an effort to expand the boundaries of belonging in the community and the car culture.
46. Like Chicana lowriders, queer Chicanx lowriders have also found ways of making themselves visible within the larger car culture. One of the most exciting visual projects that connects queerness and lowriding is the photography exhibition *The Q-Sides*, on view at San Francisco's Galería de la Raza in 2015. Artists Vero Majano, Amy Martinez (a.k.a. DJ Brown Amy), and Kari Orvik "reinterpret[ed] the album covers of *East Side Story, Volumes 1–12* through a re-staging and re-imagining of queer inclusion within the traditionally heterosexual public image of lowrider culture" ("Q-Sides"). Given the vital role of music in the construction of lowrider performance, the artists' strategy of using the popular, easily recognized albums as a tool for resignification connects the queerness of their photography subjects to a longer history of the culture. For a more in-depth analysis of the role of classic R&B, doo-wop, and soul music in lowriding culture, see Thayer.
47. The organizations that partnered with the No Papers, No Fear Ride included local immigrant rights groups, churches and religious organizations, labor groups, civil rights organizations, and community advocacy groups.
48. Laura Enriquez and Abigail Saguy observe the use of the coming-out strategy at the Immigrant Youth Justice League, a Chicago-based group whose advocacy brings the queer practice of coming out to the media discourse of describing undocumented immigrants as living in the shadows. Enriquez and Saguy write, "After the success of their first 'Coming Out of the Shadows' event . . . [the group's] leaders brought the concept of 'coming out of the shadows' to a nation-wide meeting of undocumented youth organizers to consider instituting this language nationally" (121).
49. For a profile of various LGBTQ+ artists and the role that being queer played in their coming-out as undocumented, see Rupersburg.
50. Blackmer Reyes and Curry Rodríguez trace the history of testimonio beyond its Latin American origins, to its use by US Chicanas and Latinas to bear witness to the oppression faced by their communities.
51. For Delgado Bernal and colleagues, testimonio is more than just a form of storytelling; it brings together "process (methodology), product (inclusive of text, video, performance, or audio), and a way of teaching and learning (pedagogy)" (364).

52. The students were advised by Marshall Ganz, who had organized with Cesar Chavez and the United Farm Workers in the 1960s, and were supported by the NAACP when the Ku Klux Klan planned a counterdemonstration against the walkers (Jobin-Leeds and AgitArte 88–89).
53. In *When We Fight, We Win!*, Greg Jobin-Leeds and AgitArte use the name assigned to Isabel Sousa-Rodriguez at birth. To respect Isabel's gender identity, I use her affirmed name.
54. In hindsight, Isabel Sousa-Rodriguez remembers the action as painful and "a pretty horrible experience for both Felipe and me on a personal level because it forced us both back into the closet. . . . [We] needed to have taken more of a bold stand and stand up for ourselves. . . . I just remember us feeling, 'Oh well, we're here fighting for immigrant rights. Let's not make things complicated.' But really, on a personal level, it was affecting us a lot and it hurt us a lot" (qtd. in Jobin-Leeds and AgitArte 92).
55. Another important erasure is the history of Indigenous struggle referenced in the name of the action, the Trail of DREAMs, but never addressed in the action's narrative. Jobin-Leeds and AgitArte cite previous civil rights marches, including the 1965 Selma to Montgomery marches, led by Martin Luther King Jr., and the 1966 farmworkers' march from Delano to Sacramento, led by Cesar Chavez (93). In discussing the action, we should not ignore the historical reference to the Trail of Tears, the forced relocation of Indigenous people from the southeastern United States to lands west of the Mississippi after the 1830 Indian Removal Act. Among the nations affected were the Seminole of Florida, who fought the US government's military forces for six years in an effort to remain on their ancestral lands. In his essay on the conflict, Cameron B. Strang argues that "many Native Americans in Florida opted to wage war against the whites who were attempting to relocate them because removal from Florida and the defilement of their ancestors' graves threatened the bonds that connected living Indians to dead kin and Floridian space" (974). Given the Seminole people's challenge to the nation's arbitrary construction of borders and territorial boundaries and their fight against forced removal, it seems like a missed opportunity to ignore this connection when discussing the Trail of DREAMs.
56. In his story on the action, Ed Pilkington reports, "When the bus riders asked local Latinos to join them in rallying outside the sheriff's office, they were told that the inhabitants of Sylva were too scared of retribution to speak out in public. But by the end of the protest, many local residents had come and joined the rally."
57. In her 2012 blog post "In Admiration: Learning about the Civil Rights Movement," Rider Maria Cruz Ramirez Jimenez discusses the impact of the meetings with civil rights veterans on her activism and her understanding of the interconnectedness of their histories.
58. Given the level of security around the hearings, and the presence of law enforcement, the Riders' choice to make very public proclamations of their undocumented status in such a venue was incredibly dangerous. Fortunately, all four Riders were escorted out without being arrested. The alternative, of having

others speak for them, made the risk worth taking. Gerardo Torres recounts, "I remember feeling like I was taking away the power that they had taken from me, without me knowing that I had lost it. The power to defend myself and speak for myself." Through this act of peaceful protest, the Riders asserted the authority of their coming-out testimonio to insert themselves into a hearing before a governing body with the power to influence the lives of undocumented immigrants. At the end of the hearing, all of the Riders were permitted to enter the hearing room, and two undocumented individuals, one from Alabama and one from Arizona, testified before the panel. For Torres, "We at least got a corner at the table. I hope that very soon we can be at the center of that table, at the same level as the rest." Their ability to claim a spot at the table was aided by the empowerment they found in performing their coming-out testimonios. With each recitation, the Riders became more comfortable with claiming authority over their narratives as they found strength and pride in advocating for their community.

59. In the actos of Teatro Campesino, farmworkers would often play the role of the villainous *patrón* (boss) or labor contractor.
60. For more information on the Georgia Latino Alliance for Human Rights, see the organization's website at https://www.glahr.org/.
61. In a 2014 interview, Adelina Nicholls, the executive director of GLAHR, discussed the importance that art and theater have played in the work of the organization. For Nicholls, art "is a way of making community within the movement itself, and of expressing it through theater and art. Obviously none of us are actors, or even took acting classes. It is street theater, with a direct message. And it comes from the same communities that are being affected by the detentions. . . . Art and street theater are part of the group's internal development, as well as to inform others—done by the very people affected by abuses, and telling others how to protect themselves against it" (Rees).
62. Favianna Rodriguez notes that "wheat-pasting, up until a decade ago, wasn't as illegal as it is now, even though the paste that you use can easily be pulled off. It is nevertheless considered vandalism." She further explains that the presence of the Democratic National Convention and the president enabled law enforcement to declare the city a site of a special event, and thus to institute security measures that infringe on the rights of individuals (*Migration*). Her explanation makes clear the danger the group faced in performing their artistic activism.
63. For a brief history of Martin Niemöller's quotation and his very complicated relationship to Nazism, see Marcuse.
64. State law enforcement divisions often partner with federal immigration authorities to share the immigration status of arrested individuals with ICE. In Charlotte, arrested individuals are screened for documents and, if they are not citizens, are reported to ICE by local authorities. According to Mecklenburg County Sheriff Chipp Bailey, his office "is just a broker of information. 'The sheriff's office does not deport people. We merely report them to ICE'" (Crump).
65. In *Migration Is Beautiful*, "the first two parts . . . offer viewers a brief primer on the issue of immigration and the growth of anti-immigrant sentiments. [Favianna] Rodriguez explains the importance of the butterfly metaphor, the

campaign to spread the message that 'migration is beautiful and inevitable,' and takes the camera to Arizona to discuss the reality of life for immigrants under anti-immigrant policies" (K. Puga). The third installment specifically focuses on the artistic support for the Ride. The documentary aired as part of the *Voice of Art* series on iamOTHER, a YouTube channel for Pharrell Williams's record label and "cultural movement dedicated to Thinkers, Innovators and Outcasts" (@iamOTHER). Williams executive produced the film.

Conclusion. Mentoring and Imagining Visions of Change

1. Allgo is a statewide organization that incorporates the arts into its organizing model. The group "nurtures and celebrates queer people of color" through a focus on "cultural arts, wellness, and social justice programming" ("Who We Are: Our Mission").
2. The Faculty of Color Working Group was developed to help BIPOC faculty "navigate the particular challenges they face" in the academic workplace, including "myriad inequalities, institutional microaggressions, and bad-faith policies" around recruitment and advancement. Through its mentoring network and programs, the group establishes "sustainable, integral, and evolving supports that [will not only] work to ensure . . . healthier daily lives and professional outcomes among BIPOC, but will also fundamentally orient and strengthen the institutions at which they work" ("Who We Are . . .").

Works Cited

"About V-Day." *V-Day*, 9 Sept. 2020, https://www.vday.org/about-v-day/.

Alfaro, Luis. "Notes on Performance / 26th, May of 2017." *Facebook*, 26 May 2017, https://www.facebook.com/theluisalfaro/posts/pfbid02bL6fvxNr9e8CX9yqovgGbiwPbVUe9QpvQHZRMguSrVwNaTx9SD3o4o6pT9vbtJ2Wl.

Allen, Zita. "Labor Leaders Announce Immigrant Workers Freedom Rides." *New York Amsterdam News*, 7 Aug. 2003, p. 4.

"America's Concentration Camps?" *Code Switch*. Hosted by Shereen Marisol Meraji and Adrian Florido, *NPR*, 3 July 2019, https://www.npr.org/transcripts/738247414.

Anthony, Adelina. *Las Hociconas: Three Locas with Big Mouths and Even Bigger Brains*. Kórima Press, 2013.

Anzaldúa, Gloria. "Border Arte: Nepantla, el lugar de la frontera." *The Gloria Anzaldúa Reader*, edited by AnaLouise Keating, Duke UP, 2009, pp. 176–186.

Anzaldúa, Gloria. "Speaking in Tongues: A Letter to Third World Women Writers." *This Bridge Called My Back: Writings by Radical Women of Color*, edited by Cherríe Moraga and Gloria Anzaldúa, Persephone Press, 1981, pp. 165–174.

Arsenault, Raymond. *Freedom Riders: 1961 and the Struggle for Racial Justice*. Oxford UP, 2006.

Associated Press. "Levi Strauss Closes Last Two U.S. Plants." *NBC News*, 8 Jan. 2004, https://www.nbcnews.com/id/wbna3909407.

Atkin, Jerry. "We Make the Road by Riding (*Se hace el camino al viajar*): Stories from a Journal of the Immigrant Workers Freedom Ride—Portland to New York, September 23 to October 4, 2003." *Radical History Review*, no. 93, 2005, pp. 200–216, https://doi.org/10.1215/01636545-2005-93-200.

"Aug. 24, 20212—Undocubus Rally Atlanta," *YouTube*, uploaded by Erik Voss (erkvss), 25 Aug. 2012, https://www.youtube.com/watch?v=hK1w0if5M5E.

"Austin: Fandango y Nueva Familia." *YouTube*, uploaded by NDLONvideos, 9 Aug. 2012, https://www.youtube.com/watch?v=jMawIG9oQDU.

Basu, Srimati. "V Is for Veil, V Is for Ventriloquism: Global Feminisms in *The Vagina Monologues*." *Frontiers: A Journal of Women Studies*, vol. 31, no. 1, 2010, pp. 31–62.

Benjamin, Ruha. *Imagination: A Manifesto*. W. W. Norton, 2024.

Beverley, John. "The Margin at the Center: On *Testimonio* (Testimonial Narrative)." *MFS: Modern Fiction Studies*, vol. 35, no. 1, 1989, pp. 11–28.

"Bio: Gerardo Torres." *No Papers, No Fear Ride for Justice*, 19 July 2012, http://www.nopapersnofear.org/blog/post.php?s=2012-07-19-bio-gerardo-torres.

Black, Naomi. *Virginia Woolf as Feminist*. Cornell UP, 2004.

Borchelt, Gretchen, et al. *Break Them Down: Systemic Use of Psychological Torture by US Forces*. Physicians for Human Rights, 1 May 2005, https://phr.org/our-work/resources/break-them-down/.

Brigida, Danielle. "Spreading Milkweed, Not Myths." *Medium*, 19 Apr. 2017, https://medium.com/usfws/spreading-milkweed-not-myths-5df8c480912d.

Broyles-González, Yolanda. *El Teatro Campesino: Theater in the Chicano Movement*. U of Texas P, 1994.

Bush, George W. "Humane Treatment of al Qaeda and Taliban Detainees." Memorandum for Vice President Dick Cheney et al., 7 Feb. 2002, https://www.aclu.org/documents/memo-president-bush-white-house-senior-executive-branch-officials-regarding-humane-treatment.

Butler, Judith. *Gender Trouble: Feminism and the Subversion of Identity*. Routledge, 1999.

Bybee, Jay S. Classified Memo ["Interrogation of al Qaeda Operative"]. Department of Justice memorandum to John Rizzo, acting general counsel of the Central Intelligence Agency, 1 Aug. 2002, https://www.justice.gov/sites/default/files/olc/legacy/2010/08/05/memo-bybee2002.pdf.

Bybee, Jay S. Unclassified Memo ["Standards of Conduct for Interrogation Under 18 U.S.C. §§ 2340–2340A"]. Department of Justice memorandum to White House Counsel Alberto R. Gonzales, 1 Aug. 2002, https://www.justice.gov/olc/file/886061/dl.

Caldwell, Ryan Ashley. *Fallgirls: Gender and the Framing of Torture at Abu Ghraib*. Ashgate, 2012.

Carter, Rodney G. S. "Of Things Said and Unsaid: Power, Archival Silences, and Power in Silence." *Archivaria*, vol. 61, 2006, pp. 215–233, https://archivaria.ca/index.php/archivaria/article/view/12541.

Carwan, Guy, and Candie Carwan, editors. *Sing for Freedom: The Story of the Civil Rights Movement Through Its Songs*. NewSouth Books, 2007.

Catsam, Derek Charles. *Freedom's Main Line: The Journey of Reconciliation and the Freedom Rides*. UP of Kentucky, 2009.

Chappell, Ben. "Lowrider Publics." *The Routledge Companion to Latina/o Popular Culture*, edited by Frederick Luis Aldama, Routledge, 2016.

Chappell, Ben. *Lowrider Space: Aesthetics and Politics of Mexican American Custom Cars*. U of Texas P, 2012.

"Charlotte to Greet No Papers No Fear Ride for Justice Upon Arrival." *No Papers, No Fear Ride for Justice*, 2 Sept. 2012, http://nopapersnofear.org/blog/post.php?s=2012-09-02-charlotte-to-greet-no-papers-no-fear-ride-for-justice-upon-arrival.

Chavoya, C. Ondine. "Customized Hybrids: The Art of Rubén Ortiz Torres and Lowriding in Southern California." *CR: The New Centennial Review*, vol. 4, no. 2, 2004, pp. 141–184.

Cheng, Sealing. "Questioning Global Vaginahood: Reflections from Adapting *The Vagina Monologues* in Hong Kong." *Feminist Review*, vol. 92, 2009, pp. 19–35.

Chew, Huibin Amelia. "What's Left? After 'Imperial Feminist' Hijackings." *Feminism and War: Confronting U.S. Imperialism*, edited by Robin L. Riley et al., Zed Books, 2008, pp. 75–92.

Chishti, Muzaffar, et al. "The Obama Record on Deportations: Deporter in Chief or Not?" *Migration Policy Institute*, 25 Jan. 2017, https://www.migrationpolicy.org/article/obama-record-deportations-deporter-chief-or-not.

Cotter, Holland. "Feminist Art Finally Takes Center Stage." *The New York Times*, 29 Jan. 2007, https://www.nytimes.com/2007/01/29/arts/design/29femi.html.

Crump, Steve. "Undocumented DNC Protesters Run the Risk of Deportation." *WBTV*, 1 Sept. 2012, https://www.wbtv.com/story/19433269/undocumented-dnc-protesters-run-the-risk-of-deportation.

Cruz, Daniela. "We Dream at All Ages." *No Papers, No Fear Ride for Justice*, 7 Aug. 2012, http://www.nopapersnofear.org/blog/post.php?s=2012-08-07-we-dream-at-all-ages.

Danner, Mark. *Torture and Truth: America, Abu Ghraib, and the War on Terror*. New York Review Books, 2004.

Daybell, James. "Women's Letters, Literature and Conscience in Sixteenth-Century England." *Renaissance Studies*, vol. 23, no. 4, 2009, pp. 516–533.

de la Fuente, Flavia. "The Metrics of Change." *No Papers, No Fear Ride for Justice*, 8 Aug. 2012, http://nopapersnofear.org/blog/post.php?s=2012-08-08-the-metrics-of-change.

Delgado Bernal, Dolores, et al. "Chicana/Latina *Testimonios*: Mapping the Methodological, Pedagogical, and Political." *Equity and Excellence in Education*, vol. 45, no. 3, 2012, pp. 363–372, https://doi.org/10.1080/10665684.2012.698149.

D'Emilio, John. *Lost Prophet: The Life and Times of Bayard Rustin*. Free Press, 2003.

Derrida, Jacques. "Archive Fever: A Freudian Impression." Translated by Eric Prenowitz. *Diacritics*, vol. 25, no. 2, 1995, pp. 9–63.

"DNC Time: Protests Lead the Way." *WFAE*, 31 Aug. 2012, https://www.wfae.org/politics/2012-08-31/dnc-time-protests-lead-the-way.

Edmonds, Penelope. "Unofficial Apartheid, Convention and Country Towns: Reflections on Australian History and the New South Wales Freedom Rides of 1965." *Postcolonial Studies*, vol. 15, no. 2, 2012, pp. 167–190, https://doi.org/10.1080/13688790.2012.693043.

Edquist, Samuel. "Archival Divides: Archives as Contested Realities and Metaphors." *From Dust to Dawn: Archival Studies After the Archival Turn*, edited by Ann Öhrberg et al., Uppsala Rhetorical Studies, 2021, pp. 102–129, https://www.diva-portal.org/smash/get/diva2:1640945/FULLTEXT01.pdf.

Ehrenreich, Barbara. "Foreword: Feminism's Assumptions Upended." *One of the Guys: Women as Aggressors and Torturers*, edited by Tara McKelvey, Seal Press, 2007, pp. 1–6.

Eisenstein, Zillah. "Resexing Militarism for the Globe." *Feminism and War: Confronting U.S. Imperialism*, edited by Robin L. Riley et al., Zed Books, 2008, pp. 27–46.

Enloe, Cynthia. "Feminist Readings on Abu Ghraib." *International Feminist Journal of Politics*, vol. 9, no. 1, 2007, pp. 35–37, https://doi.org/10.1080/14616740601066317.

Enriquez, Laura E., and Abigail C. Saguy. "Coming Out of the Shadows: Harnessing a Cultural Schema to Advance the Undocumented Immigrant Youth Movement." *American Journal of Cultural Sociology*, vol. 4, no. 1, 2016, pp. 107–130, https://doi.org/10.1057/ajcs.2015.6.

Ensler, Eve. "I Still Don't Get How You Could Put a Leash on a Human Being." *One of the Guys: Women as Aggressors and Torturers*, edited by Tara McKelvey, Seal Press, 2007, pp. 17–22.

Ensler, Eve. *The Vagina Monologues: The V-Day Edition*. Villard, 2001.

"Eve Ensler's Tribute to Afghan Women Is a Sold Out Success at Madison Square Garden." *Feminist Majority Foundation*, 12 Feb. 2001, https://feminist.org/news/eve-ensleros-tribute-to-afghan-women-is-a-sold-out-success-at-madison-square-garden/.

Fager, Jeff. Interview with Jenni Matz, 6 June 2016. *The Interviews*, Television Academy Foundation, https://interviews.televisionacademy.com/interviews/jeff-fager.

Fay, George R., and Anthony R. Jones. Report [*AR 15–6 Investigation of the Abu Ghraib Prison and 205th Military Intelligence Brigade*]. US Military, Aug. 2004, https://www.thetorturedatabase.org/files/foia_subsite/pdfs/fay_jones_kern_report.pdf.

"February 10th, 2001 Is V-Day!" *V-Day*, 9 Jan. 2001, https://www.vday.org/node/1520.html.

"The Feminist Future: Coco Fusco." *MoMA*, 11 Feb. 2018, https://www.moma.org/multimedia/video/16/161.

Flegal, K. M., et al. "Overweight and Obesity in the United States: Prevalence and Trends, 1960–1994." *International Journal of Obesity and Related Metabolic Disorders*, vol. 22, no. 1, 1998, https://doi.org/10.1038/sj.ijo.0800541.

Flores, Marco. "Letter to My Mother." *No Papers, No Fear Ride for Justice*, 18 Sept. 2012, http://nopapersnofear.org/blog/post.php?s=2012-09-18-letter-to-my-mother.

Flores Niemann, Yolanda, et al., editors. *Presumed Incompetent II: Race, Class, Power, and Resistance of Women in Academia*. Utah State UP, 2020.

Foley, Elise. "DNC Protest Leads to Arrest of 10 Undocumented Immigrants." *HuffPost*, 5 Sept. 2012, https://www.huffpost.com/entry/dnc-protest-undocumented-immigrants_n_1858331.

Folkenflik, David. "Iraq Prison Story Tough to Hold Off on, CBS Says." *Chicago Tribune*, 5 May 2004, https://www.chicagotribune.com/2004/05/05/iraq-prison-story-tough-to-hold-off-on-cbs-says/.

Franco, Marisa. "Farewells and Full Moons." *No Papers, No Fear Ride for Justice*, 1 Aug. 2012, http://nopapersnofear.org/blog/post.php?s=2012-08-01-farewells-and-full-moons.

Franco, Marisa. "Pricila Get Some Love from Labor." *No Papers, No Fear Ride for Justice*, 1 Sept. 2012, http://nopapersnofear.org/blog/post.php?s=2012-09-01-pricila-get-some-love-from-labor.

Frost, Laura. "Photography/Pornography/Torture: The Politics of Seeing Abu Ghraib." *One of the Guys: Women as Aggressors and Torturers*, edited by Tara McKelvey, Seal Press, 2007, pp. 135–144.

Fuentes, Marcela A. *Performance Constellations: Networks of Protest and Activism in Latin America*. U of Michigan P, 2019.

Fusco, Coco. *A Field Guide for Female Interrogators*. Seven Stories Press, 2008.

Fusco, Coco. "Racial Time, Racial Marks, Racial Metaphors." *Only Skin Deep: Changing Visions of the American Self*, edited by Coco Fusco and Brian Wallis, Harry N. Abrams, 2003, pp. 13–49.

Fusco, Coco, and Guillermo Gómez-Peña. "Norte: Sur." In *English Is Broken Here: Notes on Cultural Fusion in the Americas* by Coco Fusco, 169–178. The New Press, 1995.

Fusco, Coco, and José Esteban Muñoz. "A Room of One's Own: Women and Power in the New America." *TDR / The Drama Review*, vol. 52, no. 1, 2008, pp. 136–159, https://doi.org/10.1162/dram.2008.52.1.136.

García Peña, Lorgia. *Community as Rebellion: A Syllabus for Surviving Academia as a Woman of Color*. Haymarket Books, 2022.

"Gerardo: I'm a Queer Undocumented Mexican. We Exist. We're Involved." *YouTube*, uploaded by NDLONvideos, 31 July 2012, https://www.youtube.com/watch?v=gb7XWco3HTU.

Gonzales, Alberto R. "Decision Re Application of the Geneva Convention on Prisoners of War to the Conflict with al Qaeda and the Taliban." Memorandum for President George W. Bush, 25 Jan. 2002, https://www.washingtonpost.com/wp-srv/politics/documents/cheney/gonzales_addington_memo_jan252001.pdf.

Griffin, Maryam S. "Freedom Rides in Palestine: Racial Segregation and Grassroots Politics on the Bus." *Race and Class*, vol. 56, no. 4, 2015, pp. 73–84, https://doi.org/10.1177/0306396814567410.

Grise, Virginia, and Irma Mayorga. *The Panza Monologues*. 2nd ed., U of Texas P, 2014.

Gutierrez, Gitanjali. "Declaration of Gitanjali S. Gutierrez, Esq., Lawyer for Mohammed al Qahtani." *Center for Constitutional Rights*, Oct. 2006, https://ccrjustice.org/files/Gutierrez%20Declaration%20re%20Al%20Qahtani%20Oct%202006.pdf.

Gutierrez, Jess. "Cesar Chavez." *Low Rider*, vol. 3, no. 12, 1980.

Haas, Eric. *To Respect and Protect: Expanding Our Discourse on Immigration*. Rockridge Institute, 2008.

Hanley, Charles J. "Early Accounts of Extensive Iraq Abuse Met U.S. Silence." *Southeast Missourian*, 9 May 2004, https://web.archive.org/web/20130701074054/http://www.semissourian.com/story/137193.html.

Hannley, Pamela Powers, and Krzysztof Piotrowski. "VIDEO: Undocumented Protestors Arrested Outside Democratic Convention." *HuffPost*, 5 Sept. 2012, https://www.huffpost.com/entry/undocumented-protesters-a_b_1857887.

Hathaway, Oona, et al. "Tortured Reasoning: The Intent to Torture Under International and Domestic Law." *Virginia Journal of International Law*, vol. 52, no. 791, 2012, pp. 791–837, https://openyls.law.yale.edu/handle/20.500.13051/4242.

Hernández, David Manuel. "'My Fellow Citizens': Barack Obama and Immigration Policy." *Journal of Race and Policy*, vol. 6, no. 1, 2010, pp. 24–44.

Hersh, Seymour M. "The General's Report: How Antonio Taguba, Who Investigated the Abu Ghraib Scandal, Became One of Its Casualties." *The New Yorker*, 18 June 2007, https://www.newyorker.com/magazine/2007/06/25/the-generals-report.

Hersh, Seymour M. "Torture at Abu Ghraib." *The New Yorker*, 10 May 2004, https://www.newyorker.com/magazine/2004/05/10/torture-at-abu-ghraib.

Hill, Jacqueline, et al. "Understanding the Social Factors That Contribute to Diabetes: A Means to Informing Health Care and Social Policies for the Chronically Ill." *The Permanente Journal*, vol. 17, no. 2, 2013, pp. 67–72, https://doi.org/10.7812/TPP/12-099.

Holsaert, Faith S., et al., editors. *Hands on the Freedom Plow: Personal Accounts by Women in SNCC*. U of Illinois P, 2010.

hooks, bell. "Choosing the Margin as a Space of Radical Openness." *Framework: The Journal of Cinema and Media*, vol. 36, 1989, pp. 15–23.

Huerta, Jorge. *Chicano Theater: Themes and Forms*. Bilingual Press, 1982.

Huerta, Maria, and Isela Meraz. "Selma: Crossing Bridges, Building Puentes." *No Papers, No Fear Ride for Justice*, 23 Aug. 2012, http://nopapersnofear.org/blog/post.php?s=2012-08-23-selma-crossing-bridges-building-puentes.

iamOTHER. *YouTube*, https://www.youtube.com/channel/UCE560wL2ftkMrQL-40LYFUVg. Accessed 21 Jan. 2020.

"Interrogation Log: Detainee 063." *Center for Constitutional Rights*, 23 Nov. 2002, https://ccrjustice.org/files/Publication_AlQahtaniLog.pdf.

Jackson, Shannon. *Social Works: Performing Art, Supporting Publics*. Routledge, 2011.

Jobin-Leeds, Greg, and AgitArte. *When We Fight, We Win! Twenty-First-Century Social Movements and the Activists That Are Transforming Our World*. New Press, 2016.

"Juan Jose Mangandi: Our Best Kept Secret Is Our Own Community's Strength." *YouTube*, uploaded by NDLONvideos, 17 Aug. 2012, https://www.youtube.com/watch?v=C0wm98wIJCY.

"Justicia para los 32 del Sur, Joaquin's Case on Its Way to Winning." *YouTube*, uploaded by NDLONvideos, 13 Aug. 2012, https://www.youtube.com/watch?v=eeTuAQ6g-e8.

Kalhan, Anil. "Deferred Action, Supervised Enforcement Discretion, and the Rule of Law Basis for Executive Action on Immigration." *UCLA Law Review*, 22 July 2015, https://www.uclalawreview.org/deferred-action-supervised-enforcement-discretion-rule-law-basis-executive-action-immigration/.

Kamarck, Kristy N. *Women in Combat: Issues for Congress*. Congressional Research Service, 13 Dec. 2016, https://sgp.fas.org/crs/natsec/R42075.pdf.

Kendall, Brent. "Appeals Court Rules Against Trump on Canceling DACA Protections." *The Wall Street Journal*, 8 Nov. 2018, https://www.wsj.com/articles/appeals-court-rules-trump-cant-cancel-protections-for-undocumented-immigrants-who-came-to-u-s-as-children-1541701312.

Kershaw, Baz. *The Politics of Performance: Radical Theatre as Cultural Intervention*. Routledge, 2002.

Kozma, Leila. "TikTok Users Respond to the TikTok Crying Trend: This Is Not a Trend, This Is a 'Threat.'" *Distractify*, 17 June 2021, https://www.distractify.com/p/tiktok-crying-trend.

Lakoff, George, and Sam Ferguson. *The Framing of Immigration*. Rockridge Institute, 25 May 2006, https://escholarship.org/uc/item/0j89f85g.

Lewis, John. "Freedom Riders of 2003." *The Washington Post*, 1 Oct. 2003, p. 1.

Lopez, Fernando. "In Depth in Denver." *No Papers, No Fear Ride for Justice*, 2 Aug. 2012, http://nopapersnofear.org/blog/post.php?s=2012-08-02-in-depth-in-denver.

Lopez, Mark Hugo. "The Hispanic Vote in the 2008 Election." *Pew Research Center*, 5 Nov. 2008, http://www.pewhispanic.org/2008/11/05/the-hispanic-vote-in-the-2008-election/.

Lopez, Mark Hugo, and Paul Taylor. "Latino Voters in the 2012 Election." *Pew Research Center*, 7 Nov. 2012, http://www.pewhispanic.org/2012/11/07/latino-voters-in-the-2012-election/.

López, Nancy, and Vivian L. Gadsden. "Health Inequities, Social Determinants, and Intersectionality." *Perspectives on Health Equity and Social Determinants of Health*, edited by Kimber Bogard et al., National Academy of Medicine, 2017, https://www.ncbi.nlm.nih.gov/books/NBK595256/.

Lorde, Audre. *Sister Outsider: Essays and Speeches*. Crossing Press, 1984.

Luu, Chi. "The Ladylike Language of Letters." *JSTOR Daily*, 10 Jan. 2019, https://daily.jstor.org/the-ladylike-language-of-letters/.

Madison, D. Soyini. *Acts of Activism: Human Rights as Radical Performance*. Cambridge UP, 2010.

Mangandi, José. "La mano de obra inmigrante en las polleras de Laurel, Mississippi." *No Papers, No Fear Ride for Justice*, 11 Aug. 2012, http://nopapersnofear.org/blog/post.php?s=2012-08-11-la-mano-de-obra-inmigrante-en-las-polleras-de-laurel-mississippi.

Manoff, Marlene. "Theories of the Archive from Across the Disciplines." *Portal: Libraries and the Academy*, vol. 4, no. 1, 2004, pp. 9–25, https://doi.org/10.1353/pla.2004.0015.

Marcus, Jane. *Hearts of Darkness: White Women Write Race*, Rutgers UP, 2004.

Marcuse, Harold. "The Origin and Reception of Martin Niemöller's Quotation 'First They Came for the Communists . . .'" *Remembering for the Future: Armenia, Auschwitz, and Beyond*, edited by Michael Berenbaum et al., Paragon House, 2016, pp. 173–199.

Mariscal, George. *Aztlán and Viet Nam: Chicano and Chicana Experiences of the War*. U of California P, 1999.

Marshall, Lucinda. "The Misogynist Implications of Abu Ghraib." *One of the Guys: Women as Aggressors and Torturers*, edited by Tara McKelvey, Seal Press, 2007, pp. 51–56.

"The Meaning of the Mariposa (Butterfly). A Symbol for All." *No Papers, No Fear Ride for Justice*, 20 Sept. 2012, http://nopapersnofear.org/blog/post.php?s=2012-09-20-the-meaning-of-the-mariposa-butterfly-a-symbol-for-all.

"Memphis no tiene miedo. Memphis Has No Fear." *YouTube*, uploaded by NDLONvideos, 18 Aug. 2012, https://www.youtube.com/watch?v=omdMDVQ66O0.

Mendoza, Rubén G. "Cruising Art and Culture in Aztlán: Lowriding in the Mexican American Southwest." *U.S. Latino Literatures and Cultures: Transnational Perspectives*, edited by Francisco A. Lomelí and Karin Ikas, C. Winter, 2000.

Mesa-Bains, Amalia. "Domesticana: The Sensibility of Chicana Rasquachismo." *Chicano and Chicana Art: A Critical Anthology*, edited by Jennifer A. González et al., Duke UP, 2019, https://doi.org/10.1215/9781478003403.

Meyer, David S., and Nancy Whittier. "Social Movement Spillover." *Social Problems*, vol. 41, no. 2, 1994, pp. 277–298, https://doi.org/10.2307/3096934.

Migration Is Beautiful. Directed by Z. S. Grant, Black Dog Films, 2012. *YouTube*, uploaded by iamOTHER, 14 Jan. 2013, https://www.youtube.com/watch?v=LWE2T8Bx5d8, https://www.youtube.com/watch?v=LWE2T8Bx5d8, https://www.youtube.com/watch?v=iAvNHSmk9vI.

Mohanty, Chandra Talpade. *Feminism Without Borders: Decolonizing Theory, Practicing Solidarity*. Duke UP, 2003.

Molina, Alejandro Luis, and Michael Reyes. "The Freedom Ride: A Journey across the Geography of Human Dignity." *Latino Studies*, vol. 3, no. 1, 2005, pp. 132–141, https://doi.org/10.1057/palgrave.lst.8600126.

Mollett, Sharlene, and Caroline Faria. "The Spatialities of Intersectional Thinking: Fashioning Feminist Geographic Futures." *Gender, Place and Culture: A Journal of Feminist Geography*, vol. 25, no. 4, 2018, pp. 565–577, https://doi.org/10.1080/0966369X.2018.1454404.

Montgomery, Beronda L. "Mapping a Mentoring Roadmap and Developing a Supportive Network for Strategic Career Advancement." *SAGE Open*, vol. 7, no. 2, 2017, pp. 1–13, https://doi.org/10.1177/2158244017710288.

Montoya, Michael. *Making the Mexican Diabetic: Race, Science, and the Genetics of Inequality*. U of California P, 2011.

Moore, Emma. "Women in Combat: Five-Year Status Update." *Center for New American Security*, 31 Mar. 2020, https://www.cnas.org/publications/commentary/women-in-combat-five-year-status-update.

Moraga, Cherríe. "An Irrevocable Promise: Staging the Story Xicana." *Radical Acts: Theatre and Feminist Pedagogies of Change*, edited by Ann Elizabeth Armstrong and Kathleen Juhl, Aunt Lute Books, 2007, pp. 45–56.

Morales, Alfonso. "Growing Food and Justice: Dismantling Racism Through Sustainable Food Systems." *Cultivating Food Justice: Race, Class, and Sustainability*, edited by Alison Hope Alkon and Julian Agyeman, MIT Press, 2011, pp. 149–176.

Muñoz, José Esteban. *Cruising Utopia: The Then and There of Queer Futurity*. New York UP, 2009.

Murrell, Audrey J. "Five Key Steps for Effective Mentoring Relationships." *The Kaitz Quarterly*, vol. 1, no. 1, 2007, http://nl.walterkaitz.org/FiveStepsInMentoring_Murrell.pdf.

Murrell, Audrey J., et al. "The Importance of Peer Mentoring, Identity Work and Holding Environments: A Study of African American Leadership Development." *International Journal of Environmental Research and Public Health*, vol. 18, no. 9, 2021, https://doi.org/10.3390/ijerph18094920.

"No One Can Turn Us Around - No Papers No Fear Exchange with Civil Rights Veterans." *YouTube*, uploaded by NDLONvideos, 12 Aug. 2012, https://www.youtube.com/watch?v=nKwYbELwNAo.

"No Papers No Fear Delegation Makes First Stop in North Carolina [. . .]." *No Papers, No Fear Ride for Justice*, 30 Aug. 2012, http://nopapersnofear.org/blog/post.php?s=2012-08-30-no-papers-no-fear-delegation-makes-first-stop-in-north-carolina-towards-democratic-national-convention-supports-undocumented-immigrants-of-asheville.

"No Papers No Fear Ride for Justice" [blog post]. *No Papers, No Fear Ride for Justice*, 19 July 2012, http://nopapersnofear.org/blog/post.php?s=2012-07-19-no-papers-no-fear-ride-for-justice.

"No Papers No Fear Ride for Justice" [video]. *YouTube*, uploaded by NDLONvideos, 19 July 2012, https://www.youtube.com/watch?v=r2uKmu_-rk0.

Nusair, Isis. "Gendered, Racialized, and Sexualized Torture at Abu Ghraib." *Feminism and War: Confronting U.S. Imperialism,* edited by Robin L. Riley et al., Zed Books, 2008, pp. 179–193.

Nuttall, Frank Q. "Body Mass Index: Obesity, BMI, and Health: A Critical Review." *Nutrition Today,* vol. 50, no. 3, 2015, pp. 117–128, https://doi.org/10.1097/NT.0000000000000092.

Office of Professional Responsibility. *Investigation into the Office of Legal Counsel's Memoranda Concerning Issues Relating to the Central Intelligence Agency's Use of 'Enhanced Interrogation Techniques' on Suspected Terrorists.* Department of Justice, 29 July 2009, https://irp.fas.org/agency/doj/opr-final.pdf.

Olguín, B. V. "From Counter to Hegemonic: Re-Mapping Ideology in Latina/o Life Writing from the War on Terror." *Biography,* vol. 36, no. 1, 2013, pp. 179–210, https://doi.org/10.1353/bio.2013.0004.

Olson, Meg. "Nuns on the Bus: A History!" *Nuns on the Bus,* 27 Sept. 2024, https://www.nunsonthebus.org/2024/09/nunsonthebus-history/.

Omi, Michael, and Howard Winant. *Racial Formation in the United States.* Routledge, 2014.

"Only Skin Deep: Changing Visions of the American Self." *International Center of Photography,* 2003, https://www.icp.org/exhibitions/only-skin-deep-changing-visions-of-the-american-self.

Ortiz Torres, Rubén. "Cathedrals on Wheels." *Art Issues,* Sept./Oct. 1998, https://escholarship.org/uc/item/6nf108sz.

"Our History of Grassroots Organizing." *New Orleans Workers' Center for Racial Justice,* https://www.nowcrj.org/about-nowcrj. Accessed 9 May 2025.

"Our Mission." *Save OurSelves,* https://sosmovement.net/join-the-movement/our-mission/. Accessed 4 Jan. 2020.

Pelaez Lopez, Alan. "The X in Latinx Is a Wound, Not a Trend." *Color Bloq: The Stories of Us,* Sept. 2018, https://www.colorbloq.org/the-x-in-latinx-is-a-wound-not-a-trend.

Pell, Susan. "Radicalizing the Politics of the Archive: An Ethnographic Reading of an Activist Archive." *Archivaria,* vol. 80, 2015, pp. 33–57, https://archivaria.ca/index.php/archivaria/article/view/13543.

Penland, Paige R. *Lowrider: History, Pride, Culture.* Motorbooks, 2003.

Pérez, Daniel Enrique. "Toward a Mariposa Consciousness: Reimagining Queer Chicano and Latino Identities." *Aztlán: A Journal of Chicano Studies,* vol. 39, no. 2, 2014, pp. 95–127.

Pérez Huber, Lindsay, et al. "Getting Beyond the 'Symptom,' Acknowledging the 'Disease': Theorizing Racist Nativism." *Contemporary Justice Review,* vol. 11, no. 1, 2008, pp. 39–51.

Philipose, Liz. "The Politics of Pain and the Uses of Torture." *Signs,* vol. 32, no. 4, 2007, pp. 1047–1071, https://doi.org/10.1086/513022.

Pilkington, Ed. "Undocumented Latinos End Protest Tour of South at Democratic Convention." *The Guardian,* 2 Sept. 2012, https://www.theguardian.com/world/2012/sep/02/undocumented-latinos-protest-convention.

Plascencia, Luis F. B. "Low Riding in the Southwest: Cultural Symbols in the Mexican Community." *History, Culture, and Society: Chicano Studies in the 1980s*, edited by the National Association for Chicano Studies, Bilingual Press, 1983, pp. 141–175.

"Promotoras de salud con los jornaleros de Gretna." *YouTube*, uploaded by NDLON-videos, 12 Aug. 2012, https://www.youtube.com/watch?v=lS4NCRjKDH0.

"Proud of My Culture." *TikTok*, posted by Yadi1207 (@yadi.1207), 10 Dec. 2022, https://www.tiktok.com/@yadi.1207/video/7175668755622612267?is_from_webapp=1&sender_device=pc&web_id=7185979579152352810.

Puar, Jasbir K. "Abu Ghraib: Arguing Against Exceptionalism." *Feminist Studies*, vol. 30, no. 2, 2004, pp. 522–534, https://doi.org/10.2307/20458978.

"Puerto Ricans Stand Up." *Code Switch*. Hosted by Karen Grigsby Bates and Adrian Florido, *NPR*, 31 July 2019, https://www.npr.org/templates/transcript/transcript.php?storyId=746819091.

Puga, Ana Elena. "The *Caravana* of Central American Mothers in Mexico: Performances of Devotional and Saintly Motherhood on a Transnational Stage-in-Motion." *Theatre Research International*, vol. 46, no. 3, 2021, pp. 266–284, https://doi.org/10.1017/S0307883321000262.

Puga, Kristina. "An Activist Shows 'Migration Is Beautiful' Through Art." *NBC Latino*, 15 Jan. 2013, https://nbclatino.com/2013/01/15/video-an-activist-shows-migration-is-beautiful-through-art/.

"The Q-Sides." *Galería de la Raza*, http://www.galeriadelaraza.org/eng/events/index.php?op=view&id=5687. Accessed 27 July 2019.

Rakoff, Ian. "Comic Strips and the Makings of American Identity." *Humour, Comedy and Laughter: Obscenities, Paradoxes, Insights and the Renewal of Life*, edited by Lidia Dina Sciama, Berghahn Books, 2018, pp. 76–97.

Ramirez, Leticia, et al. "They Pushed Us Out. We Came Back Stronger. They Let Us In." *No Papers, No Fear Ride for Justice*, 19 Aug. 2012, http://www.nopapersnofear.org/blog/post.php?s=2012-08-19-they-pushed-us-out-we-came-back-stronger-they-let-us-in.

Ramirez Jimenez, Mari Cruz. "In Admiration: Learning About the Civil Rights Movement." *No Papers, No Fear Ride for Justice*, 16 Aug. 2012, http://nopapersnofear.org/blog/post.php?s=2012-08-16-in-admiration-learning-about-the-civil-rights-movement.

Ransby, Barbara. *Ella Baker and the Black Freedom Movement*. U of North Carolina P, 2003.

Razack, Sherene. "When Is Prisoner Abuse Racial Violence." *ZNetwork*, 24 May 2004, https://zcomm.org/znetarticle/when-is-prisoner-abuse-racial-violence-by-sherene-razack/.

Rees, Martha W. "Aquí estamos y no nos vamos—Adelina Nicholls on the Fight for Immigrant Rights." *New Politics*, vol. 15, no. 1, 2014, pp. 43–50, https://newpol.org/issue_post/aqu%C3%AD-estamos-y-no-nos-vamos-adelina-nicholls-fight-immigrant-rights/.

Reiser, Alyssa. "Our Vaginas, Not Ourselves: A Critical Analysis of the *Vagina Monologues*." *MP: An Online Feminist Journal*, vol. 1, no. 4, 2006, https://academinist.org/wp-content/uploads/2010/06/Reiser.pdf.

Rejali, Darius M. *Torture and Democracy*. Princeton UP, 2009.

Reuters. "New Guantanamo Abuse Cases Surface." *Al Jazeera*, 6 Jan. 2005, https://www.aljazeera.com/news/2005/1/6/new-guantanamo-abuse-cases-surface.

Reyes, Israel. *Embodied Economies: Diaspora and Transcultural Capital in Latinx Caribbean Fiction and Theater*. Rutgers UP, 2022.

Reyes, Kathryn Blackmer, and Julia E. Curry Rodríguez. "*Testimonio*: Origins, Terms, and Resources." *Equity and Excellence in Education*, vol. 45, no. 3, 2012, pp. 525–538, https://doi.org/10.1080/10665684.2012.698571.

Richter-Montpetit, Melanie. "Empire, Desire and Violence: A Queer Transnational Feminist Reading of the Prisoner 'Abuse' in Abu Ghraib and the Question of 'Gender Equality.'" *International Feminist Journal of Politics*, vol. 9, no. 1, 2007, pp. 38–59, https://doi.org/10.1080/14616740601066366.

Riley, Robin L., et al., editors. *Feminism and War: Confronting U.S. Imperialism*. Zed Books, 2008.

Rodríguez, Richard T. *Next of Kin: The Family in Chicano/a Cultural Politics*. Duke UP, 2009.

Román, David. *Performance in America: Contemporary U.S. Culture and the Performing Arts*. Duke UP, 2005.

Romo, Vanessa, et al. "Trump Ends DACA, Calls on Congress to Act." *NPR*, 5 Sept. 2017, https://www.npr.org/2017/09/05/546423550/trump-signals-end-to-daca-calls-on-congress-to-act.

Rupersburg, Nicole. "Queer and Undocumented: The Art and Activism of Coming Out, and Coming Out." *Creative Exchange*, 28 June 2019, https://springboardexchange.org/queer-and-undocumented-the-art-and-activism-of-coming-out-and-coming-out/.

Sánchez, George J. *Becoming Mexican American: Ethnicity, Culture, and Identity in Chicano Los Angeles, 1900–1945*. Oxford UP, 1995.

Sánchez, Rosaura, and Beatrice Pita. "Theses on the Latino Bloc: A Critical Perspective." *Aztlán: A Journal of Chicano Studies*, vol. 31, no. 3, 2006, pp. 25–53, https://doi.org/10.1525/azt.2006.31.2.25.

Sandoval, Chela, and Guisela Latorre. "Chicana/o Artivism." *Learning Race and Ethnicity: Youth and Digital Media*, edited by Anna Everett, MIT Press, 2008, pp. 81–108.

Sandoval, Denise Michelle. "Cruising Through Low Rider Culture: Chicana/o Identity in the Marketing of *Low Rider Magazine*." *Velvet Barrios: Popular Culture & Chicana/o Sexualities*, edited by Alicia Gaspar de Alba, Palgrave Macmillan, 2003, pp. 179–196.

Sandoval, Denise M. "The Politics of Low and Slow / *Bajito y Suavecito*: Black and Chicano Lowriders in Los Angeles, from the 1960s through the 1970s." *Black and Brown in Los Angeles: Beyond Conflict and Coalition*, edited by Josh Kun and Laura Pulido, U of California P, 2019, pp. 176–200.

Santa Ana, Otto. *Brown Tide Rising: Metaphors of Latinos in Contemporary American Public Discourse*. U of Texas P, 2002.

Santos, Fernanda. "A Bus Ride to Show the Cracks in Immigration." *The New York Times*, 27 July 2012, https://www.nytimes.com/2012/07/28/us/immigrants-seek-to-highlight-a-problem-through-a-bus-trip.html.

Sauers, Camille. "In 1990, a Levi's Plant Abruptly Closed on Zarzamora; These San Antonio Women Never Stopped Fighting." *MySA*, 6 Sept. 2021, https://www.mysanantonio.com/entertainment/article/Meet-the-Southside-San-Antonio-women-who-fought-16434174.php.

Schlesinger, James R. Report [*Final Review of the Independent Panel to Review DoD Detention Operations*]. Department of Defense, Aug. 2004, http://pdf.prisonexp.org/SchlesingerReport.pdf.

Schmidt, Randall M., and John T. Furlow. Report [*Army Regulation 15–6: Final Report; Investigation into FBI Allegations of Detainee Abuse at Guantanamo Bay, Cuba Detention Facility*]. US Army, Apr. 2005, https://www.thetorturedatabase.org/files/foia_subsite/pdfs/schmidt_furlow_report.pdf.

Schneider, Rebecca. *Performing Remains: Art and War in Times of Theatrical Reenactment*. Routledge, 2011.

Schwartz, Joan M., and Terry Cook. "Archives, Records, and Power: The Making of Modern Memory." *Archival Science*, vol. 2, 2002, pp. 1–19, https://doi.org/10.1007/BF02435628.

Shigematsu, Setsu. "Women-of-Color Veterans on War, Militarism, and Feminism." With Anuradha Kristina Bhagwati and Eli Paintedcrow. *Feminism and War: Confronting U.S. Imperialism*, edited by Robin L. Riley et al., Zed Books, 2008, pp. 93–102.

Simien, Evelyn M., and Danielle L. McGuire. "A Tribute to the Women: Rewriting History, Retelling Herstory in Civil Rights." *Politics and Gender*, vol. 10, no. 3, 2014, pp. 413–431, https://doi.org/10.1017/S1743923X14000245.

Spade, Dean, and Aaron Belkin. "Queer Militarism?!: The Politics of Military Inclusion Advocacy in Authoritarian Times." *GLQ: A Journal of Lesbian and Gay Studies*, vol. 27, no. 2, 2021, pp. 281–307, https://doi.org/10.1215/10642684-8871705.

Stone, Michael Cutler. "Bajito y sauvecito (Low and Slow): Low Riding and the 'Class' of Class." *Studies in Latin American Popular Culture*, vol. 9, 1990, p. 85.

Strang, Cameron B. "Violence, Ethnicity, and Human Remains During the Second Seminole War." *The Journal of American History*, vol. 100, no. 4, 2014, pp. 973–994.

Striff, Erin. "Realism and Realpolitik in Eve Ensler's *The Vagina Monologues*." *The Journal of American Drama and Theatre*, vol. 17, no. 2, 2005, pp. 71–87.

Strings, S., et al. "The Association of Body Mass Index and Odds of Type 2 Diabetes Mellitus Varies by Race/Ethnicity." *Public Health*, vol. 215, 2023, pp. 27–30.

Subcommittee on Military Personnel, Committee on Armed Services, US House of Representatives. *Diversity in Recruiting and Retention: Increasing Diversity in the Military—What the Military Services Are Doing*. 116th Congress, 1st Session, 10 Dec. 2019, https://www.congress.gov/116/chrg/CHRG-116hhrg41929/CHRG-116hhrg41929.htm.

"Sylva: We'd Like to See the Sheriff . . . Today." *YouTube*, uploaded by NDLONvideos, 1 Sept. 2012, https://www.youtube.com/watch?v=yuGS1g3uhfM.

Taguba, Antonio M. Report [*Article 15-16 Investigation of the 800th Military Police Brigade*]. US military, May 2004, https://irp.fas.org/agency/dod/taguba.pdf.

Tamas, Sophie. "Autogeography: Placing Research in the First-Person Singular." *Routledge Handbook of Gender and Feminist Geographies*, edited by Anindita Datta et al., Routledge, 2020, pp. 511–518.

Taylor, Diana. *The Archive and the Repertoire: Performing Cultural Memory in the Americas*. 2nd ed., Duke UP, 2003.

Taylor, Diana. "Theater and Terrorism: Griselda Gambaro's *Information for Foreigners*." *Theatre Journal*, vol. 42, no. 2, 1990, pp. 165–182, https://doi.org/10.2307/3207753.

"Teatro de los Glahriadores en Atlanta: No papeles no miedo." *YouTube*, uploaded by NDLONvideos, 27 Aug. 2012, https://www.youtube.com/watch?v=Dz06lCLlgPc.

Thayer, Allen. "Classic Lowriders: Low, Slow and Soulful." *Utne Reader*, May/June 2012, https://www.allenthayer.com/home/2020/7/rockinyoueternally-xnzla-yfp3f-hbww5.

"Timelapse: The Making of the (Undocu)Bus." *YouTube*, uploaded by NDLONvideos, 25 Aug. 2012, https://www.youtube.com/watch?v=Mh_jA0ykyyw.

Torres, Gerardo. "Fearless and Speaking for Ourselves." *No Papers, No Fear Ride for Justice*, 18 Aug. 2012, http://www.nopapersnofear.org/blog/post.php?s=2012-08-18-fearless-and-speaking-for-ourselves.

Tovar, Virgie. "All Food Is Good Food with Mia Feuer." *Rebel Eaters Club*, season 1, episode 1, 24 Feb. 2020.

"UndocuBus Ride: A Journey from Arizona to the DNC." *YouTube*, uploaded by Race Forward, 5 Sept. 2012, https://www.youtube.com/watch?v=9_236XsMN8Y.

"Undocumented Activists Arrested Outside DNC After Cross-Country Journey for Immigration Reform." *Democracy Now!*, 5 Sept. 2012, http://www.democracynow.org/2012/9/5/undocumented_activists_arrested_outside_dnc_after.

"Undocumented People Arrested in Civil Disobedience Watch President's Speech [. . .]." *No Papers, No Fear Ride for Justice*, 6 Sept. 2012, http://nopapersnofear.org/blog/post.php?s=2012-09-06-undocumented-people-arrested-in-civil-disobedience-watch-presidents-speech-announce-next-steps-after-presidents-speech-call-on-dnc-to-be-on-right-side-of-history-end-merger-of-police-with-immigration-enforcement.

"V (formerly Eve Ensler), Founder." *V-Day*, 31 Aug. 2020, https://www.vday.org/about-v-day/eve-ensler-founder/.

"V's 'The Vagina Monologues' Performed at Madison Square Garden." *Jewish Women's Archive*, 10 Feb. 2001, https://jwa.org/thisweek/feb/10/2001/eve-ensler.

Valdez, Luis. *Early Works: Actos, Bernabé, and Pensamiento Serpentino*. Arte Público Press, 1994.

Walker, Alice. *In Search of Our Mothers' Gardens: Womanist Prose*. Harvest Books, 2003.

Walker, LaNitra. "Women's Role in Mob Violence: Lynchings and Abu Ghraib." *One of the Guys: Women as Aggressors and Torturers*, edited by Tara McKelvey, Seal Press, 2007, pp. 189–198.

War Department. *Field Service Regulations, Administration*. US Government Printing Office, 1943.

Wasko, Jean. "The Angel in the Envelope: The Letters of Jane Welsh Carlyle." *Modern Language Studies*, vol. 27, no. 3/4, 1997, pp. 3–18, https://doi.org/10.2307/3195389.

"We're Here." *HBO*, https://www.hbomax.com/shows/were-here/761317f7-afa5-44bd-9045-4d7bc8b786ea. Accessed 9 May 2025.

"'When I See Injustice I Tend to Move Against It' - Selma, Alabama." *YouTube*, uploaded by NDLONvideos, 23 Aug. 2012, https://www.youtube.com/watch?app=desktop&v=edVyMqu_hf8.

"Who We Are . . ." *Faculty of Color Working Group*, https://www.focwg.org/. Accessed 1 Aug. 2023.

"Who We Are: Our Mission." *allgo*, https://allgo.org/about-us/#. Accessed 9 May 2025.

Wong, Kent, and Carolina Bank Muñoz. "Don't Miss the Bus: The Immigrant Workers Freedom Ride." *New Labor Forum*, vol. 13, no. 2, 2004, pp. 60–66, 147.

Woolf, Virginia. *A Room of One's Own*. Harcourt, 2005.

Woolf, Virginia. *Three Guineas*. Harcourt Brace Jovanovich, 1966.

World Health Organization. "Social Determinants of Health." *World Health Organization*, https://www.who.int/health-topics/social-determinants-of-health. Accessed 20 Nov. 2023.

Ybarra-Frausto, Tomás. "*Rasquachismo*: A Chicano Sensibility." *Chicano and Chicana Art: A Critical Anthology*, edited by Jennifer A. González et al., Duke UP, 2019.

Yoo, John C. Memo ["Military Interrogation of Alien Unlawful Combatants Held Outside the United States"]. Department of Justice memorandum for William J. Haynes II, general counsel of the Department of Defense, 14 Mar. 2003, https://www.aclu.org/documents/memo-regarding-torture-and-military-interrogation-alien-unlawful-combatants-held-outside.

Zagorin, Adam, and Michael Duffy. "Inside the Interrogation of Detainee 063." *Time*, 20 June 2005, https://time.com/3624326/inside-the-interrogation-of-detainee-063/.

Zambrana, Ruth E. *Toxic Ivory Towers: The Consequences of Work Stress on Underrepresented Minority Faculty*. Rutgers UP, 2018.

Index